Princess Grace

Other books by Gwen Robyns

The Friendly Potato
Light of a Star—A Biography of Vivien Leigh
Royal Sporting Lives
Royal Ladies
Wimbledon

Also, in collaboration

Margaret Rutherford

Princess Grace

by

Gwen Robyns

David McKay Company, Inc.
New York

Library of Congress Cataloging in Publication Data

Robyns, Gwen.
  Princess Grace.

  Includes index.
  1. Grace, Princess of Monaco, 1929-   I. Title.
DC943.G7R6   944′.949′080924 [B]   76-17294
ISBN 0-679-50612-8

Little Flower, you're a lucky one
you soak in all the lovely sun
you stand and watch it all go by
and never once do bat an eye
while others have to fight and strain
against the world and its every pain of living.

But you must, too, have wars to fight
the cold bleak darkness of every night
of a bigger vine who seeks to grow
and is able to stand the rain and snow
and yet you never let it show
on your pretty face.

—Written by Grace Kelly as a child

Foreword

Whenever I begin work on a biography I search for the key—the key that will unlock the character of the person I am writing about, which is so necessary if one is to understand the motivation of his or her life. There is no point in simply asking the person concerned. He or she has no way of knowing, no extra perceptory faculties through which to recognize such a deliquiscent characteristic.

With the actress Vivien Leigh I found the key in her own words—searing, ruthless, honest—"Scorpions burn themselves out and eat themselves up and they are careless about themselves—like me."

When I wrote Margaret Rutherford's autobiography for her, this beloved woman had already slipped into her own autumnal world of shadows. One day as she sat in the garden in lonesome, depressive silence, she suddenly leaned forward in her wheelchair and spoke:

"Do you believe in fairies? When did you last see a miracle?"

I smiled gratefully. I had the key.

With Her Serene Highness Princess Grace of Monaco it was different. The canvas was broader, blurred by international barriers and indefinable royal obstructions. Once upon a time she was an ordinary little American girl with knobby knees and a shy, whimsical smile. Now she is a royal princess—a renowned beauty and personality. How and why did this metamorphosis take place?

For a year I searched: day after day listening to her family, sniffing the streets of Philadelphia, New York and Los Angeles where once she walked freely. I sat long into the night, conversing with her friends, and mingled with the film world who had worked, and played, with her. Perseveringly, I probed trusted members of her staff who, over the years, have observed her in the family life of the palace in Monaco. And I learned from sifting through the Princess's own elusive and original thoughts.

As people talked, the platitudes and clichés tumbled out. All were perfectly true—but none offered a clue. It was not until I sat in the cool luxury of producer John Foreman's house in Beverly Hills that I suddenly knew my quest was over.

It was nearly midnight on a Sunday in June, 1974.

Hollywood is a crisp, early-to-bed city in contrast to Rome with its decadent night hours. In Los Angeles Sunday is a day for barbecuing 'round the swimming pool, catching up with parental duties and boozing with friends. By 9 P.M. the last guests have gone, and in the blue twilight the curtains are drawn.

I knew this. I knew it all. Selfishly I sat on, sipping wine and fencing with words. At 11:50 P.M., when Foreman's brown beauty and pale blue denims were beginning to crumple, there came a revealing moment.

I almost wept with gratitude. He had given me the key.

Thank you, John Foreman.

There are many others who have helped with this book. Because it is not an official biography their help was vital. They do not need to stand up and be counted. Their words are here—testimony to the charismatic affection Princess Grace arouses within everyone who meets her.

To the Kelly family, one and all, I am grateful for bringing to life the Princess's happy childhood.

I would especially like to thank Madame Nadia Lacoste of the Monaco Palace Press Bureau; Gant Gaither for permitting me to quote from his book *Princess Grace* (Holt), which was written at the time of her marriage; Peter Hawkins for permission to quote from his authorized biography of Prince Rainier (William Kimber); Carole Browne for her help and encouragement; and the editor of the *Philadelphia Bulletin* for allowing access to the *Bulletin*'s fine library.

But one person stands out beyond the others. When all doors were closed, all hopes abandoned, all dreams unfulfilled, he alone trusted me.

viii

I owe so much to Vane Ivanovic, the distinguished consul general for Monaco in London. He never once failed me.

G.R.
—London, New York, Philadelphia,
Los Angeles, Paris, Monaco, Oxfordshire

Princess Grace

One

"There is a mystique that surrounds Grace and always has from the beginning. It is the act she put together for survival."

Producer John Foreman was talking to me late one Sunday night in the intimacy of his den in his home in Beverly Hills, California.

"Only Grace could have created Grace Kelly. It must have been a concept in her head. No one else did. No manager, no agent, no producer, not even her family.

"She made up the idea of Grace Kelly, and having made it up she was the only one who knew how to make it operate. She can make Grace Kelly do Grace Kelly things that nobody else can do. She did it then and she does it now. She is unique."

Foreman has known Princess Grace of Monaco since she was a young actress in New York, and has watched her survive, conquer the most arduous obstacles in Hollywood, and reach the pinnacle of success via her sheer will power.

"To have one's act together is the best thing anyone can possibly have in this business of surviving. It means a coloring in personality that you have put on yourself to afford the best protection.

"Grace's act, which has stood her in good stead all these years, is one of the most efficient I have ever seen because it affords her the chance to make friends immediately and have people help her instantly and be glad of the opportunity. She is also absolutely consistent in her behavior and utterly dependable. For quite a few of us, and for many years, she gave us a perfect place that one can relate to, and this is why we admire her so."

Having one's act together is not only a consistency of character, but also a combination of knowing one's own limitations and never

1

breaking one's own code of behavior at whatever level one has previously set for oneself. Thus, it becomes the essence of good manners, since it protects other people from outbursts of emotion.

Princess Caroline was untruthfully quoted in an English magazine article as saying: "My mother is a Nordic beauty. She is very beautiful but this type of beauty can sometimes be rather cold." To begin with, Princess Caroline has never said this about her mother, whom she admires tremendously. Also, nothing is further from the truth as seen through my eyes, which have spent a lifetime studying the world's most beautiful women. Grace's economy of emotion in public is part of her act and her own personal way of never embarrassing anyone—of keeping the situation one which she can control. And her golden coloring is never cold.

In private she is warm, outgoing, unfailingly thoughtful, and she loves to giggle. Few of her staff or friends have ever seen her visibly angry. "I go away to be horrible by myself," she says. As a child this state of mind was called "the sulks"; now it is more likely to be described as "one of her moods," which everyone around her is fully aware of—and respects.

This, then, is the clue to the character of Princess Grace. It began when, as child with a maturity far beyond her years, she conscientiously set a pattern for the lifestyle that she intended to follow. And she has never deviated from it.

It was coincidental, but turned out to be fortuitous timing, that she arrived in Hollywood at a time when the lives of many stars were going through an untidy period. This was the era of Elizabeth Taylor, Ava Gardner and Marilyn Monroe. With courage and abandon their lives spilled over daily into the gossip columns, leaving them pathetically vulnerable.

Elizabeth Taylor had her professional act together as no one else had since Garbo. She knew her acting capabilities, and within those boundaries kept strictly to her limitations. It has made her a very rich woman, but it has also cost her five marriages.

Ava Gardner did not care. Once she had the Hollywood situation summed up, she used it like a piece of lingerie and threw it away when the lace began to fray at the ends.

Marilyn Monroe had her act together on one level: She knew how to exploit sexuality better than anyone else ever has. But her private life was in shambles. So many days were wasted because she could not cope with even the smallest problems of living. She was totally incapable of administering to her own life and personal affairs.

If you walked into a room to meet her, you never knew what to expect—she was slovenly, sloppy, dirty, disagreeable, funny, bewitching, sensuous, beautiful, enchanting. She was so inconsistent that her friends found it unnerving because they never knew where they stood.

Grace Kelly could, and still can, always be counted on for an optimistic, enthusiastic and humorous reaction to the circumstances in which she finds herself. She alone created her public and private images, maintained them and has never tarnished them by either word or gesture. Her consistency and professionalism of temperament made her if not the most gifted film actress in Hollywood at least the most respected.

Grace Kelly deliberately left behind the security of a wealthy family life in Philadelphia; refused financial help from her parents; and, with only her act to protect her, in five brief years left an indelible mark on Hollywood history.

She not only chose the most difficult career—the most competitive and the most heart-breaking—but she climbed to the top in Hollywood strictly on her own terms. She never conceded—and it was a gamble that paid off.

There were other girls just as pretty—she had not yet acquired real beauty—just as talented, just as hard working. Why did she succeed where others failed? Why was she also mentally, physically and emotionally able to slip into the role of royal princess in the oldest and one of the most difficult ruling houses in Europe without any outward sign of stress?

One comes back to this key—her act—which never lets her down, as well as her own resilient toughness.

Although Princess Grace has not made a film in twenty years, her impact has not diminished. She keeps up with all the American picture news through trade magazines and is still regularly sent scripts which she reads avidly. Were she to break her self-imposed vow not to act in commercial films again, she could certainly command the highest financial deal of any film star alive today.

For twenty years after her retirement, Garbo remained the in-cult among her fans, but among the young people today she would rate as little more than an interesting curiosity. With Princess Grace it is different. Her glamor is still gleaming brightly. As John Foreman explained: "The producer who could go to the studio or bank with a commitment for her to appear in a film would get immediate finance. There is not one actor in the business, from Marlon Brando to Paul Newman, who would not be enchanted to work with her."

Oddly enough, Grace Kelly and Marilyn Monroe never met, although they were a stone's throw apart on at least two occasions. Once they were both on the same plane flying from New York to Los Angeles. While Marilyn was receiving the "star treatment" in first class up-front in the plane, Grace sat up through the night in the economy class reading a book. It was the kind of scoop that every Hollywood reporter would have given his eyeteeth to get. It also proves the truth in what Grace Kelly used to say about herself: "When Ava Gardner gets into a cab, the driver knows straight away that she's Ava Gardner. I'm sure it's the same with Marilyn Monroe and Elizabeth Taylor. But not me. I'm never Grace Kelly. I'm always somebody who looks like Grace Kelly."

In New York when her engagement to Prince Rainier had been announced and they were both appearing in public for the first time at the dazzling Monte Carlo gala ball, Marilyn was a block away at Madison Square Garden riding a pink elephant in the Barnum & Bailey Circus. Next morning the New York newspapers had double headlines recording the events.

It is interesting, too, that both Grace Kelly and Marilyn Monroe appeared as storybook princesses in movies: Grace in *The Swan* with Alec Guinness, and Marilyn in *The Prince and the Showgirl*. The difference was that Grace married a real live prince and now lives in a palace, and Marilyn died a mysterious, lonely death in a small house in Los Angeles.

Grace had her act together. . . .

The marriage of Prince Rainier of Monaco to Grace Kelly, the golden girl of America, hit a tired, disillusioned world like a galaxy of stars. No one disputed the Prince's urgent need to find a bride who would bear an heir to the throne of Monaco. No one debated that an injection of healthy American blood was a desirable addition to the house of Grimaldi. But the sheer creditability of this romance between the dashing Prince and beautiful girl made a sugar-spun fairy tale come to life.

It is what every little girl dreams of when she sits alone in her own private world. For Grace Kelly, who used to beg her older sister,

Peggy, "Please let me be the princess" when they played "let's pretend" games, it was a dream come true.

What makes Princess Grace the remarkable woman she is is her ability to have transcended the sugar story and created for herself a unique niche in the world. This she has done as few other women could have.

Though both would probably deny it, Princess Grace and Queen Elizabeth II of England have much in common. Outwardly they are reserved, shy, sincere and lonely to a point of almost being misunderstood on occasion. But privately, within their own chosen worlds, they are fun, sensitive, quick-tongued and can be wildly funny.

Both, too, have accomplished the almost impossible task of being full-time royal personages as well as involved mothers concerned with every aspect of family life. In addition, each in her own way is a perfectionist, although the Queen's canvas is broader and her personal interests less feminine than those of Princess Grace.

The main difference between them is that the Queen is a dedicated countrywoman, her real interests revolving around rural living, whereas Princess Grace is a fringe country girl who relishes ballet, film, the theater, art world and people of metropolitan living.

Princess Grace's esteem in Monaco is remarkable. The fact that she is always referred to by Monegasques as "Our Princess" is understandable after twenty years; but so deep is their love and respect for her that they totally resent anyone who knocks her image. Any criticism of the Princess immediately becomes a personal insult to the citizens of Monaco.

When *Time* magazine last year wrote a professionally slick article on Princess Caroline called "The Super Kid from Monaco," which also included some snide remarks about Princess Grace, it was the talk of Monaco.

"How could they do this to our Princess—and her own countrypeople, too?" they questioned me.

Princess Grace also brought to Monaco a profound sense of responsibility. This, too, is part of her act. The Monegasques found her a sincere person who, for her royal status, was prepared to give more than she expected in return. This they had not anticipated.

"She brought us life. The whole place changed from the moment she arrived. Her ideas were fresh and charming. For instance, she arranged that every Monegasque mother who gives birth to a baby is sent a medal commemorating the event. Her daily personal interest in running the Red Cross as its president is astonishing, and even when she is abroad she is in constant contact, making decisions by telephone. A day nursery for the children of working mothers, help for the old, our wonderful International Flower Show, the crafts centers, the formation of the International Arts Festival—to which top artists from all over the world are invited—are all due to the Princess.''

Behind the scenes her acts of kindness are prudent and private.

Being a princess of Monaco is also a form of role-playing, so her strict personal discipline as an actress makes her present royal situation tenable, habitable and livable. She is doing another job, only this time with the help of a loving husband, Prince Rainier.

Princess Grace has also brought Monte Carlo glamor, and spares no effort to dress up for the galas and to be seen on every possible occasion. Despite being a very private person, she considers all this part of her job, and whenever possible likes to include the Prince and her children.

Princess Grace does not have an easy self-assurance, but what she has acquired over the last twenty years is a deep well of defensiveness from which she draws when there is need.

At forty-five years of age, Princess Grace is probably more beautiful than she has been at any other time in her life. Her bone structure is inherited but, knowing her responsibility, she works hard keeping herself at the pinnacle of health and form. She looks about ten pounds heavier than when she married, and if she gains a pound or so is distraught and immediately goes on a diet.

"Whenever I gain weight people always think I am pregnant. Then I know it is time to diet again. I don't know whether it is a compliment or not, but when I read how many times the Continental Press wrote that Queen Elizabeth was pregnant, I managed to take it light-heartedly as I am sure she did.''

Grace's skin is flawless without a trace of lines, and her eyes clear blue and frank. The Hollywood highlights have disappeared from her hair, which is now a soft butterscotch. No photograph that I have seen does her beauty justice.

As the fierce summer sun of Monaco affects her, she tends to wear dark sunglasses or floppy straw hats.

She has a hatred of crowds and, like many persons forced into public view for much of their lives, suffers from claustrophobia.

6

She has developed techniques whereby people are kept from coming too close to her. She is mindful of the time early in her marriage when admirers tried to snatch souvenirs such as buttons from her coat. Once, in fact, when she was expecting Caroline, a woman rushed forward to lay her hands on the Princess's body "for good luck."

In Paris she is always recognized and has a special quick-step technique. The moment she sees a crowd gathering, she quickens her walk, rushing from one counter to another, where her own assistants help her hastily. Thus, she is in and out of the shop before there is time for real chaos. Hovering discreetly in the background is always a family chauffeur who watches over her like a faithful nanny.

She enjoys the anonymity of shopping in London where, she says, the people have "such good manners." In New York, she has comparative freedom and spends hours in her favorite store, Bloomingdale's.

What she dislikes intensely are the *paparazzi* (free-lance photographers) who flood in from Italy and pester the family wherever they go.

Walking through the streets of Monaco to the hairdresser, Alexandre, or to her favorite patisserie (as she frequently does), she is allowed the privacy she craves, and the Monegasques only recognize her if she stops to speak to them.

I spoke with a taxi driver in Monaco as we drove up the winding road to the palace. Perhaps he best summed up the feelings of the Monegasques about their American Princess.

"Is good princess," he said. "The first year we did not know if Hollywood princess or real princess. Now we know she is real princess.

"But she is more than that. She is good mother and she lives her religion. That is more important than being princess. We all family people and we know she has to be in Paris to be with daughter Caroline and visit her mother in America. But it is not the same when she not here.

"Princesse Grace belongs to us and we belong to her."

Two

Much of the tensile strength and moral fiber that we see in Princess Grace today stems from her early forebears. On both sides of her family she comes from energetic, rugged and resolute stock.

On her father's side are the Kellys, who brought to America not only the vivid, handsome looks of Ireland, but also a splendid capacity for hard work.

Grandfather John Henry Kelly, a twenty-year-old County Mayo farm boy, sailed across the Atlantic on the *City of Boston* in 1867 to a new life in America. Soon after his arrival he caught the eye of seventeen-year-old Mary Costello, also from County Mayo. She had been sent to America to live with her grandmother and aunt in Rutland, Vermont, when she was only eight years old. John and Mary soon married.

Mary Costello Kelly matured into a woman of strong principles, with both a strict belief in the tenets of the Roman Catholic Church and an invincible Irish tongue. To the ten strapping children she bore she was always known as "The Dowager."

Soon after the birth of their first child, named John (who died at the age of ten from sunstroke), they moved from Rutland to Mineville, New York. Later they moved to Vermont and finally to Philadelphia, where the family settled down for the next hundred years.

Although John Henry Kelly began his married life as a laborer, a job that his magnificent body could easily cope with, he went on to build a flourishing insurance business. That tradition, along with Mary Kelly's blood in Princess Grace's veins—and her fierce

8

family loyalty—are deeply etched in the royal family life in Monaco today.

When a neighbor once asked Mrs. Kelly, "Do you have more love for your sons or your daughters?" Mary Costello Kelly puffed up like an outraged pigeon.

"That's no question to put to a mother," she replied. "But since you have asked I will tell you the truth. There's a great pride in the love I have for my sons, God bless them. But there's a special tenderness and understanding in my heart for my girls." It could have been Princess Grace speaking today.

In his book *That Kelly Family* (A. S. Barnes and Company), John McCallum quotes Mary Kelly as saying:

"The trouble is that in most families the mother is afraid of her children. I have never stood in fear of mine even though I would have given my heart's blood for them. They are the whole world to me. But I've never been afraid of them. Why should I be? For their own good they must be taught to respect me as their superior. Not that I demand their respect just because I happen to be their mother. You can demand a *show* of respect, as long as you are the stronger. But the thing itself must be *earned*. I will never stop trying to earn the respect of my children."

Just a hundred years later her granddaughter, Princess Grace of Monaco, was to tell English journalist Dennis Holman, "Handling a child you love is based on instinct, on your own upbringing and on the upbringing of others you have known.

"You just try to do your best.

"There are no rules except to help your children to realize that you are not perfect and that you, too, can make mistakes. Let them see your weaknesses so that they realize that you are human and forgive you.

"All of us, when we are young, think our parents are perfect. It is better that, as we grow older, we do not get a rude awakening."

Though Mary Kelly disliked personal publicity, in 1924 the *American Magazine* chose her to write an article entitled "Oh, There Ought to Be a Million Mothers Like Mary Kelly." And of Princess Grace in 1974, *New Reveille* wrote "No One Rules This Royal Roost!"

The spirit is the same.

One of Mary and John Henry Kelly's daughters, Grace—an

actress after whom Princess Grace is named—was to die of a heart attack at a skating party when she was only twenty. Four of their six sons were to become celebrated figures, each in his own right.

Patrick became a leading figure in the construction business and made his mark as a polished after-dinner speaker.

The next oldest in the family, Walter, became known in England and in America as "The Virginia Judge" due to his original vaudeville act. Princess Grace was only nine years of age when Walter died, but his fame was such that the whole Kelly family was brought up on anecdotes about Uncle Walter.

His celebrated act, "The Virginia Judge" was created from a chance visit to the Newport News police court where he sat enthralled as Judge John Dudley Brown, a serious-looking Virginian, dispensed justice with a whimsical blend of homespun philosophy and humor. Walter was so entranced with the hilarious repartee that went on between Judge Brown and "the accused" that he spent the next days in court jotting down notes. From this, then, was born the act that was to bring him fame throughout America, Australia and England.

The turning point in Walter's career was the night he substituted for Marie Dressler on Broadway. He had been engaged to act with this great comedienne in a musical production, but on the opening night she was ill with an acute attack of laryngitis. Just a quarter of an hour before the curtain went up, the producer, Percy Williams, grabbed Walter and said that he had to go out and do his "Virginia Judge" act.

The management offered the customers their money back but suggested that they stay and see "the brilliant new comedian, Walter Kelly." Most remained in their seats; and that night, as he went into his patter and brought to life all of the warm-hearted characters of the Newport News courtroom, Broadway history was made and Walter Kelly became an overnight star.

Some of Walter's gift for patter seems to have rubbed off on his niece. Princess Grace has a keen ear for dialect and can give an impromptu performance with superb mimicry of any event that amuses her. She also has a rare gift whereby she can repeat almost verbatim any conversation which she has recently heard. Thus, learning lines as an actress was never any problem for her.

But perhaps the uncle who was to most influence the young

actress Grace Kelly was George. Like all the sons whom Mary Costello Kelly raised, George had a body of steel. Before World War I he worked in an iron works, but his heart was always on the stage. He continued his job after the war for three months while he took a night course in acting.

From there it was just a step to the footlights. But it is not as an actor that America remembers George Kelly today, but as a playwright of considerable talent. From writing his own vaudeville sketches he moved on into full-length plays. His first, *The Torch Bearers*—in which years later young Grace Kelly was to make her professional stage debut at Bucks County Playhouse—was an instant Broadway hit. This was followed by even greater successes: *The Show Off* and *Craig's Wife*, which won the Pulitzer Prize.

All of George Kelly's plays were inspired by Philadelphia neighbors from The Falls, and much of the appeal of these works was that every small community could identify with his characters.

When *The Show Off* opened on Broadway, the Kelly clan arrived in New York from East Falls. There was his father, John Henry Kelly, "The Dowager," and brothers and sisters Walter, Mary, Ann, Elizabeth, and Jack with his new girl friend, Margaret Majer. The family gathering was a tradition that Jack and Margaret (who were later married) were to continue whenever their own daughter, Grace, had an opening night.

George made his home in California for many years, and whenever Grace had time she would enjoy sitting for hours with this grand old gentleman, listening to his advice—not only as a playwright, but also as a wonderful human being.

During the preparation of this book I had hoped to speak with George Kelly. He was by then old and frail and had returned to Philadelphia to be with his family. On the day we were to meet he was not well, but took great pains to send me this message:

"I am so proud of my niece, Grace. She was not only a very fine actress but is a human being with considerable qualities. Had she stayed on the stage and continued her career, I think we would have seen some very fine performances from her."

He was to die a few weeks later.

John B. Kelly (Jack—named after his late uncle), so good-looking that President Roosevelt was to say he was the handsomest man he had ever seen, was once invited to Hollywood to take a screen test. Although he made a name for himself in business, sports and politics, he did not achieve fame on the stage.

As a young boy he worked for his brother Patrick, carrying hods in his brick contracting business. In the evenings he spent his time on the Schuylkill River, where he became so proficient at sculling that he went on to win a medal at the Olympics. His rejection at Britain's Henley Regatta on the grounds that, as a former laborer he was not a gentleman, made sporting history.

When Philadelphia's Democratic party was reviving in 1935, Jack Kelly ran for mayor. He lost by 47,000 votes and never ran for office again, but he always retained an interest in politics.

Jack was twenty-three when he first laid eyes on a pretty blonde, blue-eyed schoolgirl, Margaret Majer, at the Philadelphia Turngemeinde Athletic and Social Club. He came from the East Falls section and she was from Strawberry Manson. Neither took each other very seriously at the time, but Jack occasionally picked Margaret up from school or the club and walked her home. She told him that she intended to enroll at Temple University and study physical education; he confided his ambitions to become an international sculler. But it was not until after Jack returned from serving in World War I that their courtship began in earnest.

In 1924, nine years after they had first met, Margaret Majer and John B. Kelly were married at St. Bridget's Church, and the whole of the Falls of Schuylkill turned out for the event. By then Margaret had become a magazine cover girl along with having gained a degree in physical education. In addition she had just been hired by the University of Pennsylvania and was to be the first woman physical education instructor of coeds.

Today Margaret Kelly is a remarkably pretty seventy-seven years old. She has the looks and energy of a woman twenty years younger and keeps her hair slightly more golden than her daughters'. The eyes are still china blue and the skin as delicate as an apricot. Princess Grace has inherited her mother's clear-cut bone structure, which comes from the Majers' Teutonic background.

Mrs. Kelly has always been known—even to the children—as "Ma Kelly." During the summer when she moves to the old family house at Ocean Beach, Ma Kelly (as everyone still calls her) rises with the sun, swims every morning and keeps herself remarkably trim despite recent ill health.

She had just returned from a visit to Monaco when I met her. It was a very pretty scene as she was sitting in her luxurious Germantown apartment in Philadelphia, surrounded by flowers. We talked about Princess Grace:

"If I did give my daughter anything it is very hard to say what it was, you know. I think perhaps discipline played an important part. I had a good stiff German background. My parents believed in discipline and so do I . . . no tyranny or anything like that, but a certain firmness.

"Grace was so timid as a child that she was reluctant to go downtown by herself. She would say to me, 'Mommy, please come with me. I am afraid to go. I don't know anybody.'

"I think she is still a bit timid, but now she goes out and gets things done—mostly by an act of will. She is very determined. I'm terribly proud of her, you know.''

To understand the environment of the Kelly family, it is necessary to know about Philadelphia itself. Princess Grace does not come from an old main line Philadelphia family like the Biddles or Stotesburys or Cadwalladers, as is popularly believed. Nor do the Kellys take their place in the social structure along with these other well-known families.

The affluent families of the eastern seaboard towns of America are largely descended from the first English settlers, and to this day this well-defined class system remains. They consider themselves to be better than the rest not only because of birthright but because of their own splendidly isolated culture. Bostonians regard themselves above all others in the hierarchy, but the Charleston, Baltimore, Philadelphia and New Orleans families do not accept this, and any family that can trace its ancestry in the United States for two hundred years is aristocracy indeed.

Pennsylvania was founded by that eccentric Quaker aristocrat William Penn in 1682, and his influence is still felt today. Though Philadelphia had a Catholic population way back in the eighteenth century, these people are still in the minority. Boston did not have its Catholic community until the nineteenth century.

I discussed the anomalies of the Philadelphian social structure with Professor E. Digby Baltzell of the University of Pennsylvania, who is one of America's foremost sociologists of the upper classes. He told me:

"The Kennedys have far more ability, since they came from a

culture that stressed the intellect, stressed leadership, stressed dominance. For all his ability, you did not feel that Jack Kelly had any dominance here in Philadelphia.

"I think he could have very well been a great political leader in the city if he had come from Boston—but he did not. I think by the same token only a Philadelphian would have given up a top career in the movies to become the wife of a minor royalty in Europe. I could not visualize a Kennedy doing this."

One might say in comparison that the Kennedys are a clan, the Kellys a family. But a major difference between the families is that the Kellys are a great athletic family whereas the Kennedys gained their status in politics.

Although the Kellys are about as conspicuous in Philadelphia as the 30th Street Station, it is interesting to note that in his scholarly book *The Philadelphia Gentlemen—The Making of a National Upper Class,* Dr. Baltzell mentions hundreds of families by name but there is no entry about the Kellys, who have given so much to the city of Philadelphia.

The Philadelphia Social Register is itself a feudal phenomenon in which the name of Kelly does not appear. It has certain basic filters through which names must pass and one of these filters guards against the inclusion of anyone who is not essentially white Anglo-Saxon Protestant. The Kellys were originally Irish immigrants, and the stigma remains to this day.

One of the strangest anachronisms is the Assembly Ball that Philadelphians have been attending since Washington attended it. As it is an historical institution, it is open to those of the Episcopalian and Protestant faiths, but not to those practicing Catholicism, which in Philadelphia is not so much a religion as an indication of ethnicity and race. Equally curious is the fact that one does not mention being on the Assembly list as it is tantamount to announcing one's rank in a country of hereditary titles.

For all their beauty, good manners and intelligence, the Kelly girls never attended the Assembly Ball. The only way they could have been invited was either to have married into one of the founding families or to have taken up residence in another county where they could have received an out-of-town invitation for one year.

Grace Kelly would undoubtedly have been invited had she married an early beau, Bill Crozier, as many people predicted. His was one of the socially acceptable families. It is birthright and breeding, not money, that counts in the old families of Philadelphia.

All this may have been important to the Kelly family twenty-five years ago, but knowing their disdain of snobbism, I doubt it. Jack Kelly's dream was to celebrate the bicentennial anniversary of the founding of Philadelphia by bringing the Olympics to his doorstep. Margaret Kelly has carved her name in pure gold in the city's history by her incalculable contribution to Women's Medical.

These, then, are the reasons for Mr. Kelly's remark upon the announcement of the engagement of his daughter, Grace, to Prince Rainier of Monaco: "I told the Prince that royalty didn't mean a thing to us. I told him that I certainly hoped that he wouldn't run around the way some princes do. And I told him that if he did, he'd lose a mighty fine girl."

After a trying and painful illness, Princess Grace's father died at his home on June 20, 1960.

An event which happened in the Kelly family at that time was that after having four daughters, Kell's wife gave birth to a son on May 16. Although Mr. Kelly had been ill for some time, his first outing was for the baptism of the baby boy bearing his name.

Princess Grace was in Philadelphia at the time and was able to accompany her father to the ceremony. One of the last pictures taken of John B. Kelly was, in fact, snapped by the Princess when he was holding the baby.

Three

Grace Patricia Kelly was a puny little girl. From infancy she was susceptible to colds, had sinus trouble and was constantly disturbed with asthma. She was, in fact, sickly during a great deal of her childhood; and, because of the asthma, she spoke with a whiny voice which she later overcame through speech training lessons. Today her voice is low and gentle with English overtones.

There were many days in the family's fifteen-room brick house at Henry Avenue, Germantown, when Grace had to be kept in bed while her rumbustious brothers and sisters were allowed out to play. But if she minded, she never showed it.

"We all knew from the beginning that there was something special about Grace," her mother told me. "She was a shy child, but there was a kind of inner tranquility and quiet resourcefulness. She never minded being kept in bed and would sit there with her dolls for hours on end. When you passed near, you could hear her talking very quietly to them. She was making up little plays for the dolls. Grace could change her voice for each doll, giving it a different character. Yes, she was a very patient and calm child. She loved attention but did not cry if she didn't get it."

All the Kelly girls loved dolls and each amassed a large "family" during her girlhood.

"Grace loved her dolls," recalled Mrs. Kelly, "but somehow managed to play with Peggy's and Lizanne's and keep her own in brand-new condition—she just did not want to dirty them."

Lizanne was not only the challenger but also the holy terror of the family. To tease her bigger sister she would steal Grace's family of dolls until Peggy intervened. Once in a fit of temper, she locked

Grace in a closet and went off to play. It was not until some time later that Mrs. Kelly became suspicious that Grace was missing and began looking in the cupboards. There she found Grace completely happy. She had found some dolls in the cupboard and was quietly playing "mother-and-baby."

From those early days on, Grace was always a squirrel and hoarded everything that made up her personal life—letters, badges, programs, snapshots and even old clothes. These traits remain with her today and she still wears clothes that she had, including one much-loved skirt, before her marriage twenty years ago.

One of the favorite family stories about Grace is that when she wanted to stay away from school she would solemnly announce the fact at breakfast. She would then sit back and wait for the family to talk her out of it—the point being that she did not really want to skip school.

Neighbors in Germantown remember Grace Kelly as an ordinary American child with knobby knees, skinny legs, and a shining smile—but less pretty than her two sisters, Peggy and Lizanne. Grace's was a round little face with plump cheeks; calm, lollipop-sized eyes; and straight, silky, ash blond hair pulled starkly to the side, as was the fashion, and held with a big ribbon bow. There was certainly none of the true beauty that was to show in her face in later years and make her one of the most arresting women in the world today.

The Kelly home provided an exceptionally agreeable atmosphere in which to bring up children. There was sufficient money to give the children the security they needed; but much more than that, Margaret and Jack Kelly were passionately involved and active parents, and although kind and concerned they did not fuss over their children. Each child was allowed to develop naturally like maple saplings in the forest.

Indeed, if there were any marital differences in the Kelly family—and Jack was quite a lad—they were never aired publicly. Above all, it was a united and wholesome Catholic family, a family of "Beautiful People," long before the jet set discovered and mutilated the phrase. They had the same healthy charisma of the Kennedys, but none of the built-in arrogance nurtured in Boston. In later years the two families were often to be compared, but they are as unalike as boeuf tartare is to the wholesome hamburger.

The Kelly backyard was always filled with the sounds of children—their own and all of their friends' from east of the Schuylkill River. The backyard had a family vegetable plot, which all the children worked in during the war years; a swing; sandbox; tennis court; walk-in dollhouse; boys' den; plenty of bats, rackets, glasses of milk, cookies and fruit. (This was in the days before the ubiquitous swimming pool.)

The Kelly family world was not made up of blacks, yellows or whites. It was made up of human beings, and all children were welcome. It was a lesson so indelibly printed in the Kelly children's minds that fifteen years later, when an American television crew moved into the Principality of Monaco, Princess Grace reacted true to the family standard. There was a scene planned using the children of friends and members of the staff. The director noticed three little black children, the family of one of the palace staff, who had intermingled and were playing with the others. Someone immediately went over to Princess Grace and explained:

"Your Serene Highness, the film is to be shown in the South and it won't do to have black children playing with white children. At least while we are filming we don't want them there."

"We do," Princess Grace answered without hesitation, and there were no more complications.

Keeping a kindly eye on the Kelly's backyard in Germantown was Godfrey Ford—"Fordie" to all the children. Fordie was hired as a handyman in the Kelly house, but by the sheer force of his personality he became part of the family. He was part-time parent, nursemaid, father confessor, referee, chauffeur and confidant. That he was black was totally irrelevant. His daughter Ethel shared in the Kelly children's playtime.

When Grace Kelly became a famous film actress Fordie obliged *Newsweek* magazine with his reminiscences of her.

"Every Thursday night when the nurse was off, I used to put the kiddies to bed. Before bedtime Gracie used to ask my opinions, I'd tell her what I thought, and she'd usually follow my advice. . . ."

It was Fordie who taught Grace to drive in front of the house. Chuckling with delight, he loved to tell how she finally got her license "but she was never any good at parking." Even today Princess Grace hates to drive a car and just as Fordie said, is not very skilled at parking!

When Grace Kelly married the charming Prince of Monaco and

became a part of the royal household of Monaco, Fordie was not in the least surprised. His girls were only fit to be princesses.

The girls had a large dollhouse in the Kelly backyard where they played with their doll families. When brother "Kell" (Jack) decided to turn the shed at the bottom of the garden into the headquarters of the "Tomato Men," Peggy immediately retaliated by pinning a notice on the outside of the dollhouse: "No Boys Allowed." The Tomato Men were a group of Kell's friends who took their gang name from the fact that a large patch of the garden was given over to the growing of tomatoes for the family's daily use and home preserving. As some boys today use snowballs, bicycle chains, or even knives, the Tomato Men used tomatoes.

Opposite the Kelly house lived Howard Wikoff, who formed his own gang called the Potato Men. When the rival gangs came into combat, small sisters were apt to get in the way. On one such occasion, Gracie caught a tomato right between her eyes. In an instant this tiny waif turned into a fighting shrew and began slamming the boy who had fired it. Only the swift action of Fordie saved a first-class fistfight.

It was Ma Kelly herself who was responsible for the disbanding of the Tomato Men. One morning she went out into the garden to find a sizzling fight in action between the boys and the girls. They had all raided the tomato patch and, with armfuls of tomato ammunition, were pelting each other. Their faces and clothes were stained with red tomato juice and the garden was bare. Ma Kelly roared into action and read them the riot act. The Tomato Men were no more.

Both Mr. and Mrs. Kelly were keenly interested in and knowledgeable about building healthy bodies. Jack had gained his experience during his rowing days and Margaret during her period as women's physical education instructor. Apart from advocating plenty of sun, fresh air and exercise as a means of keeping fit, they kept a sharp eye on the children's diet.

Mrs. Kelly worried most over "little Gracie," and there were special conspiracies to build her up. As Mr. Kelly was often out for dinner, Mrs. Kelly carved the meat, which she did even when he was home. Today Kell remembers vividly how his mother meticulously saved the meat juice from the roast for Grace, a favoritism that he resented bitterly at the time. Grace was made to dunk her bread in it and was not always appreciative of its nourishing qualities. Another of Mrs. Kelly's ruses to get Grace to eat up her bread and butter was to sprinkle it with white sugar.

In a household of such noisy extroverts Grace could easily have been stifled. That she was not is entirely due to her inner tenacity and toughness. Years later she was to say to a group of fellow actors:

"Sometimes I have to wait a long time for things I want very much. I don't always get them, but something inside won't let me give up easily."

These were not new thoughts. They were formed way back in those childhood days and she never wavered from them. Grace compensated for whatever she lacked in physical prowess with her imagination. She lived in her own dream world and peopled it with her own creations—reality and fantasy were totally interchangeable.

As her husband was frequently away from home attending to his business or civic work, Mrs. Kelly was the mainstay of the family life. With her strict German upbringing, she had a healthy respect for old-fashioned virtues, and was determined that her children should be brought up with a social conscience and concern for others less fortunate than themselves. Today these principles are so much a part of Princess Grace's character that she in turn is now passing them on to her own children.

Religion has always figured prominently in the Kelly family life, and before each meal the children were always asked to say grace. To this day all the children remember their mother's homespun grace said before each meal.

Peggy: Bless us, Oh Lord, and these Thy gifts we are about to receive from Thy bounty through Christ our Lord.
Kell: Do unto others as you would have others do unto you.
Grace: Politeness is to do and say the kindest things in the kindest way.
Baby Lizanne: Amen.

The family food was always nourishing and wholesome, and the children were not allowed to leave the table until their plates were cleaned. They were constantly reminded of less fortunate children in the world—"the starving Indians, the poor little black children in the South and the millions of Chinese orphans."

20

Of the children Grace was the slowest and most fastidious eater. There were those awful red cabbage days which made her small face sad, and her mouth turn down. How she suffered! The family still remembers the night she refused to eat the horrible calves' liver, packed with its beastly minerals. She was in anguish as her mother made her sit for two hours at the dinner table as punishment.

Although the household always had domestic help, the girls were expected to keep their rooms tidy and make their own beds. If they failed to hang up their clothes, they were fined a nickel from their twenty-five-cent-a-week allowance.

All the children had their own jobs to do and the girls were trained to be proper housewives. There was nothing sentimental about this operation. It was merely that Mrs. Kelly had not found anything better to teach the same discipline and values that she was given as a child and which had been handed down from her German parentage.

During the long summer holidays the girls were taught to cook, sew, knit and crochet. While Peggy and Lizanne both loved to cook, Grace preferred knitting. However, she, too, enjoyed cooking, and one of her specialties, a good German dish, was curly cabbage and pork. She also knew the secret magic of how to make a white sauce "real creamy."

Those childhood habits persist today and in the library of the ocher fairy-tale palace at Monaco or at the family *mas* at Mount Agel on the hilltop in France, Princess Grace always has close at hand some knitting or embroidery which she is working on. Her greatest triumph has been an embroidered waistcoat for Prince Rainier with a romantic flower design made in colorful petit point. Princess Grace always maintained that she would "finish the vest in Heaven" when, in fact, it took her only two years. While the family is alone in Paris or at their weekend house, she often does the cooking. Her large collection of cookbooks dates back to those early days of her first flat in New York, and includes not only traditional French and American cuisine but Mexican, Chinese and Indian recipes.

The Kelly children's life was healthy and vigorous. Daydreaming and idleness were definitely not encouraged. Saturday was a family day when Margaret and Jack oversaw the physical development of their children. In the winter the whole family used to go to the Penn Athletic Club at Rittenhouse Square, where the senior Kellys were active members. The children would spend the morning taking swimming or other athletic instruction, which was followed by a luncheon treat. After this they usually went to the movies or a circus, if one was in town. Once the whole family was invited to have lunch with the performers in their tents. While they goggled at the sight of bearded ladies and midgets and bare-thighed trapeze artists, the least concerned seemed to be little Gracie. Later, when the family asked her if she wasn't impressed, she just shrugged her shoulders. "That's show business" is all she said.

Although she did not have the stamina of her more athletic sisters, Grace put on a brave face while keeping up with them.

During the summer months the whole family went to the Jersey coast where they had a summer home in Ocean City—and still have to this day. Ocean City, just below Atlantic City where the respectable Philadelphian families brought their children, is a great wide stretch of beach with a small footpath. The houses are sprawling, unpretentious and splendidly childproof, and the good-neighbor spirit flows from house to house.

To all the children at Ocean City Jack Kelly was a hero. Wasn't he the superman who brought the first surfboard back from Hawaii? As the waves in Ocean City were not so dashing as those in Hawaii, Jack would perch Peggy and Grace on the board and coax them to ride in on the surf.

"Baby, you sit right there and take whatever comes your way," he would say to little Grace. "There's nothing to be afraid of."

And because his children felt that their father was strong and totally reliable, he was able to instill in his children a complete freedom from fear which has remained with them throughout their lives. It is a kind of independence of spirit that only consistently loving and caring parents can transfer to their children.

There were also acrobatics on the beach with Jack swinging little Grace round and round, holding her firmly by the ankle and arm. Again, if she was afraid, she never showed it. She knew that her father would never let his child down, either physically or emotionally.

On family boat outings in Atlantic City, the Kelly clan often passed a nudist camp. Ma Kelly would have none of that nonsense, and used to order the children to the other side of the boat.

"And there we were on the other side of the boat . . . with binoculars," Grace Kelly recalled.

Early in their lives the Kelly sisters were made aware of the Women's Medical College. One of Mrs. Kelly's lifetime crusades, it was to be significant throughout their teenage years. Raising funds for Women's Medical was as normal to the Kelly children as Sunday mass at St. Bridget's Church. It was something they expected and accepted.

Peggy had her own personal schemes for raising funds. One of her favorites was to set up a flower stall at the front gate and inveigle passers-by to buy bunches of flowers.

"When we didn't have enough of our own, I would tell my little sister Gracie to go and steal the flowers next door. She was very clever at it and would secretly pick bunches of violets in the neighbors' gardens and sell them right back to them. I don't remember that we were ever found out once."

Grace was particularly good at selling, and few could resist her large innocent eyes and beguiling smile that lit up her whole face— much as it can do today when she is happy.

To this day people in Germantown talk of the time when the Kelly family put on a circus to raise funds for Women's Medical. Peggy was ten, Kell just eight, Grace six and Lizanne a toddler. The tennis court was transformed into a circus arena and neighbors like the Levys were "pressurized" into paying generously for the tickets.

"But we raised two hundred and fifty dollars and were extremely proud of Gracie that day," says Peggy.

Of course, everything was improvised and someone even made a movie of the day. Peggy was an authoritative, if somewhat bossy, circus master; Kell did a strong man act; but it was "little Gracie" in a white tu-tu who stole the show. She was the tightrope walker. It did not matter to anyone that in fact the "rope" was a line drawn on the ground. With all the aplomb of an Olga Korbut, she balanced her way along the rope, steadied, did a neat pirouette turn and tripped back.

The clapping was like music to her small ears.

When Grace was just eight years of age, she was taken with her friend Alice Waters to see the movie *Madam Curie*. The two small girls returned home in a daze of romanticism, and immediately decided to set up their own laboratory in Alice's basement. Carried away by the Curie saga, they transformed tables into laboratory benches, filled soda pop bottles with colored water and collected odd bits of junk that became make-believe laboratory equipment. Once their preparations were complete, the two girls lured a neighborhood boy, Rusty Koelle, down into the cellar.

"We are about to blow you up," Grace announced calmly as she fired a shot of soda water into a green concoction. A screaming Rusty escaped from his captors as the girls dissolved in giggles.

Friday afternoons after school were favorite times for Grace and Alice. They were allowed into the Waters' kitchen where they would take out the *Boston Cook Book*, looking for something to make. They would read and discuss all sorts of receipes but the cooking usually ended up to be plain, old-fashioned vinegar toffee.

The two girls were fast friends as only small girls can be. They hated to be parted and could spend hours just talking. At the time, Mr. Kelly was running for mayor of Philadelphia and Alice's father was also in politics, but both fathers had a tough time using the telephone in the evening. The girls just talked and talked.

When Grace was eight years old, her first romantic hero entered her life. He was Douglas Fairbanks, Jr., who had been invited to a party by her parents. Grace and Alice immediately fell in love with him and both girls blushed when he kissed them good-night.

Years later when she was a famous film star, Grace mentioned the story to a newspaper reporter who wrote about it. Friends of Douglas Fairbanks's sent it to him, and for years he carried the tattered snippet in his wallet until it fell into shreds. It was to be many years later before he finally met Princess Grace again, and she reminded him of her first kiss. He has since become a friend of both the Princess and Prince Rainier.

Another of Grace's friends at the Ravenhill Academy, a strict Philadelphia convent, was Dottie Langdon. Today she remembers Grace as "painfully shy and often withdrawn. She was always quiet-spoken, very feminine and sensitive to the point that she would cry at the drop of a hat.

"I don't mean that she was a crybaby. It was just that she felt things deeply. The Kellys had two huge boxers named Wrinkles and Siegfried. Once Siegfried was sick and had to be taken to the vet. When Grace described his sickness to her friends, she bawled like a baby."

As a schoolgirl Grace was above average, but not ve
math or the sciences. They were simply not in her line of
preferred English, story writing and creative games
French songs at parties in a small, sweet voice.

The Ravenhill girls were all taught to write in a squar
script which most of them never lost. Today Princess Grace
retained the same style of writing—elegant and feminine, with clean
bold outlines. Her note paper carries the royal cipher in aquamarine,
which has always been her favorite color.

Grace's older sister Peggy, a lovable extrovert with beguiling
Irish charm, was invariably the leader of the girls in the Kelly
backyard. It was Peggy who decided to rewrite *Cinderella* so that
she and her friend, Edie Godfrey, could play with relish the main
characters—the ugly sisters. Grace was given the role of Cinderella who, in Peggy's script, had nothing to do except sit and
look sad.

When Mr. Kelly asked Peggy, "I hear some of your school
chums are coming out. Do you want to come out, too?" she stormed
back, "I am out. Do you think I have to use those women who sell
mailing lists of boys' names to mothers and fathers of girls to get me
a date?" The result was that the question never came up for the other
girls, and thus Grace never had a coming-out party.

When she was twelve years of age, Grace was allowed to become
a "pink girl," a predecessor of the candystriper, which was considered a very special privilege for a young girl at that time. It meant
that she was a wartime hospital volunteer and could carry food trays
to patients in the hospital, thus relieving the more senior staff.

Grace loved her hours of duty, not so much because of the work
itself, but because it gave her an outlet for her sense of theater. On
one occasion she was asked to take a meal to a man whose eyes were
bandaged following an operation. Grace was enthralled, and not
only offered to feed the patient, but to brighten his life.

"You are now tasting rare green turtle soup imported directly
from the king's palace in Barcelona," she told the bewildered
patient as she spooned out the thin, watery soup. The grisly chop
became venison from the king's private park; and when she came to
dessert, she was at her best.

25

"And now," she exclaimed in a breathless voice, "two waiters are lighting the brandy on your crêpes suzette. My, how the flame burns! Can't you smell it? Now they are putting them on your plate from a gleaming silver dish. Gee, it smells divine."

Thus, tapioca pudding became a dish fit for a king, and a war veteran gave his heart to the small voice at his side.

Four

It was in 1947, when she was just seventeen years old, that Grace Kelly made her first trip to Europe. In the previous year Kell had, been in London with his father and had gained a second in the Diamond Skulls. This year Mrs. Kelly, with Grace and Lizanne, went along with Kell and Mr. Kelly. The girls had many new dresses for the trip—eight of which Mrs. Kelly had made herself—and accompanying saucy straw hats. Mrs. Kelly's stylish millinery could compete with any other hats at Henley that year.

Grace, with her pretty feminine looks, was like maple syrup to the contingent of boys from the Kent School of Connecticut and the Tabor Academy of New England.

"They pursued her with some vigor as Lizzie was a little too young," recalls Kell.

The family stayed at The Red Lion Hotel in Henley which today boasts a plaque: "Grace Kelly slept here." With their exuberant good looks the Kellys were the most attractive family at Henley—a Norman Rockwell cover from the *Saturday Evening Post* come to life.

In their luggage was a supply of meat, as Britain was still on rationing. Mr. Kelly was so concerned for Kell's health that he even brought bottled water over in case the London water would upset his son. Pictures appeared in the British newspapers of Kell and his sister with this modest supply of food. Like Jack Kramer, who had done exactly the same the year before while he was training for Wimbledon, the Kellys were consequently in for some unfavorable publicity about the meat.

"The only reason we did it was because we had heard that there was such a shortage of meat and we did not want to worsen the shortage,'' Kell remembers.

For middle-aged Jack Kelly, Kell's winning the Diamond Skulls brought more than paternal pride. It was a vindication of his own humiliation suffered when the Henley Stewards had rejected his entry into the Diamond Skulls twenty-seven years earlier. Twice national champion of America, he had been advised by Russell Johnson, secretary of the American Rowing Association, that the rules were changed in England and his entry would be honored. He stepped up his training and was all set to go to England when he received a cable from the Henley Stewards rejecting his entry.

In Jack Kelly's own words to his mother: ''They won't let a man who has worked with his hands row against their *gentlemen.* They claim that a fellow who works with his muscles has an unfair advantage over an aristocrat.''

Even though he evened up the score some time later by beating the English Diamond Skulls champion at the Olympic Games, he never completely forgot the Henley snub. With his liberal way of thinking it was a difficult thing to dismiss. ''Sport is a great leveler,'' he always said. But this did not seem to be the case in his first acquaintance with the rigidity of the English establishment.

The Kelly family had been brought up on the Henley disaster, and if they appeared more united than ever on the Diamond Skull day, there was certainly justification. John B. Kelly was fond of passing along to his children Grandmother Kelly's wisdom. That day he told Kell: ''A licking is not a failure. You are never done unless you let yourself stay licked.''

Mr. Kelly related his thoughts of that day to a British reporter:

''It's something like 'Sorel and Son,' an old story, but true,'' said Jack gravely. ''When it finally came to me today, there weren't any words that could do justice to my feelings, and there aren't any now. Now that it is all here I feel a tremendous feeling of pride for Kell. He's the one that matters, not the thwarted ambition of an old guy who once got his fingers publicly slapped over here because he was born without a silver spoon in his mouth.''

The irony of the situation was that among young Kell's titles was also Pennsylvania State Apprentice Bricklaying Champion.

Only the change of the absurdly archaic rules at Henley made Kell's win possible. The family was elated, and among the first to congratulate Kell was his sister, Grace, who had followed the race from the towpath.

Following the race, Mrs. Kelly took the girls on a holiday to Switzerland. It was to be a kind of compensation for Grace, who felt she had let the family down when she failed the Bennington entrance examination because of her poor math.

While Mrs. Kelly, Grace and Lizanne toured Europe, hundreds jammed the dockside of New York to greet Mr. Kelly and his son, holding the Diamond Cup chalice, upon their triumphant return to the United States.

Five

Grace Kelly made her first amateur stage debut when she was twelve years of age. It was at the Old Academy Players in East Falls where she had been given one of the lead roles in *Don't Feed the Animals*. The whole family was excited as they filed into their places in the front row. Jack Kelly's shining head was seen towering proudly above the audience, but Mrs. Kelly, outwardly so cool and confident, was inwardly nervous as a cat for Grace.

In the middle of the performance Grace's stage-mother muffed her lines. The whole Kelly family stiffened as they watched Grace, with characteristic coolness, drop her handbag, turn her back to the audience and give her stage-mother her lines while she stooped to pick up the bag. It was the kind of instinctive stage presence and quickness of mind that only a very experienced performer possesses.

Quick to spot what had happened, Jack Kelly turned to his wife and said, "We've got a trouper on our hands."

The director of the play, Ruth Emmert, was not surprised. All through rehearsals she had watched the tall girl and noted her poise. In fact, she had thought that Grace was fourteen and was amazed when she learned her real age. Grace swore her to secrecy in case her youth might prevent her from getting the more mature roles in other productions. Her attention and complete absorption were also amazing in one so young. She was never late for rehearsals, and could be relied upon to raid her mother's wardrobe and even furniture in her zeal for props if she felt she could help in this way.

After one of her opening nights a leading critic in Philadelphia wrote next day, "Grace Kelly, John B's pretty daughter, made her

30

pro stage debut last night in Uncle George Kelly's comedy hit *The Torch Bearers*. For a young lady whose previous experience was slim, Miss Kelly came through this footlight baptism of fire splendidly. Although father and mother beamed at Grace from the front row and other friends were scattered through the house, it was largely a theatrical crowd this girl faced on her break-in. From where I sat it appeared as if Grace Kelly should become the theatrical torchbearer for her family.''

Actually Grace Kelly made her stage debut—although it turned out to be a very short run—some months earlier. She had been chosen to act in *The Women*, and no one in the entire cast had worked harder than "the little Kelly girl," as she was called. Two days after the play opened, Grace appeared at the dinner table flushed and with small red spots sprinkled all over her face.

Mrs. Kelly took one look and asked, "Gracie, what are those spots on your face?"

"Nothing, Mother, they are nothing," Grace protested, trying to hide her face from the light.

But, being the experienced mother that she was, Mrs. Kelly took another look and announced firmly, "Off to bed young lady. You've got the measles."

Turning to her eldest daughter, Mrs. Kelly said in her matter of fact voice: "Now Peggy, you've got to take over Grace's part."

There was no use remonstrating. Tears were of no avail. When Ma Kelly said something she meant it, and off to bed went Grace to have her measles in sheer misery while Peggy took over the script.

Word perfect, Peggy played Grace's role, while the real heroine languished crossly in bed.

Because of her height and her totally feminine approach to life as compared to that of her tomboy sisters, Grace Kelly, at twelve years of age, had begun to take notice of her looks. It was part of the natural growing-up process in such a sensitive and introspective girl. She spent hours on the garden swing pushing her legs down and swinging with force. When her schoolgirl friends asked why, she explained pertinently, "If you swing a lot, it'll make your legs pretty."

Fortunately the swinging left her with elegantly tapered legs and not with the bulging muscles which could have resulted. When she sat she was also careful not to cross her legs. "It makes your calves look fat" was her matter-of-fact explanation.

During my stay in Hollywood I talked to the directors and photographers who had worked with her, and they all told me that it was uncanny how Grace Kelly knew just what to do with her body. She was never known to be ungainly and always knew exactly how to place her legs and feet.

Besides teaching her children athletics and swimming, Mrs. Kelly—who had taught everything from athletics to dancing at the University of Pennsylvania before her marriage—was determined that her girls should have well-coordinated bodies. Ever since she was tiny, Grace had attended ballet classes and was far above average. Had she not grown so tall it is very possible that she would have made ballet her career instead of acting. The fantasia of the ballet world totally captivated her.

Unlike the rest of the family, Grace took no particular interest in competitive sports. She played them because it was part of the family's daily life, but showed no burning zeal like the rest of the children. At school she played hockey and basketball; at summer camp, swimming and tennis. As an active member of the Girl Guides, she worked hard and enjoyed collecting the various badges of achievement. During the war when metal was short, the Guides of East Falls made a door-to-door collection for coat hangers. Grace collected more than anybody. Whatever she chose to do as a child she did well, which runs true to her character today. She has a totally professional approach to everything whether it is making dried flower collages as gifts for her friends or organizing a Red Cross fête.

Just as the game of Consequences had been the fashion in Margaret Kelly's youth, the "Slam Book" featured highly in Grace Kelly's crowd. She was just thirteen at the time when Jack Oechsle, one of Kell's friends, made out a questionnaire which he called the "Slam Book." It was sealed and not opened until ten years later. Grace's entry read:

Favorite sport, swimming; favorite actor, Alan Ladd; favorite actress, Ingrid Bergman; favorite color, purple; favorite comedian, Bob Hope; favorite pet hate, school. To the question "Do you want to be married?" she had written a firm "yes."

At thirteen, when the metamorphosis usually occurs in girls, they begin to take on their final shape as women, and Grace was no exception. She had the basis of all the traits that have carried her through her successful life. She also showed a glimmer of beauty—shining, healthy good looks that begin with superb bone structure and end with an inner light—the misnomer for which has often been "sex appeal."

As Peggy says, "She never went through a gawky stage. Not too tall, nice and thin, no skin problems. She went from Girl Scout to belle of the ball without us noticing it, in her sweet and quiet way. She had a million beaux."

She had already begun to be aware of her limitations and her achievements, and suddenly she found that boys liked her.

They liked her for many reasons: the romantic, corn-colored silky hair; the shy smile (punctuated with dimples at each end of the mouth which are still there today) that occasionally broke into a generous grin; the peaches-and-cream skin; and the willowy body which, though on the skinny side, looked great in the flared-skirted swimsuits of the time. There was also that enigmatic quality of self-preservation that was to take her unscathed through the Hollywood jungle.

But mostly they liked her because she could listen. As Howard Wikoff explains, "Gracie had a pleasing way about her. She didn't talk too much, just listened. Instead of showing off and chattering all about herself like most teenagers, she was attentive to her dates. She made each escort think he was King Bee. And you know, some girls never learn that."

She was popular because she made her date feel comfortable and a little bit like a hero. As Jack Oechsle explained, "If you wanted to sit, she'd sit; if you wanted to dance, she'd dance. And if you took her to a party she wouldn't float off with another fellow. She was your date and she remained your date."

Even then Grace Kelly loved to dance barefoot. Whenever the Mills Brothers came on the Gramophone with their "Paper Moon," Grace was off, living in a dream world of her own.

One of her first dates was with a boy named Harper Davis, a friend of her brother Kell. Both boys went to the exclusive William Penn Charter School; and when Harper confided to Kell that he did not have a girl to take to the school dance, young Kelly suggested sister Grace. Peggy was a few years too old, and Lizanne far too young.

At first Mrs. Kelly hesitated. Grace was still young and vulner-

33

able. Was she too young to begin the complicated business of dating with all its ramifications? Ma Kelly discussed it with her husband, who laconically answered, "Well, she has to start sometime. And she couldn't have a nicer boy." Mrs. Kelly agreed.

On the Friday of the dance, Grace kept within ear distance of the front door. When the bell finally rang, she dashed to the door to receive a box of orchids—her first corsage.

"Flowers for me? What a bore!" is how the family remembers this momentous occasion. But once the door was shut she rushed the box to the refrigerator. It was to be the beginning of a long line of corsages which, after each dance, she placed in a cellophane envelope between the pages of an encyclopedia. Each one was then pasted into an album and carefully labeled with the giver's name and the event. The albums still exist today.

This was that once-upon-a-time era when school dances still had a quixotic air about them. Grace was clad in a sensible coat over her first long party dress when Harper Davis, handsome as a window display mannequin in his first dinner jacket, called to collect her. It could have been a scene straight from any of those pleasant, naïve family films that Hollywood was making at the time. It had the same quality of decency and prettiness about it.

Mrs. Kelly was waiting up when Grace finally came home and burst into the room positively glowing.

"Oh, Mother, I had a wonderful time."

But within a few months, at just nineteen years of age, Harper Davis contracted multiple sclerosis. He died when he was twenty-six. His death left a searing impression upon Grace. It was her first real contact with death—of someone her own age and from her own world. She was desolate.

This was also the time of writing poetry. Locked away from the boisterous Kelly world, Grace was enclosed within her own remote thoughts. They were fresh, charming verses—"some serious, some little gooney ones"—and they also had an unexpected impishness which punctuates much of her conversation among friends today. This one was written when she was fourteen years old:

> *I hate to see the sun go down*
> *And squeeze itself into the ground,*
> *Since some warm night it might get stuck*
> *And in the morning not get up.*

Grace's parents had hoped that she would continue her education at Bennington College. They passionately wanted their children to have every possible advantage that education could provide. Jack Kelly himself had had very little formal education, leaving school in his early teens to work, first as a water boy and later as a bricklayer's apprentice in his older brother's business.

"It was a tough time to get a place in college as there were so many GIs wanting to enroll. Also Grace wasn't up to par because of her arithmetic," Mrs. Kelly truthfully recalls.

No one was less disappointed than Grace. In her own indomitable way, she had decided that the only further schooling that she wanted was at the American Academy of Dramatic Arts in New York.

Hints had been dropped all around the family so that when Grace finally approached her father it came as no surprise. Mr. Kelly listened patiently and explained that it was a dangerous profession, even if one was ever lucky enough to reach the top.

"You can't be halfway about it," he said. "While others play you will have to be getting your rest so that you will look nice the next day. And once you have reached the top, you will become public property. There will be no privacy. The public will make demands on you. Are you ready to pay the price?" These were words that Grace Kelly has never forgotten.

Grace set off for the audition at the Academy in New York with stars in her eyes. If she was nervous, none of the family was aware of it. Just as today she kept her emotions tightly locked inside.

In handwriting that has blurred with time, her first appearance at the Academy (which was then housed in Carnegie Hall) is recorded in the audition book for 1947. It gives her name "Grace Patricia Kelly" and her address as "Philadelphia." She weight 126 pounds, stood 5 feet 6½ inches tall in her stocking feet, and her proportions were recorded as "good." The information then jumps to her nationality, "American Irish," and her general education, "Stevens School."

Grace played a scene from her initial success *The Torch Bearers* and also a few lines of Portia from *The Merchant of Venice*. Mr. Distell, her auditioner, noted after her name:

Voice: Not placed
Temperament: Sensitive
Spontaneity: Good youthfulness

Dramatic instinct: Expressive
Intelligence: Good
General remarks: Good, promising, youthful.

Grace Kelly was accepted and enrolled in every class for which she was eligible, including fencing. Years later when she was to make the film *The Swan*, she requested that Sandor Nage, her fencing master from the Academy, go to Hollywood to steer her through the fencing scenes. There was no need for a stand-in and the scenes were stylishly executed.

The Academy gives no academic training of any kind. It is purely a school for actors. One boast of the Academy today is that Charles Jehlinger, who was its director for over fifty years, taught the Stanislavsky method before Stanislavsky did.

Among the list of distinguished actors who have been trained at the Academy are Spencer Tracy, Robert Redford, David Hartman and John Cassavetes.

Shy Grace found the improvisation classes a strain at first. Being straight from a girls' school, she found it slightly odd to take part in classes emphasizing freedom of the body and she frequently blushed. Recalling it years later, she was to say:

"We would be assigned to go to the Bowery and observe a drunk and then come back and act out a drunk. One of the oddest assignments we had was to go to the zoo and watch a llama. I never quite figured out why because very few of us have ever been called on to play the part of a llama. But I am sure it must have been helpful if the school thought so."

It was the Academy, too, which cured Miss Kelly of her poor posture. "I was a sway-back," she confessed many years later. "When I was lying as flat as I could, this teacher used to get down on the floor and say, 'I can see air.' This meant that I'd have to try and lie even flatter."

The teacher's methods must have been effective because her carriage is one of the most arresting things about Princess Grace today. She not only stands straight and tall, but she stands without a hint of a sway-back.

The Academy was beneficial in other ways, especially for a girl as private as Grace Kelly. She began to slowly shed her inhibitions and enjoy more of life, as a flower enjoys spring sunshine.

In the entrance hall of the Academy, now housed in a handsome red brick house designed by Stanford White, hang pictures of the Academy's most illustrious students. Among them is one of Grace Kelly at her first rehearsal. The same photo appears in the school's brochure with the words, "I am very grateful for the two years I spent at the American Academy and the knowledge I gained there as an actor and a person. Grace de Monaco."

It is doubtful whether the blue-jeaned students of today ever bother to look at her photo, but ex-actress Frances Fuller, the present director, is extremely proud of this former pupil.

"Grace was always shy. She was almost humble. I am wondering if that part of her shyness might have been the aura of her Uncle George. The fact that he was someone that she looked up to and respected so. She was desperately determined to succeed, too. We once found her rehearsing nonstop for eighteen hours."

It was Frances Fuller who finally suggested to her husband, Worthington Myler, that Grace Kelly was ready for professional work.

"I was handing on a lot of young talent to him as he was producing and directing in television and had several shows. One of the best known was called *Studio One* and I worked with him a lot on the scripts. He had asked my opinion about a part and as I had not spotted anyone else I thought was right, I asked him to see Grace.

"I had an intuition even then that she would go a long way. I instinctively sensed ability and the perseverance necessary to make a good actress. Grace was not just a pretty face.

"I had the same reaction about Anne Bancroft and I recommended her to my husband. I stood in the back of the theater and watched her all alone—rehearsing—and the intensity of her concentration hit me. Grace had the same dedication and spiritual toughness even then.

"It was my husband who tutored Grace in her first stage kiss. She had to be told how to kiss, she was so shy. She stood too far away and he had to teach her to lean forward. But she was lovely in the role."

Frances Fuller follows all her girls through their professional life and had this to say about Grace Kelly.

"Didn't you feel that her development was extraordinary through the years? But not due to any particular effort on her part. She worked at what she was asked to do and did it well and the rest of it was her good breeding and considered restraint within herself. It

37

wasn't until *The Country Girl* that you really began to see the accumulation of her learning and maturity. I thought she was tremendous in it.

"Mr. Jehlinger used to say, 'Give me ten percent talent and ninety percent ambition and I'll go with it.' In her quiet way Grace obviously had a great deal of determination, and with enormous dignity set about building up what was to be her strength.

"Grace has always had an air of mystery about her and probably still has to this day. She holds back all the time."

During Grace's graduation party at the Academy, John Cassavetes—himself then a fledgling actor and a year behind Grace—overheard someone comment, "That Grace Kelly is such a pretty little thing. Isn't it a shame she's too shy ever to amount to anything?"

Six

Twenty-five years ago, there was only one proper place for a young girl to live alone in New York. For thousands of parents throughout America, the Barbizon Hotel for Women at Sixty-third Street and Lexington Avenue—"the silk stocking district," as this fashionable locale was called—was a fortress against the perils of that wicked city. It was not only a home-away-from-home, untouched by scandal, but no men were allowed into the private section. If a girl was ill and needed a doctor, he had to practically produce his medical certificate before being admitted to her bedroom. A stethoscope hanging out of a young man's pocket was the oldest gag known at the Barbizon and never got him past the elevator door.

It was to this bastion of virtue that Mrs. Kelly sent her daughter during the period of Grace's study at the Academy of Dramatic Arts. The Barbizon, a tawny twenty-two-story brick building, was built in 1928 and is still "home" to seven hundred women. In the days when Grace Kelly lived there, every girl had to produce three character references before she was accepted and the waiting list was a hundred names long.

Today the Barbizon is like a dowager duchess who has spilt the soup on her bosom. It is skimped, shabby, unloved. The once elegant duck-egg blue foyer where girls in swirling New Look dresses met their beaux is now bustling with an army of blue-jeaned girls with bossy, liberated buttons.

The Barbizon has always been owned and operated by men, and in the forties was managed by Hugh J. Connor, a cherubic man who learned the complicated art of hotel management at New York's Roosevelt and the Waldorf-Astoria hotels. At the Barbizon he was as cozily concerned about his girls as an uncle is about a favorite visiting niece. When they were sick he personally sent flowers, and if a girl ran short of cash he acted as an unofficial paymaster until her next check arrived. Broken hearts were often mended in his small office behind the reception desk where he handed out advice like petit fours on a silver platter.

The Barbizon had style in those days and every afternoon waitresses in black, with starched white aprons, served tea in the lounge where the girls were allowed to bring their dates if they had been issued special passes. There was a sun deck, gymnasium, swimming pool and a library of three thousand books as well as beauty, dress and book shops. It was a complete woman's world.

No one profited more from this camaraderie of the campus atmosphere than Grace Kelly. It was her first time away from the family and her first taste of carefully controlled freedom. For a while she shared a suite with Jean Drouillard and Bettina Thompson, who also attended the American Academy of Dramatic Arts. The following year she roomed with Prudence ("Prudy") Wise, who later became her secretary. In her last year, when her modeling fees jumped from $7.50 to $25 an hour, she had a single room and bath. But so unobtrusive were her two years there that when I stayed there last year, no one could remember what rooms she had lived in. I saw the shoebox-sized, chintzy rooms where Dorothy McGuire, Barbara Bel Geddes, Gene Tierney and Cathy O'Donnell had lived, but no one could remember which had been Grace Kelly's. Nor do any of the present veterans, who have lived at the club for the last thirty-five years, even remember her attending a "clothes auction"—a custom that when a girl left to get married, she sold her wardrobe to the highest bidders. As many of the girls were models and had to have an extensive wardrobe, clothes swapping was another common occurrence. Grace Kelly never participated in either of these activities.

Many of the girls came from rich, protective backgrounds like Grace's, but others had a hard time struggling along on student grants or meager allowances from their parents. "Money Talks" were another craze when girls would gather in a bedroom, sprawled over the bed and furniture, to gnaw pencils and make elaborate financial calculations which were never, of course, put into practice.

They were charming, beguiling grown-up children. Drugs and

drink had no part in their lives. Mr. Connor's safe was filled with such forbidden fire hazards as curling irons, electric kettles and electric rings that the girls had smuggled in to use in their rooms for late night snacks and hot chocolate.

"Grace kept a great deal to herself. We always thought that she was very shy," Mr. Connor remembers today. "I used to see her in the dining room most nights sitting alone with her glasses on and reading a book through her dinner."

When *Collier's* sent a photographer and writer to do a feature on the hotel, the girls all dressed up in party dresses and invited their young men to be included in the pictures. In one photograph, looking down from the mezzanine floor over the wedding cake balustrade—quite alone—was an exceptionally pretty girl. Her name was Grace Kelly.

During those days at the Academy, classes were split up into mornings, afternoons and evenings. With plenty of time to spare between her classes, it was the most natural thing that Grace Kelly should drift into modeling to earn some extra money. She was quite determined to pay her own way instead of being dependent upon her parents. Besides, she had the looks, the figure and the Barbizon certainly offered a conducive ambiance, with the many models who lived there. It was fun, and perhaps self-consciously it was a challenge to have to step out into real life. Once she began modeling, she enjoyed making her own money and was clever at saving it, which is still true today. She would have succeeded no matter what career she chose in life, because Grace Kelly from early in her childhood understood that hoary axiom, "A girl's best friend is money in the bank."

Of her modeling career she was quoted as saying years later in an interview in *Newsweek,* "The money was very nice and that's what makes it all worth while."

Grace also did television commercials for everything from Electrolux vacuum cleaners to "the skin a fellow loves to touch." About this phase in her career she was later to crack, "I was terrible. Honestly, anyone watching me give the pitch for Old Golds would have switched to Camels."

While the other girls spent their money on frilly "New Look" petticoats and fashionable ankle-strap shoes, Grace Kelly chose the kind of clothes that were to become almost a uniform for her, and even today remain her favorite way of dressing. She wore skirts and

41

sweaters of Botany wool (which became cashmere as her finances improved), sensible walking shoes, and no hat.

After her marriage Prince Rainier pointed out to her that she would have to wear a hat on formal occasions now that she was a royal princess. She chooses simple knitted hats in winter and plain straw in summer, but mostly her hair continues to shine in the sun and wind.

Everything about Grace Kelly, now Princess Grace of Monaco, exudes fastidiousness. In those Barbizon days there was always a look of freshness about her—the American-finishing-school, ladylike look. From schooldays onward she wore white cotton gloves, which were to become her trademark when later she went to Hollywood.

At the photographic studios with her soft, natural hairstyle, prim glasses and neat clothes, Grace Kelly looked more like an efficient secretary than a model. Once behind the cameras, however, it was a different situation. She bloomed. She knew exactly what to do with her face and became known as "the girl with a hundred faces."

While the photographers enjoyed her perfect white teeth and flawless complexion, which never needed retouching in close-up color shots, art directors of the leading magazines loved her wide-eyed, wholesome looks. She typified everything that was healthy and American. Doris Day and Grace Kelly have probably done more for publicizing clean, American womanhood than any other film stars. *Redbook, True Romance, True Story* and *Cosmopolitan* all used Grace Kelly's face week after week . . . smiling, radiating, glowing—the all-American image.

Whenever she could, Grace went to the theater. She preferred its intimacy to the movies, and it is probable that she both absorbed and inherited this interest from her two uncles, George and Walter Kelly.

During her second year at the Academy, she invited one of her acting friends home for a weekend. It was a risky thing to do in a family of teasers, but he meant enough to her at the time for her to brave a family ribbing.

Mrs. Kelly took one look at the effete young man at her daughter's side, and decided to ask Kell to do her a favor.

Recalling the story recently as we had breakfast together in his luxurious penthouse in Philadelphia, he told me:

"She [Mrs. Kelly] asked me to bring over on Friday night three of my bigger and better-looking friends. One was the Olympic Butterfly champion and looked a bit like Kirk Douglas, another was a big-looking guy, a weight-lifting type, who was my partner in rowing races and was also a life guard at Ocean City. There was another chap who was also a big, tall, swimming type.

"I gave them the word that this fellow was a bit of a creep, which I had deduced from my mother's description. When they came into the room, they gave Grace's guy the grip and in a second had him on the floor.

"My sister was so mad at me for bringing these animals home and embarrassing her that she was quiet for a month. At the time she was commuting to New York every day, leaving by the 7 A.M. train and returning about 7 P.M. I had rowing practice every evening and would just be getting in when she returned so we sat down together to have our dinner alone. For a month we ate in silence with a very occasional 'yes' or 'no' to any question I asked her. It took a long time before she forgave the rest of the family, too."

In her youth Grace was never as close to her athletic brother as were her sisters. They simply had different ideas about life and its values. Kell also had the unnerving habit of disapproving of the more aesthetic type of boyfriends that she continued to bring home.

Throughout her life Grace Kelly has developed a round, if somewhat fastidious, taste in her friends. In men she likes intellectuals and creative thinkers—directors, writers, designers, musicians, artists, actors, politicians.

"I considered one of these actor guys she brought home as a wee bit effeminate and not my type," Kell explained. "At a family dinner we had one Saturday night at the Philadelphia Club, my parents asked me to join them. I explained that I had a date and they said, 'Bring your girl along,' which I did. She was a former beauty queen and had an outstanding figure, to say the least, and liked to show it. She also wore a lot of make-up, which none of my family did.

"She was about two years older than I was, had been divorced and had a six-year-old child, which, of course, my parents were not aware of. Nevertheless I walked her straight through this crowded dining room at the Country Club and every man snapped his head around. As I arrived at our family table my father and Peggy's husband gave me the eye and looked approvingly. All the women in the family scowled and sulked.

"Next day when we were going to St. Bridget's Church on Sunday as usual, Grace got on my back. 'You insulted your mother by bringing that woman to the club,' she said.

" 'All I can say,' I replied, 'is that every man in the room thought she was great, which is more than could be said of your escort.'

"We had quite an argument about that particular incident.

"Don't let Grace's frosty beauty fool you," Kell told me. "She can be physically tough, too. I remember one of my Marine friends showed Grace some ju-jitsu holds. She was pretty quick learning them. Once, years later, she went up to a photographer, Howell Conant, a friend of hers, put her arm round his neck and before he could say a word had tossed him on his back. That was our Gracie for you.

"I would say that we [Kell and Grace] have been closer, almost, in recent years than we were when we were young. I can't say that any one of my sisters was particularly closer than another to me, but because of some personal problems I think my sister Grace has been a little more understanding of my situation."

As I've see and heard again and again, compassion and loyalty have always been an integral part of Princess Grace's character.

Seven

After two years away from the enveloping aura of the Kelly clan, Grace was even more convinced of what she wanted to do. It was not that she did not enjoy the family enclave, but she found at times it could be smothering. There was also a world outside of Philadelphia where she knew instinctively that she belonged.

From modeling she was soon making $400.00 a month at the rate of $25.00 an hour, which was enough in those days to keep any girl happy. Even in the prime of her career as top cover girl in 1919, Mrs. Kelly had never earned more than $5.00 an hour. Grace also did fashion shorts for newsreels which took her to Paris and Bermuda, and were highly profitable. During her second year of work she refused any financial help from her family and paid her own way. Like her Uncle George, she was wildly independent about money matters and still is.

Later in life Grace was to say that she made as much money in modeling as in pictures. This may be true simply because, unlike the big stars of today—Elizabeth Taylor, Barbra Streisand, Marlon Brando—she had never been given a cut on the profits from the highly successful films she made.

Photographer Ruzzie Green remembers her at that time as ''what we called 'nice, clean stuff' in our business. She was not a top model and never would be. She was the girl next door. No glamor, no oomph, no cheesecake. She had lovely shoulders but no chest. Grace was like Bergman in the 'clean way.' She could do the mush stuff in movies like *Rear Window* and get away with it.''

Others remember her at this period as ''terribly ladylike—almost sedate—with her tweed suits, sensible shoes and white gloves.''

When Grace finished her two-year course at the Academy, she was ready to test her acting wings. Each year two students from the Academy were chosen by Theron Bamberger to appear at his Bucks County Playhouse in New Hope, Pennsylvania. In the spring of 1949 Grace Kelly was chosen, and as a coincidence it was Uncle George Kelly's hilarious comedy *The Torch Bearers* in which she was to play.

Such is the fragmentation of time that when I visited the picturesque Bucks County Playhouse last year, no one clearly remembered Grace Kelly. There were those who recalled "the pretty girl who taught one of the stagehands to swim" and others who recollected "a charming shy girl who cried a lot." Her performance there was not a sensation, but neither was it a disaster.

Back in New York Grace made the rounds of the casting offices. She read for thirty-eight parts, including the role of the ingenue in *The Country Girl*, which was later cut from the movie script. She read for almost everything that was being cast. Remembering this period she said later, "People were confused about my type but they agreed on one thing. I was in the 'too' category—'too' tall, 'too' leggy, 'too'. chinny."

When I discussed this recently with Frances Fuller of the American Academy, she was not incredulous. "I can quite believe that. Grace was just one of a number of girls trying to break into the theater or television. The difference between her and many others is that she never gave up. She went for interview after interview, always arriving on time, impeccably turned out. Of course she must have been disappointed time after time, but she never let it make her bitter. She just plugged on."

Grace Kelly was lucky in that unlike other girls she knew she could pay her rent. There was even money for daily ballet lessons and voice production at the New School, under its director Sanford Meisner.

It was during the period when she was taking lessons with Sanford Meisner at the Neighborhood Playhouse that the New York office of Fox Studios telephoned her agent and asked if she could meet the director Gregory Ratoff immediately. This volatile Hungarian was then an impressive name in Hollywood and did not like to be kept waiting.

Grace was in her usual working uniform—a shirt and skirt with flat shoes—but she hurried directly over. Years later she was to describe the incident in the *Saturday Evening Post*.

"All the other girls looked cute and sweet in high heels. I looked so terrible, my agent was embarrassed. But when Mr. Ratoff saw me, he said, 'Perfect.' This was a switch. My whole life people had been telling me I was imperfect.

" 'What I like about this girl is that she is not pretty,' Mr. Ratoff said. My agent insisted, 'But Mr. Ratoff, she is pretty.' Mr. Ratoff would not be talked out of it. 'No, no, no, she is not,' he said . . . 'Take off your coat.'

"When I took it off and he saw my old skirt and shirt he was in ecstasy. 'Magnificent,' he said. 'Cannot you spik with the Irish accent?' "

Although she had never spoken with an Irish accent she replied, "Yes, I will try." She then went home and worked on it conscientiously. She did, in fact, test for the film which was to be called *Taxi*, but the producer did not like her.

It was quite evident that Gregory Ratoff definitely wanted Grace Kelly for the part of the Irish immigrant girl. Just as Alfred Hitchcock later, he obviously perceived the untouched sensual potential behind the sugar-icing looks. His producer, however, thought differently. Grace Kelly lost the part to Constance Smith, who on the surface, with her blue-black hair and Celtic eyes, probably looked the part better and may have handled the accent more naturally. In those early days an accent did not come easily to Grace Kelly's finishing school voice.

Years later this same test was seen by John Ford, who was looking for a quiet English lady type for his new film, *Mogambo*. The shirt and skirt and her English style got her the part that was to be a milestone in her life—in every way.

There were also the exciting times when work came in a rush and within a fortnight she played such diverse roles as a schoolgirl and the saucy music-hall singer in black mesh stockings in *Lights Out*.

Her theater break finally came when she was asked to read for the grim daughter's part in Strindberg's *The Father*.

It was a Wednesday evening, November 16, 1949, at the Cort Theatre when Grace Kelly made her Broadway debut.

Also in the cast of *The Father* were two distinguished performers, Raymond Massey and the late Mady Christians, whose work

Grace Kelly admired. She was later to say that she got the part only because both Massey and Christians were tall, and flat shoes suited her role. She revered their professionalism and spent many hours in Mady Christians's dressing room listening and learning while the older woman talked. The two veteran performers in turn enjoyed Grace's fresh and unspoiled good manners, so rare in the acting profession.

As was the Broadway custom in those days, after the opening night performance of *The Father* there was a cast party. Grace brought along her parents, who were distinguishable from the guests by their debonair looks. On seeing them, Raymond Massey was intrigued. Why was his old friend from rowing days, Jack Kelly, there? He went over to greet him and was astonished to learn that Grace was his daughter.

She had told no one in the cast about her parents or background. This is a classic example of the very private person that Grace Kelly is. Today she is still tremendously reticent about her family life.

Even though the show soon closed, Grace Kelly felt that as a budding actress she had now outgrown the Barbizon. She wanted her own place where she could invite the small circle of friends whom she had by now collected. She moved into a smart, two-room apartment, number 9A, in Manhattan House at Sixty-sixth Street and Third Avenue—a shiny, white house for which "Kelly for Bricks" had supplied the building material.

Intensely feminine about the atmosphere in which she relaxes—it can best be described as organized chaos—she moved all her girlhood treasures from Philadelphia to the new apartment, and "Kelly's place" was created. On a gleeful shopping spree she not only bought everything for the kitchen but, like most women, created her own individual and pretty bathroom. She chose shocking-pink towels with a deep pile and had them embroidered with her own monogram—GPK. At that time when a bachelor girl purchased her own initialed towels it was a sign that her bank account was in a healthy state and that she had arrived.

To complete her apartment Grace acquired a parakeet she named Henry, who could not easily be farmed out to friends when she went to the Coast to make a picture. On one such occasion John Foreman moved in with his cat to keep Henry company. When he heard that Mrs. Kelly was calling at the apartment, he popped the cat into a cupboard. But Ma Kelly was not to be fooled. The moment she entered the door she sniffed and remarked, "There is a cat in this place."

She walked from room to room, but fortunately did not open any cupboards. When she left, John and the cat resumed their carefree, chaotic, bachelor existence.

Friends who went to Grace's apartment at that time remember the large, circular table of ebony Formica which operated on a spiral and served as both a coffee table and a dining table. No one seems to especially remember her cooking, but it was probably the beginning of her boeuf stroganoff days.

Word games became a favorite at Kelly's place. One, especially, was a game devised by Alfred Hitchcock for Lizabeth Scott. The idea was to drop the first letter of a name—Ickey Rooney, Reer Garson, Rank Sinatra, Ary Grant, Ing Crosby, Ette Davis, Orgie Raft—and see what you get!

It was also at this time in her life that she took up photography. Everyone and everything was photographed. She was so delighted with this new interest that she even developed her own negatives, sloshing around in a dark bathroom.

(Though Prince Rainier was originally the family photographer, he has been replaced by Princess Grace, who has recorded every age and every nuance of their children's lives.)

This was a bubbling time in New York. Everyone was young and hopeful. The theater was thriving and television was the exciting new medium. There was a constant party atmosphere in those days, and Grace Kelly, actress and potential film star, was very much a part of it. Most of her friends were less well-off than she, so everyone went to Grace's place where there was always food and champagne "splits" in the refrigerator.

On nights when she was alone, Grace was perfectly happy to read, sew chiffon scarves or other frills to accentuate her wardrobe, or even work on her crochet. She was, and still is perfectly satisfied in her own company.

During this formative acting period, another woman entered Grace's life—one who was to guide her destiny through the next few but formidable years. She was Edith van Cleve of the powerful Music Corporation of America. Today this bright, spritely woman lives in semi-retirement in New York with the knowledge that she guided at least two remarkable names in cinema history—Grace Kelly and Marlon Brando.

"Grace was still at the Academy when I first saw her. A man, I believe called Richardson, telephoned me that he had a lovely-looking girl whom he thought had great potential for pictures," she recalls, "and he thought that I ought to see her. She was going to play that afternoon in *The Philadelphia Story*. I went to see her and I agreed with him one hundred percent. She was lovely looking: dressed beautifully, moved well, spoke well and had everything that I thought would eventually be right for pictures."

It has been one of Princess Grace's greatest assets that no matter what eventual relationship is established, her first impression is quietly impressive. Her own special propulsive and incandescent beauty is enigmatic and beguiling.

"I don't remember what she wore the first day she came to the office. I am sure that it was something very simple and in exquisite taste. She always had that," says Miss van Cleve, "but she did have a model's hatbox with her.

"We discussed her future and she agreed with me that she was not ready to go to Hollywood. In fact, I had the distinct impression that she would have preferred a stage career. And I don't think her family was very keen on Hollywood, either. She certainly had no wish to take up a long contract. She was never an eager-beaver girl, if you know what I mean."

Shortly after Christmas in 1950, Grace landed a part in the play *Alexander*, by Lexford Richards, which was to appear in Albany, New York. With her fine bones and chiseled good looks, it was a part tailored for her—that of a society girl turned singer appearing in a smart New York night club. It gave a glimpse of the extrovert that she was to play so memorably in the film *High Society* just a few years later. The play went into rehearsal for two weeks, followed by a two-week run. Grace was quickly a favorite with the cast, but had kept slightly distant simply because this was her nature. At the closing night party when one of the actors played an electric guitar, she suddenly threw off her high-heeled pumps and danced barefoot. As she twirled with her full skirt sweeping the air, she ran her hands through her chignon and a cascade of butterscotch-colored silky hair fell around her shoulders.

Ernestine Perrie, the production stage manager, is said to have exclaimed loud enough for the whole party to hear, "There it is! I've

50

said all along there was fire beneath that surface of ice! That Kelly has stardust in her hair. You'll see!''

Producer John Foreman also has vivid memories of a Kelly flamenco. As we talked in his Los Angeles home late one night he described it.

"Grace Kelly never did anything that she wasn't qualified or capable of doing. One night at a party I saw her turn different music on and dance a flamenco as well as Ava Gardner in *The Barefoot Contessa*. It was a kind of surprising thing coming from Grace. At what point had she rehearsed this so that she knew it would work? The fact is that it did work and we all applauded her.''

The fact that Grace Kelly danced an impromptu flamenco on two occasions is unimportant; but the flair with which she pulled them off adds to my belief that she never makes a move without first having thoroughly thought it through. She knows exactly what she is doing all of the time, and this I believe to be the key to her character. Warm, generous, but never impetuous, her every gesture and thought is a controlled reflex. I'd bet that at some time she actually practiced a flamenco!

John Foreman also has his own clear memory of the Kelly impact.

"I had just become an agent at M.C.A. in the television department. I went to meet this girl and we had lunch at the Plaza Hotel. Even in those days it was surprising to see a girl come to lunch with a hat and gloves on. I remember the hat had a little veil. I thought at the time, 'This is a strange dead-assed girl.' But by the time the lunch was over I decided that she wasn't strange or mousy at all. She was somebody who had her act together. She was—and is—a very special lady.''

When the definitive story of New York television is told, the name of Grace Kelly will bring to mind the early fifties along with Maria Riva, Mary Sinclair and Felicia Monteleagre. They were the stars.

In 1950, when Grace won her first TV acting job, she produced one of her most significant early shows. Fred Coe, then producing the original *TV Playhouse*, was seeking an unknown but talented actress for his production of *Bethel Merriday* by Sinclair Lewis. He spotted Grace in her small part in *The Father*, and immediately sent word that he wanted to see her.

Fred Coe believes that as an actress Grace Kelly was lazy. He is quoted as saying in an interview at the time of her wedding,

"Perhaps it is because she is such a beautiful woman and things came to her relatively easily. But I think that she has never fully shown her real talent.

"I remember she was always a little removed—not a snob, but she had her eyes set on a very high goal very early in her career. There was a feeling of security and great determination about her. It's easy to say this now, but I thought even then that she had a queenly quality about her."

Grace Kelly subsequently did other *Playhouse* shows and went on to appear in most of the live dramatic series.

Sandwiched in between her theater and television roles Grace accepted her first role in a film. It was to be made in New York and called *Fourteen Hours*. In this film she had a short but tantalizing part as the lady negotiating a divorce across the street from a man on a ledge. There was nothing spectacular about it at all except for two things: With the money she earned she bought her first mink stole; and as a result of the film, some high school girls in Oregon formed the first Grace Kelly fan club. She was totally bewildered when she heard the news of the club and characteristically commented, "Why would anyone want to choose me for a fan club?"

Grace was never overly concerned about money either, even when she became a star. Edith van Cleve remembers arguing about money for her during the time she played in Philadelphia.

"I was having a little trouble getting it, I told Grace.

" 'Don't worry, please,' she said, 'because the Playhouse in the Park is one of my father's projects. I want to do whatever is best for the theater.' "

The night that Grace Kelly opened at the Playhouse in the Park in Philadelphia, John B. Kelly—spellbound with pride—and all the family were in the audience.

"For a short period Grace joined the Elitches Garden Theater in Denver, which at the time was one of America's most important stock companies. She was interviewed in New York by the Gertlers who ran the theater. I had already had a film offer for her from the Coast to play in an experimental Western, *High Noon*, but I did not tell them," says Edith van Cleve. "I then had a further telephone call to say that Grace was wanted for two pictures. By now the Gertlers were getting slightly pressing as they always liked to have their contracts signed up before leaving New York to go back to Denver.

"I telephoned Grace and said, 'Now we have to decide between these two things. The salary on the movie will be $750.00 a week and all the Gertlers pay for an ingenue is $125.00 a week. In spite of this I want you to go to Denver because you will play big roles and it will be great training for you. You are still so young, and when you do go into movies the technique that you have learned there, and knowing what you are doing, will be invaluable.'

"Without hesitation Grace replied that she would do whatever I wanted her to. So I told the people in Denver that she would go there even if she had to leave the company earlier than September. I was perfectly honest and said that she had another offer which might come up but I believed that the movie wouldn't go on time. The picture was supposed to start early in the summer and the Gertlers began in June and went through till September and the company was supposed to stay intact.

"I gambled on the movie's delay, of course, because I thought it was more important for her that summer to get big roles in a good company.

"The picture did not go on time, which is exactly what I had hoped. This gave her all the summer in Denver, where she opened in *For Love of Money*—a great role for an ingenue.

"I knew Grace would succeed because very few people had her distinction and beauty. This distinction she has is very rare: She's a lovely, cool, dignified young woman and very unactressy. She is nothing like other people. It is a very special quality."

Edith van Cleve is a tough, forthright woman who has been around the film world a long time. When I spoke with her, I felt that had she any reservations she would not have minced her words. Her final summing up of Grace Kelly was this:

"She was loyal, direct, simple, straightforward and honest. I never saw her complain about anything. I never saw her have a tantrum. And I never remember hearing her talk about money. She always remembered everything. When she went abroad, she always returned with a small gift and even today every Christmas she sends me a card with pictures of the children. I keep them each year so I can compare how they are growing up. I never had anyone I enjoyed working with more than I did her."

Eight

Grace Kelly's first movie on the Coast was *High Noon*. It was a superb choice with which to launch her film career for three obvious reasons. Gary Cooper was at his peak—strong, reliable, a top box-office draw. The script was stringent, believable and featured a new kind of heroine. Stanley Kramer was the producer and Fred Zinnerman was the director, the man who knew exactly how to handle cool ladies and get the best out of them. He was later to remark that Grace Kelly was the only actress to have ever applied to him for a job wearing white gloves.

Yes, it was a strange trio of human oysters: Gary Cooper, the original quiet American, whose sum total of conversation was to look down from his golden heights and mumble "yep" or "nope"; Fred Zinnerman, a strangely withdrawn man; and Grace Kelly, as shy as a mountain violet.

This being the case, it was truly hilarious when Zinnerman, on noticing Grace's almost painful shyness, took her to one side and counseled, "You ought to learn how to speak to people and what to say to them when you meet them."

High Noon is the story of one man, Sheriff Kane, who has the moral, mental and physical courage to stand alone against the lawless. The people in this shabby little Western town had vowed to stand close to their sheriff, but at the moment of confrontation they faded away like lizards in the desert, leaving him to face it alone.

There are great action shots when, with quick thinking and quick shooting, the sheriff disposes of three of the outlaws who had come to kill him. Grace Kelly, the sheriff's pretty wife, whose Quaker upbringing made her abhor killing, picks up the gun and kills the fourth. It was a moment of subtle underacting, but also one of the most illustrious ones ever caught on the screen.

As the film fades Sheriff Kane, tall as a Redwood pine, slowly puts his protective arm around his wife as they walk to the wagon and ride off. Superb cinema. Superb performances.

High Noon gained for Gary Cooper his second Academy Award, and for Grace Kelly further proof that she was not just a pretty face but a true actress.

Yet, she was never an instinctive actress, but had to think herself into her roles. Only when she felt that it was right for her was she comfortable with the part. Her role in *High Noon* suited her perfectly because she could identify with it. Moreover, she could look the part of the chaste Quaker wife with enough undercurrent to keep the box office interested. As one Hollywood surveyor put it, "a face which reminds me of a cool, fast stream in a mountain hideaway."

Out on the Coast M.C.A.'s bright boy Jay Kanter routinely covered the various studios which included the Stanley Kramer Company. He told me how Grace Kelly came to get the part.

"I knew Fred Zinnerman and Carl Foreman were doing a Western called *High Noon*, and we talked about the various people for the different roles. It was a breakthrough in Westerns as it had a moral and intellectual appeal and the cast had to be absolutely right. They told me what sort of actress they wanted for the part of the sheriff's wife. It was a smallish role but extremely important to the climax of the picture. As a matter of fact, Gary Cooper had not been cast in the picture at that time.

"I had already had a letter from Edith van Cleve about this new girl. We all had a very high regard for Edie's ability as an agent and knew that she wouldn't be recommending anybody who wasn't a good actress. If I remember, in addition to her glowing account, Edie also sent a couple of pictures."

At that particular moment in Hollywood it was difficult for any young actress or actor to get an important role in the film business without granting the studio some sort of an exclusive arrangement for his/her future services. It was to prove a nightmare for many budding stars who found themselves at loggerheads with their studio and unable to get a release. Today it is quite different simply because the structure of the major studios is not the same.

"Grace was absolutely firm that she did not want to be tied down to a seven-year contract so this was the first hurdle, but somehow we got round it so that the way was open for her to come out.

"I remember picking her up at the Denver airport where she had been playing with a stock company [the Elitches Garden Theater]. She said, 'Hullo.' Just meeting her for the first time was quite an experience. She seemed to have it there in one look."

On the way to the hotel, Grace Kelly and Jay Kanter stopped off to meet a friend of Jay's—the late Arthur Jacobs—on hindsight, a carefully planned ruse, I suspect. The result was that Jacobs handled Grace's publicity for many years. It was also during this time that she met Rupert Allen, who has taken care of her personal publicity, including her wedding, ever since. Any special occasion in Monaco involving Princess Grace or her children will find Rupert Allen managing affairs behind the scenes.

Jay Kanter and I were talking in the flower-filled den of his Beverly Hills home. Outside by the pool the children were preparing a barbecue. It could have been a typical Los Angeles film set. He walked round and round while he was speaking. It was as if he was groping for the exact words in which to describe something special. He did not want to make a mistake.

"It's not that you suddenly look at somebody and you go religious or anything like that. I don't know what it is. There was this girl and she was as attractive as one could be. From the film business's point of view she had a freshness about her, but she also looked as if she knew where she was going and there was no turning it off. She went about it in her own way. I don't know what it is about people. They begin to affect you and you start to talk about them. Yes, I think that is what Grace had more than anyone."

The word I feel that Jay Kanter was searching for is charisma. This melodious Greek word has a special meaning for each person. To me it signifies the kind of personal magnetism, or aura, that some people have which draws others to them.

To the outside world Grace Kelly—film star or Princess of Monaco—may appear cool, aloof, remote; but to close friends who have been permitted to penetrate her façade of diffidence her charisma is bewitching, enslaving.

All her leading men, including such mature stars as Clark Gable, Bing Crosby, Ray Milland, James Stewart and William Holden, were to fall in love—some a little more, some a little less—with

Grace. But no one could have foreseen this the day she stepped off the plane at the Los Angeles airport.

During the making of *High Noon* Mr. and Mrs. Kelly insisted that Lizanne and Peggy go to Hollywood to be with Grace. It was a pattern that was to prove successful and be repeated during all her early films. At no time did she live alone. When her sisters were unable to be there, Prudence Wise (her friend from Barbizon days who became her secretary) accompanied her.

The three Kelly sisters—and any one of them could have been the starlet—stayed at the Chateau Marmont for the three weeks during which Grace was filming.

Today the Chateau Marmont sits on Sunset Boulevard like a flamboyant, cabochon rudy in a Woolworth necklace. It, too, is shabby and living on glorious memories of the past. In the days when the Kelly sisters lived there and the whole world listened to the heartbeat of Hollywood, it was bustling with stars. Bette Davis always stayed there and still does today. Myrna Loy and Boris Karloff are names remembered and revered by the few remaining original staff.

The huge entrance hall with its grand piano, fake baroque furniture and overwhelming vase of artifical flowers looks as if it was part of a derelict film set. Even the swimming pool which once gurgled with lovely young stars is seldom used. The Chateau Marmont is part of the living death of Hollywood today.

Grace, Peggy and Lizanne had a suite, which meant that they could "prepare" their own meals if necessary. Each morning as the alarm clock went off at six o'clock, there was a scurry for Grace to get ready in time to drive out to the M.G.M. studios. And punctually in late afternoon the sisters would be there to collect her.

In the evenings they would meet with some of the men who had been with Grace at the American Academy of Dramatic Arts and all would go to dinner at a small restaurant.

"We knew that the boys did not have much money and we girls did have a dollar or two," relates Peggy. "So we had a game. We had a lovely old friend from San Francisco down and we pretended that she was a very wealthy old aunt—which she wasn't—and we said it was she who paid the bill.

"Grace was never late getting home at night as she had to learn her lines for next day. We used to hear her practicing and she always set off in the morning word perfect. She was very particular about that.''

On the weekends they played tennis with these same friends, many of whom later became very fine actors.

Grace Kelly herself was never entirely happy with the film *High Noon*. She has always been disarmingly honest with herself and was to say, ''Everything is so clear working with Gary Cooper. When I look into his face I can see everything he is thinking. But when I look into my own face I see absolutely nothing. I know what I am thinking, but it just doesn't show. I wonder if I am ever going to be any good. Maybe I had better go back to New York and make my face show.''

Director Fred Zinnerman had much the same opinion. The talent was there, but as with a diamond the facets needed to be polished. Edith van Cleve later met him at a party at Bette Davis's home. He went directly to her to speak about her protégée.

''She is going to be a star—no doubt about that. But she ought to have a little longer in the theater.''

Even though the critics noted Grace Kelly's performance kindly in the accolades they wrote about *High Noon,* she herself was disappointed and still unsure that she would finally make the top grade. Her character is an intriguing mixture of humility and compulsive drive.

No on was more delighted to get back to her beloved New York than she was. And once more ''Grace's place'' was open.

Nine

By now M.G.M. had offered Grace Kelly a seven-year contract starting at $750.00 a week. She accepted as it seemed the right step to take at this stage in her career. She was just twenty-two years old, had very little actual film experience and was virtually unknown to the movie public around the world. Despite all this, she was quite determined in her demands and specified in her contract that she was to have a year off every two years, enabling her to return to the theater, and live in New York instead of hanging around Hollywood as most of the stars were required to do. Astonishingly, M.G.M. agreed to her demands.

When *High Noon* was finally released, Grace Kelly was invited to the gala opening at the Lee Theater in Fort Lee, New Jersey. It was her first public performance as a screen personality and she carefully chose a dress of black taffeta and aquamarine net from Bonwit Teller, that refined New York store for stylish shoppers.

As always she looked incredibly pretty as she cut a cake and made her first professional speech. Also included in the program was a fashion show and to everyone's horror out tripped a model wearing the identical dress as worn by the film star. Heads immediately turned to Grace Kelly to see what she would do. With the utmost charm, her eyes twinkling with fun, she made a deep curtsey to the model. Everyone sighed with relief as what could have been an embarrassing situation was turned into a complete victory for the young film star.

At least one other time in her life, Princess Grace was to be in a similar situation, although in a very different setting; and again she was to demonstrate her adroit way of handling potentially embarrassing situations.

A few years after her marriage, Princess Grace developed the habit of slipping down to the beach at Monte Carlo in the early morning, several hours ahead of the time the international set stirred their heads for their first glass of orange juice. The sea was usually empty except for another occasional early bird. On such a morning the Princess was happily swimming around when a wave took her close to another woman swimmer. They bobbed to the surface face to face and found that they had on the same swimsuit. Simultaneously Princess Grace and Countess Mannerheim (formerly of Sweden and now of Monaco, who told me the story) burst out laughing, and nodded to each other before another wave swept them apart.

There is a similar story of the Duchess of Windsor who arrived at a party in Paris only to find another guest wearing the identical dress. The other woman tactfully went home and changed.

When director John Ford was looking for an English type for the secondary role in *Mogambo*, he thought of Grace Kelly and saw the test she had made for *Taxi*.

"She's no mere beauty," he said. "That girl can also act."

Mogambo was to be a remake of that successful chestnut *Red Dust*, with Clark Gable in his original role as the white hunter. Veteran writer John Lee Mahin had completely updated the original script, which had been set in Malaya with Jean Harlow playing "Honey Bear," the brash chorus girl, and Mary Astor the "good woman."

For *Mogambo* Mahin set the scene in Africa and revitalized Honey Bear's lines to suit Ava Gardner. The role of the lily-cool English lady, Linda Norley, who had a passionate love affair with Vic Marswell (Clark Gable), fell to Grace Kelly. Her opening lines were nothing short of banal as she stepped off the river boat and met Mr. Gable. "How do you do, Mr. Marswell? I find Africa so exciting and thrilling."

In Mervyn Le Roy's office in Beverly Hills, tall, gangling John Lee Mahin—with his sun-withered face crowned by a baseball hat—talked to me of the part he wrote for Ava.

"Ava got the good lines. Grace just had to look the part, but she did it so convincingly that she almost stole the picture from Ava."

Oddly *Mogambo* (which means "passion" in Swahili) was to be a catalytic experience for all its main characters. For Ava Gardner it meant playing the role that she had been obsessed with for twenty years, ever since she had seen *Red Dust* as a girl; for her husband Frank Sinatra it was the realization that their self-destructive marriage could never be repaired; for Grace Kelly it meant an awakening as a woman and the self-assuring knowledge that she was now really on her way to stardom; and for Clark Gable it was proof that age does not wither a man's virility.

Before leaving for Africa, Grace explained in an interview that she wanted the part in *Mogambo* for three reasons: to work with the legendary director John Ford, to act with Clark Gable and to take advantage of a free trip to Africa.

The dramas began almost before the airplane took off. In his biography *Ava*, Charles Higham (W.H. Allen) places the scene.

"On October 21 she [Ava Gardner] gave a weekend house party at Frank's house, inviting Bappie [her sister]; Ben Cole, Ava's business manager; and Lana Turner, another client of Cole's and an old friend of Ava's. One night all but Ava and Lana left the house to go to another party. Frank came home unexpectedly.

"There are many versions of what happened next. Whatever the reason, Frank flew into a rage and demanded the two women leave the house. The quarrel became so violent that neighbours complained and called in Police Chief Gus Kettman to settle the matter."

Ava Gardner; Morgan Hudgins, the publicist of the film; and other members of the vast company set off to Africa by plane. At Zurich, where they changed planes, they were to pick up Grace Kelly. Hudgins describes, "We found her, lovely, blond and composed, reading quietly in the airport terminal lobby. The book, as I recall, was one dealing with the experiences of an African white hunter.

"The local photographers fell all over themselves trying to get pictures of Miss Gardner. No one paid any attention to the other young lady. How were they to know that before very long she would become probably the most celebrated, and certainly one of the most photographed, girls in the world."

For the film, which was to be shot in Kenya, Tanganyika and Uganda, M.G.M. had mounted what was to be remembered in Nairobi as the greatest camera safari of all time. The cast of four hundred and seventy-five members included eight white hunters.

There was everything from a mobile hospital to thirteen dining tents, a traveling movie theater and massive kitchens. Food and supplies were flown in daily to a special air strip which had been cleared out of the jungle. Robert Surtees, the cameraman, had special refrigerated trucks in which to keep his film.

People in Nairobi today still talk with a mixture of amusement and derision of the *Mogambo* safari. Over drinks in the bar of The New Stanley Hotel, they retell the story of how Ava Gardner bathed naked in her canvas bath in front of the native boys assigned to her quarters.

Much more amusing is the apparently true version as told by Bob Surtees to Charles Higham.

"I'll never forget Ava's reaction when she got word of this. She roared with laughter, and immediately flung her clothes off, running bare assed through the camp to the shower in front of everyone."

Grace Kelly is remembered as "the pretty girl at Gable's side who liked to go off with the chaps hunting." In her usual professional way Grace, who was then merely a contract player, settled in with her knitting, her camera and her own very special brand of naïveté.

"Don't worry about the Mau Mau," she wrote home to her parents. "M.G.M. have promised to take care of me."

British actor Donald Sinden, who was also in *Mogambo*, has remained on friendly terms with the Princess ever since. Remembering back to the film he says, "I think Grace is the only person in the world who would have done this. She arrived in Nairobi ready for the three months' location having already acquired a working knowledge of Swahili!

"On my second evening at The New Stanley Hotel, she, Clark Gable and I had dinner together, and Grace amazed us both by ordering the entire meal in Swahili. At the close of the meal she called after a departing native waiter, '*Lati ndisi*' (or it sound like that). Clark Gable sharply inquired, 'What's a *ndisi*?' We had already gathered that *lati* meant 'bring,' and the waiter replied in perfect English but with an American accent, 'It is a banana.' "

In the beginning of the film, Ava Gardner had some difficulties with John Ford, who was known more for his brusque handling of gunmen in Westerns than for his tact with the ladies. I was also told by a member of the crew that there was a certain coolness between the two leading ladies, who "circled each other like tabby cats waiting for the first one to scratch."

Ava Gardner always claimed years later that she hated making this film and hated Africa. Grace Kelly was to say that she loved every minute of it.

Ava was joined by a fretting Frank Sinatra, her husband of less than a year. For the irascible Sinatra it was a time of nervous tension. He loathed the heat, flies and constant quarrels with Ava. Added to all this he was impatiently waiting to hear if he had gotten the part of Maggio in the film version of James Jones's best seller *From Here to Eternity*. This was more than just another role—it was the chance to make the comeback he desperately needed at the time to prove himself as an actor and perhaps to save his marriage.

Film locations are strange places where human egos and emotions are exaggerated. It is as though time itself stops. There is no past, no future—just today with all its inbred passions and jealousies. Romances have the same ephemeral importance as those born on luxury cruises: Neither usually endures back in the harsher reality of daily living.

Ava and Frank spent much of their time together—loving, brooding, arguing, drinking, quarreling. Clark Gable and Grace Kelly found their own satisfactory relationship. While the rest of the camp slept safely in their tents, Gable and Kelly were often up at dawn to go big game hunting with Frank ("Bunny") Allen, the renowned white hunter who specialized in safaris for the movie industry.

Grace Kelly enjoyed the personalities of both these men, and was intrigued by the unique vastness of Africa. The space, open skies, animals and glorious sunrises were things she had never experienced before.

During the making of the film, she was once fifteen minutes late and Clark Gable, the complete professional himself, blew up at her so much that she was terrified of being late from then on.

"She was an absolute darling," one anonymous member of the crew told me. "Ava was all temperament and drama, but Grace just behaved quietly like the lady she is. If, in fact, anything went on between Gable and herself, it was all done with great circumspection and dignity.

"Quite obviously Gable liked her. Who wouldn't? She was always quietly there and never got in the way. It was probably the first time in his life that he had ever met a woman like Grace. He was obviously fascinated and seeing her in that setting cast a kind of spell over them both."

One day when Clark Gable had a scene to shoot out in the bush and Grace did not, she asked if she could go along. It was going to be a very rough ride because there were no roads, just jungle trails. The Landrover also had no springs, which would make it decidedly bumpy and uncomfortable.

Gable turned to her and said, "Oh, Grace, what do you come out here for every day? Why didn't you take it easy and go for a swim today?"

Grace turned those big blue eyes on him and said quietly, "I wouldn't have missed this for anything. I love to work on locations because I get to learn something everywhere I go."

"But you could read all about this," he bantered.

"Oh no. I want to get my own impressions so that someday I can tell all these stories to my grandchildren."

Gable never forgot that story and loved to tell it to his friends when Grace became Princess of Monaco.

That the immense African scene had a profound and even lasting effect on Grace Kelly is illustrated in another Gable story. When he returned from filming one day, he asked in the camp where she was and was told that she had gone out in the afternoon, taking a book with her.

Gable was perturbed that she was alone with so many wild animals around and went to find her, taking a favorite path she used to take to the beach to watch the sunset. He found her sitting on some rocks with the book open on her lap, quietly crying.

"Grace. What's wrong with you? Why are you crying?" he asked.

"I can't tell you. It was too beautiful. I was just reading about a panther in the snow and I look up and there was a lion walking along the beach to the water. He was out of his element too but he just walked along the water as far as I could see," she told him.

Clark Gable also admired her sporting side—necessary equipment for survival in the Kelly family. When a herd of elephants came within forty yards of her one day while she was out hunting with him, Grace remained still and composed. Some might call her special quality "pluck" as she always came through with spirit.

The film was not without its own dramas, such as when the twenty-six-year-old assistant director, John Hancock, was killed as his jeep overturned. And the shooting of some of the sequences had to be done under a specially armed guard in case of Mau Mau terrorists.

But there were also celebrations and plenty of them. Ava and Frank turned their first wedding anniversary into quite a party. "I have been married twice before, but never for a whole year," Ava was to crack.

Both Ava Gardner and Clark Gable had birthdays on location. For Ava's on Christmas Eve, Frank Sinatra arrived back in Africa triumphant at having secured the role of Maggio. In his luggage were packets of spaghetti, tomato sauce, a mink stole and diamond ring. He also brought his own little Christmas tree, which he set up complete with lights outside Ava's tent.

Grace had been secretly knitting a pair of socks for Clark Gable. But like much of her knitting, they were never finished. Shops were nonexistent so each day the week before Christmas she would steal something from him until she had enough for a large sock, which she hung up at the end of his bed.

Rumors of the Kelly-Gable romance were reaching London so persistently that ultimately one London columnist cabled Gable, "Rumors sweeping England about your romance with Grace Kelly. Please cable confirmation or denial."

When he received the cable, Gable showed it to everyone within earshot and said loud and clear, "This is the greatest compliment I've ever had. I'm old enough to be your father." No one was fooled.

Producer John Foreman recalled to me his reaction to the gossip. "We were all jealous of the men that Grace saw. This used to amuse her heartily because we were very critical of whomever it happened to be. I remember being vitally pissed off when the stories came back from Africa that an affair was occurring between Grace and Clark Gable. It took me some years to decide if indeed it happened."

Hollywood is never kind to its favorite children. The laws of libel are lax and it constantly weaves near-truths around its stars. That Gable and Kelly liked each other was evident. The rest is pure speculation.

When Earl Wilson in his pertinent column asked her on her return how many times she had been out with Gable she parried.

"Oh, I never counted. I wasn't the only girl he dated and he wasn't the only guy I went out with."

Wilson: He must be more than twice your age.

Grace Kelly: He is fifty-two. I know because he celebrated his birthday in Africa.

Wilson: Do his ears stick out so much now?

Grace Kelly: They don't stick out at all as far as I could see. Maybe he fixes them some way. I had a girl friend who had protruding ears. She put something on them to make them stick closer to her head and when she was having a date with a boy she wanted to impress very much, the glue came unglued with a loud crack. She went right to the ladies' room to fix her ears.

To an even more persistent interviewer she tossed off, "Clark liked my silences." Even the toughest of Hollywood columnists were to find that when Grace Kelly made up her mind not to discuss her personal life, she meant it.

Gable was capable of being just as discreet. When tackled point blank about the romance he answered, "Such a sweet, well brought-up girl."

When it was inaccurately reported that Gable had given her a diamond bracelet, the friendship was on such easy grounds that she promptly telephoned him and asked, "Well . . . where is it?"

Like every other tourist to Africa, Grace Kelly returned to the United States with a bracelet made from the hair of an elephant's tail. Again, when the ever-inquisitive Earl Wilson asked her about it she said, "It's supposed to bring good luck and good health. I never take it off."

"Not even in your bath?" he queried.

"The elephant didn't take it off when he took a bath," she replied sweetly.

To verify the rumors of this affair with the Kelly family is difficult. One does not want to intrude on what was obviously a personal family matter. But marriage to the much-married Gable would not have been in keeping with Grace's own religious beliefs nor probably with the family's wishes, and it is doubtful whether, in fact, it would have lasted. Her family met Gable—Mrs. Kelly had long been a fan of his—but the romance cooled off when they were both back on their own home territory.

Though so completely opposite in every observable way—the one living out her lush life in public, the other so intensely private—Ava Gardner and Grace Kelly ended the best of friends and remain so to this day.

One incident that probably brought them closer together than anything else occurred when Ava was secretly flown to a hospital in London just before Christmas where she lost the baby she had been expecting. Even though her marriage to Frank Sinatra was unpredictable, she had wanted his child.

No one could have been more understanding when she returned to the heat and forced gaiety of Africa than Grace Kelly. She reserves her personal compassion for such special occasions as this, but once given it is warm and strong and lasting.

When Grace married Prince Rainier, Ava Gardner was among the select coterie of Hollywood friends invited to the wedding and was one of the most arresting-looking women at that fashionable affair.

An odd sidelight to *Mogambo* was the heavy bill the studio received for Miss Kelly's luggage when she arrived back from Africa. Everyone was curious as to what could possibly be in the suitcases. Jay Kanter describes his homecoming to Los Angeles.

"I got this call from our man in California who is in charge of looking after the M.G.M. people. He called me up and said, 'Listen, the studio isn't one to complain and we know about these things on location but for God's sake. We have just got a bill for overweight for your friend Grace Kelly that amounts to just a horrendous amount of money (I can't remember how much now but they were really shocked).'

"They just didn't know if it was a mistake because Grace wasn't the sort of person to travel around with forty pieces of luggage. She wasn't a star of that caliber, at the moment anyway. So I called her up and I said, 'Grace, gee this is a terrible complaint and I don't think they really mean it but they are damned upset about it.'

"There was a pause and then she laughed, 'Oh, I know what it was. I sent back a couple of small trunks, I suppose they were like foot lockers, and they did weigh a lot; but do you mean to say that they sent them back by air? They were only rocks that I was collecting.'

"She was totally ignorant and surprised that all her luggage would naturally be sent back by air."

All during the filming she had been gathering the peculiar amethyst-veined rocks that one picks up in the African fields. These and other rocks became the foundation of a collection of stones that she was to expand during the next several years.

At the time, she was sharing an apartment on Sweetzer Street, off Sunset Boulevard, with actress Rita Gam. They had been friends since modeling days in New York. The one was as fair as the other was dark. While Grace was in Africa collecting her rocks, Rita Gam was in North Africa on location for *Saadia* and making her own collection. Unbeknownst to each other, they both landed home with suitcases full of rocks.

While Grace enjoyed "African sessions" with Rita Gam, she rarely spoke about it with other people as she fretted that friends would expect her to deliver a travelogue. Even her family found it difficult to chisel anything out of her. Mr. Kelly was to say at the time, "You know, the girl must have had a lot of fascinating experiences but she won't talk."

It could have been the fact that no woman had ever looked more beguiling in a solar topee; that Bill Tuttle (make-up) and Sidney Guilaroff (hair), both of M.G.M., had turned Grace Kelly into a shining beauty; that Clark Gable had given her a new assurance. But one thing was certain: She was a much more glamorous figure after her return from *Mogambo* than before.

Grace had also picked up a lot of film technique from veteran Ford while developing a "crush" on Clark Gable. Ford, the taciturn Irishman usually so short on words about his leading ladies, was publicly predicting that Grace Kelly would soon be a star.

For her performance as the cool English wife stirred to frustrated passion for white hunter Gable, she won a "Best Supporting Role" nomination for the Academy Award.

Grace Kelly had begun the final climb to the top.

Ten

Beautiful women seldom have interest in or compassion for other women. It is a fact as old as womanhood. But the dozens of men and women with whom I spoke while collecting material for this book were all unanimous in their dedication—even love—for Princess Grace and the film star Grace Kelly.

They spoke in platitudes which were often difficult to break down. I refuse to believe that the aura which surrounds any member of a European Royal Family is responsible for this loyalty. The answer lies deeper, in the very structure of the woman; in her appreciation of and reaction to all human beings, and most of all, to her friends.

Back to Los Angeles from the heady, predominantly male scene of Africa after completing *Mogambo*, Grace Kelly easily stepped back into her modest, feminine life and the two-bedroom apartment on Sweetzer Street which she shared with laughs with actress Rita Gam.

Sweetzer Street may have changed over the last twenty years, but I doubt it. The apartment blocks are square, modern, functional and unimpressive.

Rita Gam now lives in a sprawling apartment on Park Avenue with her two children from her marriage to publisher Tom Guinzburg. At the time of sharing an apartment with Grace Kelly she was married to Sidney Lumet, the producer. Now she is on her own again and looking very much like she did in those giggly days twenty years ago. She is still incredibly beautiful and does selective acting.

"We met on a Saturday in California. I was living at the Beverly Hills Hotel and she had an apartment on Sweetzer Street, a street that was full of call girls. Grace was living with her secretary 'Prudy' Wise.

"Grace said, 'Wouldn't you like to join me in sharing this flat? Prudy can sleep in the living room and we can all go to the movies together.'

"I said, 'Why not?' and moved in straightaway. It was cheaper than a hotel and as we were both working, we had the same hours."

There was a zany "My Sister Eileen" quality about life at Sweetzer Street—such as the time they all went on the prune diet, "a mad diet of prunes, steak, eggs and more prunes. Our housekeeping tended to be chaotic and once when we found we had a pruneless larder we trailed all over Hollywood in the dead of night to find a prune shop open.

"Of course, we cheated all the time, excusing ourselves as we ate a fat piece of pie or hunk of cake. Breakfast in the morning was a shambles. I guess we'd throw an egg on the pan or boil one with a piece of toast. I would drink hot water and Grace coffee. We'd be off to the studios by six-thirty or seven, just when the other Sweetzer Street ladies were coming home."

There were nights when they both slipped around the corner to get a hamburger or cheeseburger and have an early night. The refrigerator was always stacked with "splits" of champagne, which was drunk consistently—even with hamburgers. (Today champagne is still Princess Grace's favorite drink and she rarely drinks liquor.)

On Sundays the three girls usually slept late, since they all liked and needed a lot of rest. If they had not been asked out for dinner, Grace and Rita took turns cooking.

"Grace would do her spaghetti bit with green salad or if she was in a cooking mood her beef stroganoff. The next time I would do my duck à l'orange with wild rice."

When the bulges became eminent—or the girls thought they did—there would be crazy fits of turtle racing, a form of slithering along from side to side on the bottom.

There was no television, so if they were home the trio sat around talking about men, books or film gossip; or designing clothes which they had made up by a dressmaker. Since Grace by now had a stream of Hollywood bachelors telephoning, Rita or Prudy would sift the calls while she listened in. Sometimes they went for walks, but this was not entirely satisfactory owing to the other ladies of Sweetzer Street who were also out walking.

There was a kind of protective attitude between Grace and Rita, who were amazingly unspoilt for two such beautiful girls. Rita was the more emotional, and Grace had the cool, calm common sense, as this story from Rita illustrates.

"One night we were invited to a dinner party by an agent we had met and a friend of his from South America. Prudy had not been invited. We told him that we were going on to a party given by Sam Goldwyn and he said, 'That's fine. I'll send a car over and take you both on.'

"Grace told me to tell him we were driving ourselves, and how smart she was. At the dinner party when the big seduction scene started, I began talking more and more because that's what I do when I get nervous and Grace started getting colder and colder. Then the lights got dimmer. The dinner was nearly over and his hands were on my knees. I became hysterical and whispered, 'Let's go, let's go.'

"Grace just said, 'We'll go in a minute. Let's wait for the dessert because it might be good.' We did wait and we had our dessert and then the agent said, 'Now leave your car here and I'll take you over.' 'In no way,' Grace answered firmly. 'We'll drive ourselves.' So off we popped and had a super time at the Goldwyns and left those two standing.

"Grace was great fun to live with. She was never mean or cross, but always generous and fun to be with. We both kept falling in love with all the wrong men, the married ones, so the only ones we could go out with usually turned out to be the tacky ones. No, I don't remember talking about our love life intimately to each other. Remember, we were both well brought-up girls."

Prudence Wise continued to live with Grace as her secretary for several years, but was to die of leukemia, another death which affected her acutely.

All through her days in Hollywood, even after she became a star, Grace Kelly was, in fact, extremely careful to take a girl friend or sister along with her on dates. The old-fashioned word is "chaperon," but it is my deduction that it was Grace Kelly's way of combating the kind of vitriolic gossip that Hollywood is noted for. She was taking no chances. Later, when her name was linked with

Bing Crosby's, her sister Peggy was with them on their one public date.

I later confronted Edith Head, chief of Paramount's costume designing unit, with what she had once said in an interview in the *Saturday Evening Post*. "There is a lot of solid jaw under that quiet face of hers," she smiled in her quick birdlike manner. "And I was dead right. Grace always had amazing confidence."

Eleven

Grace Kelly was soon back in her beloved New York. She had never settled happily in sprawling, inhuman Los Angeles and probably had felt far more at home in Africa and Europe. Like all short-sighted people, she was distressed by the glare of the Hollywood sun. She even preferred walking in the rain in New York.

Grace had also missed that peculiar immediacy of New York where you meet friends walking on the street, or telephone them, inviting them over, and they can be there within a few minutes. Manhattan—at least the Manhattan that this sheltered girl knew— had an intimacy as well as a style all of its own. There were the stylish apartments on the East Side, with gay striped canopies and smiling, white-gloved doormen; the robust bawdiness of Broadway; the exclusiveness of the small theaters tucked away in side streets; the tall skyscrapers like melting ice cubes in the summer sun; the drifting magical mists through the early morning in Central Park; and that Aladdin's cave called Bloomingdale's, up the street from the Barbizon, where she still loves to shop today.

Despite having made two successful films, *High Noon* and *Mogambo*, Grace Kelly was far from being an international star. Directors were not crowding for her work as they would be only three years hence, and outside America she was still virtually unknown.

Back in the East with no film work in view, she was delighted to be offered the leading role in *The Moon Is Blue*, a play that was to be staged in Philadelphia's Playhouse in the Park. Any initial shyness in playing in her own hometown had now been overcome;

in fact, she enjoyed the challenge of this highly professional drama center.

It was while dining at one of Philadelphia's smart country clubs that she received a long-distance telephone call from Jay Kanter, who informed her that a deal was being set up for her at Warner Brothers to co-star with Ray Milland in *Dial M for Murder*. But even more important, it was to be directed by Alfred Hitchcock. It was a proven point that any unknown featured in a Hitchcock film had every chance of being a star overnight.

Mr. Hitchcock had, in fact, already met Miss Kelly after he had seen the test she did for *Taxi*. As Grace later described her meeting with him at Warners, "I could not think of anything to say to him. In a horrible way it seemed funny to have my brain turn to stone."

In his study within his bungalow on the Universal set, Alfred Hitchcock talked to me about that first important meeting. It was the kind of leather and oak room that fits into dozens of English country houses, but looks ill at ease in Hollywood. Shutters were drawn to keep out the harsh Los Angeles sun. The atmosphere was somber and serious. The benign Mr. Hitchcock looked like a Buddha in a Savile Row suit. He did not smile. He scarcely blinked. I could not even see him breathe. His words were strangely without animation as he talked in the flat English voice he has retained all these years about his favorite actress.

"She is a very handsome woman, extremely intelligent, extremely sensitive with a tremendous sense of humor and natural qualities that have made her what she is.

"I once had a writer who, when I said at the end of the script, 'These people don't have enough character,' answered, 'Well, you know for some people to have character they also have to have faults.' She belies that particular comment. She has character without faults."

There were long pauses as we sat looking at each other. I had read that he freezes at the word anecdote so I mumbled something about human interest stories. The Buddha clasped his hands over that great expanse of stomach and looked at me slightly reprovingly.

"I was looking for a lady for the part and there are not many ladies around who can also act. Grace was a phenomenon at that time in the film industry. I am not a believer in the sexy type. I think it should be discovered in a woman. If you take the English woman, North German or Nordic types, you know they all look like schoolteachers but I gather that they are murder in bed. The English woman is the most promiscuous type.

"In *Dial M for Murder* we needed an English type and Grace fitted that particular requirement and was the most suitable of the actresses I interviewed. An actress like her gives the director certain advantages. He can afford to be more colorful with a love scene when it is played by a lady than when it is played by a hussy. Using one actress the scene can be vulgar, but if you put a lady in the same circumstances she can be exciting and glamorous. And that is exactly what I did with Grace. Maybe she has fire and ice and great passion, but she does not flaunt it.

"You could see Grace's potential for restraint. I always tell actors, 'Don't use the face for nothing. Don't start scribbling over the sheet of paper until we have something to write. We may need it later.' Grace has this control. It's a rare thing for a girl at such an age."

When I reminded Mr. Hitchcock of a former saying of his, "The perfect actors or actresses can do nothing well but they still do nothing better than anyone else," he permitted himself a very tiny smile. "What I meant is that their personality and presence is such that it attracts attention. It's like the famous actor Sir Gerald du Maurier, who could walk on the stage and light a cigarette and yet make it interesting."

This is what he found in Grace Kelly. "Grace Kelly has a presence—a charisma. She also has reason. She is a reasonable person. I will place Grace by far the most amenable and co-operative and untroublesome actress that I have worked with. What is it that Gertrude Stein said: 'a rose is a rose is a rose.' What else can you say about her?"

Another Hollywood observer said, "Most of these dames just suggest Kinsey statistics. But if a guy in a movie theater starts mooning about Grace, there could be nothing squalid about it; his wife would have to be made to understand that it is something fine and bigger than all of them. Her peculiar talent, you might say, is that she inspires licit passion."

Hitchcock's timing was perfect. The public during the late forties and early fifties had had a surfeit of bosoms and bottoms and bulges pushed into its face, and was now ready and eager for someone with distinction, someone who looked well-bred, someone unobtainable. Twelve years earlier it had been Greer Garson, followed six years later by Deborah Kerr. And now it was to be Grace Kelly—the still center of the whirlpool.

As Van Johnson quaintly summed it up, "Hollywood went for Kelly in rebellion against a broadside of broads."

Each film in Grace's comparatively short but memorable career added an extra dimension to her acting. She wanted to learn, and her capacity for listening was endless. It was Alfred Hitchcock who lowered her voice. Although she had taken voice production lessons ever since she went to the American Academy of Dramatic Arts and had no trace left of that indigenous Philadelphian accent, it was Alfred Hitchcock who finally coached her in how to pitch her voice lower.

"The reason was," he explained to me "that in any emotional scene, the lower the voice, the more range you have to go. But if you already have a high pitch as most English women, then in the higher notes you tend to become shrill."

Grace Kelly's *Dial M for Murder* voice was the beginning of the enchanting Continental voice that millions of television viewers have come to know all over the world. When Princess Grace on two occasions last year read extracts from the Bible on the immensely popular English television program *Stars on Sunday,* it was her voice—soft and sweet as a ripe apricot—that people remembered. No one had expected it to sound so low and rich and Anglicized.

The combination of Alfred Hitchcock and Grace Kelly was, indeed, a strange one. Of all the directors who could have worked with her at that time, he seemed the most improbable. Elia Kazan might have appealed to her intelligence and brought out another dimension in her just as he did with Vivien Leigh in *A Streetcar Named Desire*. George Cukor was an obvious choice, with his ability to get inside the feminine mind. Katharine Hepburn, Garbo and Elizabeth Taylor all produced a new kind of magic under his intuitive direction. Vincente Minnelli, William Wyler and Daniel Mann were all possibilities, each capable of extracting the distilled essence of Kelly. But it was Alfred Hitchcock, the rank outsider, who took the long chance that paid off. He wanted the kind of inner brilliance that could ignite a screen; and she, in turn, needed firm handling, the hallmark of Hitchcock's direction.

Grace Kelly was always factual about herself as an actress. It was one of her most appealing traits. Neither vain nor suffering false modesty, she was aware of all her faults, including the fact that she disliked the left side of her face.

But most of all, she was willing to listen. As a director, Alfred Hitchcock liked her level-headedness, her reserve, her mystique. Though too wholesome-looking to be mysterious, she settled instead for a fragile, tantalizing perfection that occasionally irritated women but never men. And this is just what appealed to Hitchcock.

He also enjoyed her inspired ability to get to the studio on time and to never fluff a line, as well as her consideration of everyone on the set, from producer to the lowliest cue-card boy. Henry James always spoke about "the deeper sense"—something Princess Grace has always understood.

Returning to New York she was determined to have another try in a play, but although she read twice for the role of Roxanne in *Cyrano de Bergerac* (to play opposite Jose Ferrer), she did not get the part. Of course she was disappointed, as she had been many times before, but of her eternal optimism she said simply, "I've often thought to myself that if I ever let go at times like that, I'd never come up again." Self-pity has no place in her make-up.

On the same day that she heard she had lost Roxanne, she went to Radio City Music Hall to see *Mogambo*, but hurried home to take a long-distance call from her mentor, Alfred Hitchcock. He said that he wanted her to star in his new thriller, *Rear Window*, opposite James Stewart.

"The whole point was that when I cast her in *Rear Window*, there was an opportunity in that particular character [a fashion magazine editor] to dress her and make her extremely sophisticated, and all done without any of the horrible unpleasantness that you see today," Mr. Hitchcock explained to me.

I was discussing *Rear Window* with a former Fleet Street journalistic colleague when quite suddenly this timid little man had a strange glint in his eye. It was almost as if I was not present as he talked aloud. "I remember that scene in *Rear Window* when she walks across and sits on Stewart's lap. It is one of the most sensual scenes that I have ever seen on the screen." Almost punch-drunk, he shook himself out of the trance.

Under Hitchcock's manipulation, Grace Kelly bloomed in *Rear Window*. As a sleek career girl, she exuded what Hitchcock calls "sexual elegance." It was all there: from the stunning wardrobe that Edith Head designed for her to the way she spoke, walked and even combed her hair. No other woman I know of could have produced a nightgown from her handbag with such innocent and mischievous delight. You could have cuddled her for the way she did it.

The film was also notable for the scene in which she places a kiss on James Stewart's forehead. Hitchcock made twenty-seven takes of that scene, and had it been any other actor I would swear he had bribed the director. But James Stewart, who adored working with Grace Kelly, remains one of the few actors she starred with who did not tumble into love with her.

When once asked if he thought Grace Kelly was cold, he answered, "Grace is anything but cold. She has those big warm eyes, and . . . well, if you ever have played a love scene with her, you'd know she's not cold."

James Stewart has his own vernacular, which resembles a long, lazy summer afternoon; and you hope that each sentence will never come to an end. "The public is like an old setter dog in smelling out anything good, and Grace is good," he was to say. "She has class. Not just the class of being a lady—I don't think that has anything to do with it—but she'll always have the class you find in a really great race horse."

His was a protective, fatherly devotion. Years later when he heard of her intended marriage to Prince Rainier he remarked, "I'd have slit my throat if Grace ever did anything that was not like herself. If she had married one of these phony Hollywood characters, I'd have formed a committee of vigilantes."

Over a period of eighteen months, James Stewart has been disinclined to talk to me about his days working with Grace Kelly in *Rear Window.* Maybe now he is tired, bored, or old, but there was a time when it was rumored that he would arrive on the set with a bunch of flowers for her, pretending that they had been picked from his own garden.

And when he told a magazine that Grace Kelly could have played all the Garbo roles—Camille, Ninotchka and Queen Christina—this was professional devotion indeed.

Rear Window was also the beginning of a working association that developed into a deep friendship between Grace Kelly and Edith Head. Edith Head is a birdlike lady who has remained constant to her own inimitable image, much the way Anita Loos has. They are Hollywood originals.

I visited her to talk about Grace Kelly at her white dollhouse bungalow at Universal City, just around the corner from Alfred Hitchcock.

Everything about her reminds me of a witty little bird, from her neat, black, satin-smooth hair to button-bright eyes that never miss a trick. Her movements are quick and decisive, and words explode out of her. Despite all the Hollywood razzmatazz, I felt she could still be teaching Spanish and French at Bishop School in La Jolla, where she went after gaining her Master of Arts degree from Stanford. Edith Head is a whip of a woman and totally refreshing.

First we talked about Grace Kelly, the woman. "I think that Grace accepts her work of any kind for what it is. She is the total professional in whatever she does, whether it is as a model, actress or princess. She is also such a feminine-looking person that you have the feeling that she could easily be pushed about. On the contrary, I have never worked with anybody who had a more intelligent grasp of what we were doing. Under that very sweet and demure face there is great will power."

And then Grace Kelly, the actress. "You see, working with actors and actresses everyone has a different language. So many people ask me that same repetitious question, 'Who is your favorite actor or actress?' I say 'Grace Kelly' every time. Not because I am fond of her, not because she looks so superb in anything I design; but working with her is an extraordinary experience because you don't actually work for her—you work *with* her. I don't think people realize that there is a very analytical brain behind that beautiful face. I have never made sketches until I have worked them out with her. She is one of the few women I know who is completely objective. In other words, you show her fabrics and she discusses them like a professional. She knows the difference between a hoop skirt and a crinoline. She is a very professional person.

"Practically no woman in the world over the age of five doesn't have a preconceived idea of what she likes. Unfortunately little girls with blue eyes have been told by their mothers, 'You are so lovely with your baby blue eyes in baby blue dresses.' And so it goes all through. They instinctively say, 'I would rather have a square neck than a round one.' I run into that all the time with women, but the extraordinary thing—not with men.

79

"There is practically no other woman besides Grace Kelly who does in no way project her personal likes and dislikes into a character.

"You see, she came into the industry with a head start and a lot of advantages. She had culture, breeding, money, education, and was fully equipped with practically every weapon with which to fight. It was an extraordinary background for an actress. Very few people come with that."

Already Grace Kelly had begun to collect her own elite fan club of fastidious actors and actresses who genuinely admired her work and were not just blinded by her professional beauty. One such person was Douglas Fairbanks, Jr. He told me of this period:

"Many years before Princess Grace was married, some magazine interviewer asked her if she had ever been in love. As I recall the story—no doubt embellished by wishful thinking—she answered, 'Yes,' but she didn't really know the man. He was only a photograph, or a figure on the screen. On being pressed as to who it was, she replied it was *me*!

"When a dozen friends, at least, sent me copies of the interview, I naturally ballooned with pleasure and kept one copy in my bill clip until time and overuse wore it out. As we had many friends in common, particularly David Niven, I kept hoping to correct this oversight of Fate. Although it took some time, we did at last meet, and she and Prince Rainier have since become close, valued and honored friends."

Twelve

With the completion of *Rear Window*, Grace Kelly began one of the most extraordinary careers of any movie star in history. By now not only the fans but the exhibitors were solidly behind her, and she was given star billing for the first time. One advertisement simply announced, "Grace Kelly in *Rear Window*." This was all the more amazing as she was batting against the formidable favorite, James Stewart.

Even more astonishing is the fact that within the next year she was to make five pictures that all became box office successes. It is titillating to speculate how much longer she could have gone on at that pace and how much time would have passed before she would have been toppled from her pinnacle by a satiated public looking for a new celluloid heroine to preside in their fantasy world.

One of the highest accolades of that time was to be chosen for the cover of *Life* magazine. It was a privilege reserved for presidents, peace makers, warmongers and names that had been splashed across the world's newspapers.

When Grace Kelly was invited to sit for her portrait for the magazine, a young photographer named Howell Conant was assigned to her. Again, like so many of those early contacts, it was to become a lifetime friendship. Many of the finest pictures taken of her over the last years were done by Howell, who lives in New York. His pet name for her was "Queenie," an irreverance he still retains to this day.

As one of Princess Grace's friends explained to me, "It takes a long time to be accepted as a friend of Grace's. But once you are there, she never lets you down. She has a consistency of character, temperament and behavior, both in private and public life, which is the testimony of someone who really knows what loyalty is all about.''

Grace, incidentally, was not the only Kelly girl to make a *Life* cover. Kell's former wife, Mary Freeman Kelly, a pert caramel blonde, became one of America's top women swimmers, and as a result was featured on a *Life* cover. Specializing in backstroke and medley, she established three national American Athletic Union (A.A.U.) records, won the National Senior Indoor 200-yard backstroke and 300-yard medley championships, competed in the Olympic Games at Helsinki and accumulated enough cups to fill a room.

After Grace Kelly's *Life* cover, much to her amazement, a deluge of reporters descended on her. Magazines and newspapers chose their most experienced writers to gain ''in-depth'' interviews. Instead they came away totally baffled with notebooks full of slender quotes and memories of those pregnant silences. After their interviews, they knew no more about her private life than when they first met her.

It was not that she did not want to answer their questions. I'm sure that from the moment of her birth Grace Kelly had beautiful manners! It was just that she was an enigma and viewed the reporters with suspicion and quiet amusement from behind her private Iron Curtain.

Elizabeth Taylor has spent a lifetime baring her bones across the seven continents. Ava Gardner ripped open her heart with monotonous regularity until she escaped to Europe and oblivion. Year after year Marilyn Monroe exposed her soul like a tiny child with a chronic heat rash. But Grace Kelly always remained true to herself and no one was allowed to penetrate behind her calm blue eyes.

She had, and still does have, a genuine horror of talking about herself. She flatly refused to discuss with reporters what made up her one hundred fifteen pounds, and would not allow the studio to release the usual data on bust, waist and hips.

It has been suggested that her aloofness and complete contempt for publicity stunts was, in fact, a clever ruse and an updated version of Garbo's ''I want to be alone.''

Nothing could have been further from the truth. She genuinely could not understand why people would be interested in reading about her other than to appraise her acting performance in a film. As a serious-minded actress, this seemed to be the only important thing.

When Marilyn Monroe was asked what she wore in bed, she cooed breathlessly, "Chanel Number 5," and this much-tooled remark passed into Hollywood folklore. The Hollywood columnist who dared to ask Grace Kelly whether she wore nightgowns or pajamas received a laser-beam reply. "I think it is nobody's business what I wear in bed. A person has to keep something to herself or her life is just a layout in a magazine."

When another brash reporter was foolish enough to ask if she wore "falsies," she blushed and looked terrified. It was as if someone had deliberately trodden on a kitten.

Once when she was being particularly harassed while working on the film *Green Fire* during the day and appearing on the *Bob Hope Show* in the evening, she exploded to Edith Head, "If I don't feel like talking, that's my business. I'm not employed to give monologues. I'm hired to be an actress."

Rita Gam, who was to see how she suffered during those early interviews, says, "Grace was gentle. She was a gentlewoman. She was something so totally new to Hollywood. I am sure that Grace didn't ever consciously say to herself, 'I won't give any of myself to this interviewer.' She just wanted to get away from the lush self-indulgence, extravagance and vulgarity of Hollywood in the early fifties. Grace didn't have to go in for exhibitionism of any kind. She has always been a mature human being.

"People might have called it temperament, but it was really her way of taking what she wanted from life instead of letting life take her over. She is one of the few women I know who has real clarity of purpose and has taken deep and sturdy roots in her life."

During those early Hollywood days, Grace Kelly was constantly heard to remark, "Why do they want my picture? I don't think I am very interesting." And she really meant it. She was not just being coy.

Though she had an attractive pair of legs and wore a swimsuit well, she did not think that she was the leg-art type and would do anything to get out of posing in clothes that hit her above the knees. She stubbornly refused to have anything to do with the traditional cheese-cake publicity stills.

Her favorite publicity still from Hollywood days was taken by the photographer Franker. She wore a pale green chiffon pleated evening dress and was perched archly between a pair of Grecian columns.

"This was probably the real Grace Kelly," he was to say years later, "soft, graceful, elegant—a sort of diluted crème de menthe." He was equally sincere when he said, "She is the type of girl that you put on a pedestal, then you turn around and walk out of the museum."

The paradox is that while the publicity departments of the various studios worked day and night to think of suitable quotes to superimpose on the public image of their stars, no one dared to try that trick on Grace Kelly. Even then she had an unmistakable royal presence. Her dignity enveloped her like a protective cocoon.

There are few of Grace Kelly's recorded thoughts that are irresistibly quotable lifted out of context. Gimmicks of any kind did not fit into her way of life. But there was one occasion in the South of France when a journalist asked her, "What is the secret of your fatal charm for men?"

"I really don't know why men like me. I guess it is because I am a girl," she answered.

(Above) She flies through
the air with the greatest of
ease . . . Father Jack Kelly
and Grace do their own
personal act at Ocean City
beach.
Photo: Weintraub

(Below) The Kelly clan,
Ocean City style. From left:
Peggy, Jack ("Kell"), Lizanne
and our heroine Grace,
about seven years of age.
Photo: Weintraub

(Above) Grace was always at
the dockside to wish sculling
champion Kell luck before he
pushed off.

(Below) The all-American
beautiful family. From left:
Kell, Peggy, Grace, Lizanne,
and handsome John B. Kelly.

The day Grace became the
mascot of the Philadelphia
Football Club.
Photo: Saul Harrison

*Mr. and Mrs. John B. Kelly celebrate their silver
wedding anniversary in 1949 with the family. From
left: Grace, son-in-law George Davis, then married
to Peggy, Peggy, Kell, and Lizanne.*

The face that set Grace
Kelly off as an actress.

Thirteen

Without one day's rest, Grace Kelly went straight from *Rear Window* back to Paramount for the making of *The Bridges of Toko-Ri*, a sugary war film.

The part of the wife of navy pilot William Holden in *Toko-Ri* was not big enough to attract an important star but it was a cameo that required exactly the right actress to play it. The director-producer team of George Seaton and Bill Perlberg wanted an unknown with a fresh, untarnished face. It was the kind of quality role that Deborah Kerr, Audrey Hepburn or Vivien Leigh could have played, and as it happened so could Grace Kelly.

Many girls were auditioned for the role, including one who turned up in a black dress with a six-inch crucifix. Grace Kelly wore her usual "uniform": a shirt and skirt, flat-heeled shoes and gloves. Her plain-Jane impact was not exactly devastating but, as with everyone else during her life, Seaton and Perlberg warmed to her. They saw in her the exact ingredient necessary for the part—a cool exterior with inner passion.

Everything in the jig-saw puzzle fell quickly into shape. M.G.M. were willing to lend her out to Paramount for $25,000; and as her salary was only $10,000, this meant a clear profit of $15,000 for M.G.M.

By today's figures and the kind of money that revolves around Sophia Loren and Elizabeth Taylor, this was an insignificant deal. But money itself has never been Grace Kelly's criterion for work.

On hindsight *Toko-Ri* did little to enhance her acting career and did not require her to stretch herself, which encouraged her best performances. The only things remarkable about the film were that she consented to appear in a swimsuit in the Japanese bathhouse scenes, and it brought William Holden into her life. He was to again star with her in *The Country Girl*, which changed her whole professional status, and they have remained close friends ever since.

One of the most extraordinary and endearing qualities about Grace Kelly is that all the men who have been involved with her in an "affaire de coeur" have remained totally loyal and devoted. Strangely, it is through their eyes that one gets a clearer picture of this woman than from her female friends.

The men are like a bunch of copywriters in the fifties with the assignment to promote cotton dresses. "Good taste, freshness, dignity, charm, honesty, integrity, refined"—and so the words flow on.

Bill Holden is no exception. During the two pictures he made with Grace Kelly, they spent a great deal of time together on and off the set, and he knows her better than do many other people. I caught him on the wing in the Beverly Hills Hotel when he was staying there en route from his Palm Springs home to somewhere.

Though twenty-odd years have gone by, there was a lilt in his voice and the platitudes fell like autumn leaves. But these were "for real" and therefore none the less attractive.

"I have such respect for her talent and ability," he told me. "She is such a conscientious, hard-working human being. Very often beauty negates ability and talent. But this is not the case with Grace." (Hitchcock was to say something similar.) "She was so sensitive to other people's problems."

One strange remark he made which could only come from a naïve male who really understands the workings of women very little was this: "Every woman who saw her and could identify with her thought that they were beautiful, too."

Most of us are positively covetous that anyone could have so much beauty . . . and manage her life so well.

William Holden continued, "In that period in Hollywood she became a symbol of dignity. Women like Grace Kelly and Audrey Hepburn help us to believe in the innate dignity of man—and today that is what we desperately need to believe in. She is an exceptional human being. She not only had good judgment and good taste, but a tremendous ability to concentrate and was an absolute delight to work with."

On the Hollywood grapevine there was much talk about the next film, *The Country Girl*, that William Perlberg and George Seaton were to make for Paramount. David Selznick had bought it as a vehicle for his wife, Jennifer Jones, and Bring Crosby and William Holden were lined up as co-stars. Selznick had the same kind of determination to consolidate Jennifer Jones as a major star as Randolph Hearst had for Marion Davies. With Jennifer Jones the results were more laudable. When the Perlberg-Seaton team got word that Jennifer Jones was pregnant, the flap that was expected did not, in fact, arise. Because of the dowdy clothes that were required for the role of the mousey wife, Selznick thought that the picture could be finished with Jennifer Jones in the part.

Perlberg and Seaton had other plans. They just looked at each other and said simultaneously, "Grace." They became so entranced with the idea that they quietly let Grace Kelly herself in on their conspiracy. A copy of the script was "leaked" to her and she knew that this part was right for her.

But so did at least a dozen other Hollywood stars. It was a similar situation to *Gone With the Wind* and every actress rooting for the part knew it could get her a coveted Oscar. The "rooting" took place at dinner parties, through the powerful columnists and at the Sunday pool parties—wherever there were people gathered together. Mrs. Seaton and Mrs. Perlberg had never been so popular; they realized, however, it was because they might provide a possible shortcut to their husbands.

Though Mr. Seaton and Mr. Perlberg were strongly in favor of Grace Kelly, there was one obstacle—and a formidable one at that. Bing Crosby was against it. He made it quite clear that he could not see the golden good looks of Grace Kelly in the part. Nor did he think she had the acting stamina.

This was the final straw that Grace Kelly needed. The Kellys have always been fighters and Grace is no exception. She contacted her agent, Lew Wasserman, and goaded him with the facts. "You have got to let Metro release me to play this part. If you don't I'm going to quit the picture business and go back to the theater in New York."

M.G.M. made a deal. They upped her price from $20,000 to $50,000 and insisted that after *The Country Girl* was finished, she return to the M.G.M. fold and make two films for them.

With the help of Edith Head, Grace Kelly completely transformed herself. She not only changed the obvious things like making her hair dull, coarsening the set of her jowl by sticking out her bottom lip, wearing her glasses on top of her head and playing some of her biggest scenes in a sloppy cardigan, but she visibly changed. She added years to her age by slouching and gave her soft, shining eyes a despairing glaze.

After one week's shooting, Bing Crosby was gallant enough to remark to Seaton: "Never let me open my big mouth again. This girl can really act."

It was only natural that Mr. Crosby, who was then in-between marriages, took his leading lady out to dinner. As was common knowledge at the time, Bing Crosby was quietly looking around for a new wife, and Grace Kelly could conceivably have been in his mind. When Mrs. Kelly was asked about the "romance" by a punishing reporter, she retaliated, "My Gracie with Bing? I don't blame her. Bing and Clark have always been favorites of mine."

William Holden remembers the fun they had on the set making *The Country Girl*—the kind of rapport when three people feel superbly comfortable in each other's presence. The threesome hardly ever left the set and usually had tea together. Bing used to bring his bird books to show to Grace, who invariably had her head in a book.

"Grace and I were involved in a scene where Bing was just out of jail. It culminated in my grabbing her and kissing her. I forced my mouth on her mouth and my teeth clicked like a billiard ball off her teeth.

" 'Would you mind not doing that? I'm terribly afraid we'll crack each other's teeth. I'll try to hold the passion down,' she replied.

"She was always ready for a laugh. 'Listen, you have just kissed me,' she continued. I replied, puzzled, 'Yes.' 'Well, don't let it go to your head,' she quipped."

It was a tremendously happy film in that everyone gave his or her best. As the aging alcoholic matinée idol, Crosby settled down to his own pace with that streak of brilliant professionalism. William Holden gave his usual capable performance and was delighted to be working with Grace again. But it was Grace Kelly who lifted the film up into astonishing heights. She brought to the role of the slatternly wife a compulsive and moving tenderness. Clearly she had added a new dimension to her acting.

When she first arrived on the set, the technicians scarcely gave her a second glance. To them she was just another blonde, another job. But by the end of the film, Grace Kelly was their girl. There was not a man on the set who would not have done anything for her. On the final day they presented her with a plaque on which was engraved "To Grace Kelly. This will hold you until you get next year's Academy Award."

The winning of an Academy Award is, of course, not only a financial bonanza for any actor or actress which can enhance his/her contract value overnight. It is an emotional triumph—the justification for years of disappointments, frustrations, dedication and faith. Furthermore, it is an experience that can transform a life, catapulting it up into the rarefied world of being an international star.

For weeks Hollywood had been buzzing with conjecture.

Grace Kelly was quite sure, despite the studio rumors, that she would not win an Award for her part in *The Country Girl*. She herself thought it would go to Judy Garland for her diamond-brilliant comeback role in *A Star Is Born*.

Grace lunched at the restaurant at Paramount Studios on the day the Awards were to be announced. Tensions ran high as people kept coming over to her table to wish her luck. Bing Crosby was one of the first. "Good luck, Gracie. We're keeping our fingers crossed for you."

William Perlberg and George Seaton were sure that their star would win and assured her, "Everybody's rooting for you."

As the lunch progressed the tension increased. The only one who remained calm—or appeared to—was Grace Kelly. She just kept on eating her salad.

Plans for the evening were that Edith Head would join Grace, French actress Zizi Jeanmaire and Don Hartman, head of Paramount Studios, before going on to the Awards ceremony. She had made Grace's dress, which was to be the only personal one that she ever created for her. It was an aquamarine slipper satin with shoestring shoulder straps and matching cloak. Her only accessories were a pair of long white gloves—naturally—and a handmade petit point evening bag.

Edith Head recalled, "A lock of her hair had fallen down from her chignon. We were standing by a vase of flowers and as she tucked the lock in, Grace picked up a little yellow rose and pinned it into the chignon. It was a gesture that she thought nothing of. Next day it was picked up by the fashion writers everywhere who probably thought it had all been planned. You see, she does these things so spontaneously, so naturally. Everything she does, I think, has her individual stamp.''

Hollywood's Pantages Theater was packed for the occasion with that special kind of electricity which the tenseness of competition inspires. Grace watched her friend William Holden as he took the envelope to read the name. In a clear resonant voice, looking straight at her seated in the audience, he announced, ''Actress of the year—Grace Kelly.''

Every head turned as she slowly walked up the aisle, amid the clapping and congratulations, to claim her Award. Some actresses bounce up, others almost trip; but Grace seemed to float down the great aisle and up onto the stage.

No one was more delighted than Bill Holden to hand her the shiny bronze statuette. The audience was hushed as she began to say in almost a whisper, ''I will never forget this moment. All I can say is thank you.''

Tears came into her eyes as she walked off into the wings. Many stars wait a lifetime before receiving an Award, but it had only taken Grace Kelly five brief years, a record by Hollywood standards. But for her personally it was the justification to her family and herself that those early years of losing part after part had not been in vain.

Besieged by reporters and photographers waiting to photograph the new Award winners, Grace was asked to pose with Marlon Brando, best actor of the year for his role in *On the Waterfront*.

''Why don't you kiss Marlon?'' one of the photographers asked her.

''Well, I think he should kiss me,'' Grace replied. It is typical that even in this volatile moment no one could upset her public equilibrium. It was only after she had returned to the privacy of her own apartment after the party at Romanoff's that she allowed herself to cry. She cried for an hour.

Jack Kelly's proud moment that night was when he received a Western Union telegram from friends which read, ''The Country Girl has become the girl of the country.''

It was this night, too, that brash Jack Kelly was to make one of his most fatuous and tactless remarks. He had asked some friends to the Kelly home in East Falls to watch the Oscar ceremony on television. When Grace's name was announced he remarked, ''I can't believe it. I simply can't believe Grace won. Of the four children she's the last one I'd expected to support me in my old age."

It was a remark that was to be quoted in and out of context for the rest of his life. It was also the observation of a father who had little patience for anyone who was not totally obsessed by sport as he was. Peggy and Lizanne had fulfilled his hopes, but Grace, with her mediocrity of sports talent, her supersensitiveness and reserve, was the only one of his children with whom he could not communicate. Although he was to become extremely proud of her, she always remained an enigma to him.

The bronze Oscar statuette which she won that night now stands on a shelf in the salon of the private apartment in the Palace of Monaco.

Now that Grace Kelly had finally proved herself to be an actress of star quality, M.G.M. viewed their protégée with new interest. Their big plans for their meteoric star turned out to be *Green Fire,* a piece of Hollywood trivia about emerald hunting in Colombia. No one was happy on that film, including both the stars, Grace Kelly and Stewart Granger. But at least it gave Grace a chance on location to collect some more rocks to bring home.

When the film was to make its debut at the Broadway Theater, Grace was furious. On the huge poster was the figure of a woman— it was Grace Kelly's head pinned onto a bosomy, lascivious body suggestively draped in green that was certainly not hers.

"It makes me mad and the dress isn't even in the picture," she said.

Other actresses, including Elizabeth Taylor, who have received the same despicable treatment by their studios, have created such a fuss that the posters had to be replaced. Grace Kelly had her own private form of retaliation. She just stayed away from that side of town.

By now Grace was more determined than ever to find the right film for her. She was professional enough to realize her worth and anxious to avoid something as worthless as *Green Fire.*

M.G.M. now offered her Sir Walter Scott's classic *Quentin Durward.* She read the script carefully—she never makes up her mind about important things in a hurry—and decided to refuse it.

Her reason was quite simple. "All the men are jousting, but all I have to do is to wear thirty-five changes of costume, look pretty and frightened clutching a box of jewels. I'd be so bored."

With her self-protective intuition, she was right. The enchanting Kay Kendall took over the role, which added nothing at all to her film career.

Grace Kelly was next offered a Western called *Tribute to a Bad Man*, in which Spencer Tracy was to star. She went out to Hollywood from New York to discuss the proposition. After two days of talk, with that quiet voice of hers she announced that she would wait to make her decision until a final script had been prepared.

This must have been a big decision for a young actress, as working with Spencer Tracy was considered one of the great "plums" of Hollywood. Besides Marlon Brando, he was probably the greatest film actor Hollywood has ever produced and was also one of the most generous spirits in the history of films.

With her uncanny determination Grace Kelly once more turned M.G.M. down and hiked back to the composure of New York. This was too much for M.G.M., who promptly sent her a telegram suspending her until further notice.

Grace Kelly was "bewildered and disappointed," but with her characteristic coolness was to tell the press, "It's my first experience with a thing like this, and I guess that there is nothing that I can do but sit here and wait till they want me back. I feel very strange not getting a salary anymore."

With typical Kelly candor and no resentment she added, "I felt I had to turn down the roles because they're just parts that I couldn't see myself playing. I hope that they are not too mad at me. Perhaps I was spoilt by my loan-out pictures. Now Metro say that they won't lend me to other studios anymore. They feel it is time that I made one for them and, of course, they have a good talking point."

There had been, in fact, several roles at M.G.M. that Grace Kelly would have been interested in, but the studio was not in agreement.

Over in Hollywood Dore Schary, head of M.G.M., was more explicit. "We feel that Miss Kelly has certain obligations to us. After all, we were the first to give her a chance. All her offers came after she appeared in *Mogambo*. . . . Maybe she has a few complaints, but we are all willing to discuss whatever is wrong."

Fourteen

Two charming Europeans were to play a significant part in Grace Kelly's life before she met Prince Rainier. They were Jean Pierre Aumont and Oleg Cassini.

Taken in the context of Princess Grace's life and her ultimate choice of Prince Rainier, these two romances may not be important, but they do illustrate the kind of worldly man to whom she was attracted. They were the complete opposite of the all-American image with which she had been brought up, typified by the two men who had dominated her childhood—her father and her brother.

It was in 1955, during the time that she was friends with both of these men, that she did, in fact, meet Prince Rainier.

Grace Kelly had met Jean Pierre Aumont during her early acting days in New York and their friendship was to span over a period of two years. They met intermittently but it was not until 1955 that her family and friends considered him a serious contender for marriage.

Aumont had been married to the beautiful film actress Maria Montez, who had died leaving a small daughter, Marie-Christine. Though his home was in the countryside outside Paris, Aumont was frequently in America because of his acting commitments. Just as Yves Montand was to enchant Marilyn Monroe, so did Jean Pierre Aumont fascinate Grace Kelly.

He had a kind of wanton charm superimposed on golden good looks that defy age—''a wonderful man whom everyone loves,'' as Grace herself was to say.

His friends were legion, including many in the British theater. During World War II when he was serving with the Free French Forces in England, he frequently stayed with Vivien Leigh and

93

Laurence Olivier at their small, stately home, Notley Abbey. He and Vivien were to enthrall New York in 1963 in the musical *Tovarich*.

The Kelly-Aumont romance did not, in fact, reach its crescendo—at least for the public—until the Film Festival of 1955. Newsmen hungry for gossip soon latched onto the possibility of a romance between Grace and Jean Pierre, and doggedly trailed them.

When first queried about marriage, Grace was her usual reticent self, but when one newsman informed her that Jean Pierre was telling everyone of his love for her she blushed and answered, "We live in a terrible world. You can't have secrets from anyone. A man kisses your hand and it is screamed out from the headlines. He can't even tell you he loves you without the whole world knowing it."

As for Jean Pierre, he proclaimed for all the world to hear, "I adore Grace. Any man would be proud to marry her. She is a wonderful woman."

Just before she left Cannes, after bewitching everyone at the festival, Grace was handed a copy of *Life* and blushed with anger.

There in black and white was a picture sequence that might have been taken straight out of one of her films. The sun was shining, the mimosa drenching the hillsides and the champagne cool and crisp. The hero and heroine held hands. They kissed. They snuggled. There was even one picture showing Grace kissing Jean Pierre's hand. It was all perfectly innocent, joyous fun that belonged to two people.

Unbeknownst to them, a hidden camera had recorded every moment of this lunchtime love story.

In reporting the matter to its readers in America a few weeks later, *Motion Picture* wrote, "Rumors were flying through Cannes that Aumont was less surprised than Grace at the magazine's disclosures. Also, stories which had originated in Cannes were seeping back to America that the romance was nothing but a publicity stunt.

"Grace may or may not have heard these rumors, and the timing could have been just a coincidence but the night she left Cannes she told a reporter, 'Jean Pierre and I are just good friends. There is no truth to the rumors about a romance, but there would have been two years ago.'"

Grace Kelly was deeply shocked. Nothing was more likely to chill a romance with this shy girl than the public exposure of her private feelings. It was the first time her well-kept privacy had been invaded.

But all this did not deter Grace from leaving Cannes and staying over in Paris for six days where she and Jean Pierre were inseparable. Grace stayed for a few days in the discreet Raphael Hotel where Garbo and Ingrid Bergman like to hole up when they are in Paris.

During this weekend she accepted the invitation to go riding with Gordon White, a young rich English film star addict who had once been the frequent escort of Audrey Hepburn.

In the evenings Grace and Jean Pierre took in several of the current plays: *Intermezzo* at the Marigny Theatre, after which they went backstage to meet the stars, Jean Louis Barrault and Madeleine Renaud; they then proceeded to Patachou's opening at the Olympia Theatre.

After this, word seeped through Paris that they had eloped and were already married. This, of course, was impossible because it is not so simple for an American girl in France to marry a Frenchman at a minute's notice. Also, anyone knowing Grace would realize that she would never have married without at least some members of the family being present.

The pressure grew so intense that on the next Friday Grace asked her studio, M.G.M., to issue an official denial of marriage plans. But when questioned further by a persistent reporter, she would only add obliquely, "I see no obstacles to marrying a Frenchman. Love is not a question of nationality. . . . I love France and the way Frenchmen's minds work."

The greater part of the following weekend was spent at Jean Pierre's country home Les Rochers at Rueil-Malmaison. Here she had been quietly getting to know his daughter and his closest relatives, including those of Maria Montez. It was a simple family gathering.

In London the *Daily Herald* printed a story that Aumont had announced that he would marry Miss Kelly and that the marriage would take place in America.

What happened privately that weekend is pure conjecture. Even to her family and closest friends, Grace never opened her heart. But the facts are that she left the following day as planned and returned to America.

It is too easy to speculate about other people's personal affairs, but on the surface this romance had lasted two years and looked as if it would last forever. The fact that Jean Pierre was seventeen years older made it all the more tenable since Grace had always enjoyed the company of older men. He was of the Catholic faith and his nationality had obviously not deterred her, nor had the presence of his delightful daughter.

Perhaps Jean Pierre supplied the real answer when he told a reporter, "I like her very much, but things are too fast. We are being pushed by all this publicity."

Even before this romance had completely cooled down, Mr. Cassini arrived on the scene.

Oleg Loiewski-Cassini was born in Paris, the son of the late Countess Marguerite Cassini, daughter of Czar Nicholas II's ambassador to the United States, and Alexander Loiewski, a Russian diplomatic attaché.

He and his brother were brought up in the rarefied cultural world of Florence, where his mother opened a dress salon after the Russian revolution. Though Oleg Cassini himself would have preferred the more gregarious world of the diplomat or professional soldier, the family's finances made it more expedient for him to follow in his mother's footsteps. He opened his own dressmaking salon in Rome so as not to be in competition with her. His main sporting interest was tennis, which he played for Italy in the Davis Cup when tennis was still a glamorous pastime for gentlemen.

Four years later, with very little except high hopes, he and his brother Igor set out for America to seek their fortunes. They had all the urban charm, wit and international charisma to titillate New York society.

Oleg immediately set up his own dressmaking salon, while Igor became the piquant society columnist under the pseudonym Cholly Knickerbocker. They were both adored and feared as they sprinkled New York parties with their *double-entendres* showing the same exuberance Zsa Zsa Gabor employs to dissect her husbands.

When Oleg was chosen by Jacqueline Kennedy, then First Lady, to make many of her clothes, his social cachet and financial success were secured.

Both brothers were to become American citizens and Oleg served in the cavalry in World War II. Once back in private life he married twice. Both were very controversial American women: first the cough-drop heiress Merry "Madcap" Fahrney—Oleg was the fourth in what was to finally be a series of eight husbands—and second, the beautiful film actress Gene Tierney who, by coincidence, had lived at the Barbizon Hotel with that other young budding star, Grace Kelly.

Oleg loved—and still does—to be seen with beautiful women. To a girl reared on the stuff that American men are made of, he was like a draught of glacier-cool, dry Dom Perignon—pure, undiluted sophistication.

This, then, was the man who set out to attract Grace Kelly with predatory intensity such as she had never known before.

They met in a droll way. He had gone to the cinema with a friend to see *Mogambo*, and nudging his companion in the dark as the beautiful cool blonde swished her way through the jungle, he said, "This is the girl for me."

"You are not lacking in modesty, are you?" his friend snapped.

"No, I am not lacking in modesty. I just think she is the type of girl that I would like," Cassini replied.

Continuing the story to me in his New York office, Oleg Cassini recounted, "I had always liked actresses. They had a special fascination. Not because of the publicity or anything, but because of the character they needed to succeed. I had already been married to Gene Tierney with whom I had two daughters and was now heart free again."

After the movie the two men went to dinner in a small French restaurant, and as they prepared to sit down Cassini turned around to his right and saw seated next to him Grace Kelly, who was dining with the French actor, Jean Pierre Aumont.

"I had some kind of resentment for him because when I was in the Army during the war, he kept calling my wife [Gene Tierney] all the time to take her out, but I suppose all is fair in love and war.

"I managed to get myself introduced to Grace, who was polite although not particularly encouraging. But her smile was warm. I went home that night saying, 'Well, this is destiny . . . how could it be otherwise? I'm going to work on this thing.' Although I did not know her character, she invited all the things that I think are attractive in women: clean-cut good looks and a coolness of appearance."

Within the next few days, having secured Grace's address, Cas-

97

sini began to bombard her with flowers. Vast amounts of flowers were delivered daily. After one week of this floral barrage he telephoned the apartment on Sixty-third Street and with his characteristic ebullience said, "I'd like to speak to Miss Kelly."

"Who's speaking?" came the cautious reply.

"This is your friendly florist," Cassini quipped.

There was a silence and then a small peremptory voice asked, "Who are you?"

"I would like to tell you who I am, but do me the favor, as long as I promise that we have already been introduced, to meet me for lunch or dinner."

Grace Kelly said that she would think about it and then made the suggestion that as she was lunching with her sister that day would *the voice* like to join them. Sisterly solidarity in such matters was typical of the Kelly girls.

"I managed to get her aside for a while and she told me that she was going back to California. 'Well, I would like very much to get to know you better,' I persisted. 'I go there often as I have many friends there, and would you mind if I called you?"

At the time Grace had just finished a short-lived romance and Oleg Cassini's arrival hit her at the right emotional time.

During the early part of their friendship Grace and Oleg had such a rapport that they disliked being apart for any length of time. After a heavy day's filming, she enjoyed being with him in the evening to dine in the small restaurants he had a genius for finding.

Other women who have known Cassini have told me that he has that incomparably rare talent: When a woman was within his orbit he made her feel all woman and unique. He knows every nuance of how to make a woman bloom although he can be an awesome sight when he becomes jealous.

When Grace was filming *The Country Girl*, a most exacting role, she telephoned Cassini one evening at 7 P.M. at his Long Island home, which he shared with his mother and brother. She was staying at the Bel Air Hotel and wondered if he would come out and cheer her up.

"She said she needed my company. We had a field outside the house with a swimming pool at the end. I was so overjoyed at the thought of seeing her that I rushed out and took a dive in the pool. There was no water! I landed flat on my face and broke my nose, which immediately became gigantic.

"It did not bleed so I did not bother to go to a doctor. Instead I went straight on the night flight to California. I had told Grace on the telephone that I had had a little accident.

"When I knocked on the door of her apartment in the Bel Air, she opened it, took one look and closed it again. She was certainly not devoid of a sense of humor.

"We had a couple of fights at that time because several important guys, like Frank Sinatra, now wanted to be seen with her. I have a very violent temper and while I was quite willing to go back to New York, I did not feel like sitting around while she went out with someone else.

"You must remember that this was during the days of the big Hollywood studios. M.G.M. had plans and expectations for Grace so that many times I seemed to be competing against them for her time, attention and commitment."

Much of what happened in her own pre-marriage days may have colored Princess Grace's decision today that her own children must be able to have a private life of their own—one in which to select, develop and discard friendships without the continual blaze of publicity as had surrounded her own early romances once Grace Kelly became a name that belonged to the world.

Fifteen

All through her personal life and film career, Grace Kelly had an ability to bend people's wills to her advantage. She inspired everyone to throw out his protective nets and shield her from the harsh realities of life.

A point in case was the spring of 1954. It seemed certain to everyone that after her suspension by M.G.M., she would not be allowed to work for anyone until it had been irrevocably settled—in the studio's favor.

Both Louella Parsons and Hedda Hopper blazed away in their columns that they did not think it was feasible that M.G.M. would lend out their hottest property for the fourth time to Paramount for a stylish new Hitchcock thriller to be called *To Catch a Thief*, which was to be made on the Riviera. They reasoned, with some accuracy, that if she was that good, a property could certainly be found by M.G.M. in which to star her.

But batting against M.G.M. was a formidable team indeed. The threesome was made up of Grace Kelly and her two knights in shining armor: Alfred Hitchcock and Gary Grant.

Grace was so convinced that they would win that she persuaded Edith Head to begin designing her clothes for the film. "No matter what anyone says," Grace told Edith in her turtle-dove voice, "keep right on making the clothes. You'll see, I'll be in it."

The "heavies" went into action and Grace was kept informed on the end of the telephone. Paramount in the end did get their way, but it may well have been on the premise that M.G.M. wanted William Holden sufficiently for a picture that they were scheduling. Also Grace's cash price had once again gone up steeply.

There was a story at the time ricocheting around Hollywood that the Kelly family could have bought out M.G.M. had they wished. This, of course, is far from the truth, but it does give some indication of Grace's public image: a determined young woman who was now in the position to make the kind of films that she wanted and not accept anything thrust upon her.

Grace and Edith Head had a fine time choosing the glamorous clothes that the part called for—a wardrobe fit for a successful fashion editor. This was their third film together and no actress and designer worked more in harmony.

They both stopped over in Paris for the final accessory shopping. Alfred Hitchcock was generous in that he recognized two perfectionists and appreciated the need for quality of detail in any picture that he directed. It was part of his stock in trade.

Edith still remembers with immense affection their shopping sprees. "Grace had just heard about Hermès and one afternoon she said to me, 'Let's go and buy some gloves. I know where we can get the nicest gloves in the world.'

"Like two girls in an ice-cream shop, once inside we fell in love with everything we saw. We chose gloves with little roses embroidered on them, gloves with open work trim, all kinds of gloves. Grace got more and more excited, as she got the same kind of joy collecting gloves as other women did diamonds. Finally they presented her with a package and an astronomical bill. Gloves and shoes are the only things where Grace loses count of money.

"For a moment she looked confused and said, 'I haven't got that much on me.'

"We pooled our resources and it still wasn't enough. In the end they let us go back to the hotel and the gloves were delivered later which, of course, wouldn't happen today. She would have walked out with them.

"The story illustrates that in spite of all her intelligence and business ability about contracts in those days she still had this rather charming childish exuberance about her when it came to shopping.

"Two years ago I was again shopping in Paris for a Hitchcock film and picking out shoes for the star. Guess who I met? Grace was there at it again buying shoes. Our eyes met and we both laughed. The lovely thing about Grace is that she never changes with her old friends."

The film was a dream to make largely because it was such a happy crew. By now Alfred Hitchcock knew better than anyone every nuance of his new star and how to use her to the best advantage. The script about an elegant cat burglar had the right touch of fantasy and escapism, and her old friend Cary Grant was to play opposite her.

Cary Grant's friendship has been threaded throughout Princess Grace's life in a very special way. Theirs has never been a Hollywood affair in the accepted sense, but their enjoyment of each other has endured the years. Both Cary and his wife at that time, the former Betsey Drake, along with David Niven have today remained her closest friends from her former Hollywood days.

By the time Grace left for the Riviera to do the outdoor shots of the film she was so exhausted that friends close to her feared a breakdown. The culminant effect of five films in a year had begun to affect her health. She could not sleep, was apt to burst into tears and was desperate for much-needed rest. She spent any spare time alone trying to replenish her ebbing strength.

On the stopover in New York, she was besieged by the press at the airport and although surrounded by her agent, Jay Kanter, and Paramount officials, she just avoided one of those pitfalls that many an actress has tripped into.

Someone in the publicity department of Paramount had collected a gendarme's cap and cape from the costume department and suggested to Grace that she wear them as she came down the steps. It was to be a new gimmick for the film, which involved the French police chasing a cat burglar.

Tired and exhausted as she was, Grace could sniff out a cheap publicity trick and turn it to her advantage with all the charm of royal blood. "I don't think Mr. Hitchcock would like it," she faltered in her soft voice. "I would prefer not to do that." And the miracle is that no one dared suggest it again. They had received the message loud and strong that no one pushed Grace Kelly about.

It was the delicacy of the way in which she handled the whole situation that was to amaze Jay Kanter; and once more an awkward situation had been adroitly turned into a minor Kelly triumph. This attribute has prevailed during several maladroit moments over the last twenty years in her exacting role as a royal princess.

On arrival in Paris, Grace contacted Hitchcock and begged to be allowed to sleep a couple of days before making the trip south. The film by now had already run into minor troubles due to bad weather, so she was to proceed immediately to Cannes. Which, of course, she did.

Harry Ray, who was the make-up man on the film, remembers the first telephone call he had from the star.

" 'Have you any Kleenex? Could you bring a couple of boxes up to my room?' she asked.

" 'Sure,' I replied, as I suspected immediately why she wanted Kleenex, because French toilet paper is so harsh. She also asked me if it was all right if she got a little tan. Wally Westmore had given his approval and, typical of Grace, she just wanted to check that it was all right with me.

" 'Go right ahead. Don't get too much, just take it easy so that you don't get sunburned,' I told her. The part called for an American girl vacationing with her mother on the Riviera, so it seemed to me quite natural that she should pick up a little tan for the part. Besides she looked pale and tired and some sunbathing would do her good, I felt. She turned the softest apricot color, which was fine for the Technicolor the film was being made in. Her skin was just gorgeous, beautiful. All I had to do every day was to add a little mascara. It took me seven minutes flat. She was the first woman I have ever worked with that I didn't have to put foundation on.

"I have never met anyone with a skin as lovely as Grace's. Arlene Dahl has a nice skin but not as good as Grace's. I must say this truthfully. She is the most charming, nicest girl I have ever worked with in the business."

It was once again a matter of days before the whole camera crew had "fallen a little in love" with Grace. "You couldn't help yourself," Harry Ray confirmed.

Alfred Hitchcock is known to be a meticulous master, but he prefers a more civilized working schedule than do many other Hollywood directors. He never begins shooting in the morning before 9 A.M. and lets his stars have as much time off as possible for sightseeing. There is never any talk of keeping them hanging around. The man is much too professional to waste anyone's time unnecessarily.

One day when they had finished shooting at noon, Grace asked Harry Ray if he would like to come with her in her car to do some sightseeing. He agreed and said it would be fun.

"She then asked the driver if it was permissible to go up into the palace grounds and drive around.

"He replied that she could even go into the palace if she wanted.

" 'No—we don't want to go in,' she replied. 'All we want to do is to go into the grounds.'

"So he drives up this winding road to the palace. It was beautiful up there. Just beautiful. Beautiful view and the soldiers on guard there with their beautiful uniforms. I remember they were blue with some red in them and they looked just lovely," Harry Ray recalls today.

"I turned to Grace and said, 'Now isn't this just beautiful? You know there is a Prince who lives here all alone. It seems a pretty dull life to me living up here on top of a hill.'

"She turned to me and said, 'Why?'

"I said, 'For instance, Grace, if he wants to take a swim he's got to get into his trunks and a robe and get a car and driver and go all the way down that road to the beach.'

"She kind of laughed and said, 'Don't you think he might have some sort of a beach house, Harry?' And that was the end of the conversation."

(One of the first major changes Princess Grace persuaded Prince Rainier to make at the palace after their marriage was to install a large swimming pool in the private part of the grounds where they could swim without going down the hill. It was also Princes Grace's idea that a heated indoor swimming pool be built on the waterfront for the use of tourists and the local people.)

The following year, after she had been photographed with Prince Rainier at his palace for *Paris Match* during the Cannes Film Festival, she was to meet Harry Ray on a set in Hollywood. They talked nostalgically of their days on the set of *To Catch a Thief*.

"You know, Harry, I finally did meet that Prince," she said. "He was a very nice guy."

We had been talking on a sound stage at a Universal City studio. Harry Ray, with his jazzy shirt and pale marmalade hair, still makes up the stars, although he does a lot of television work these days. "I miss the glamor of the fifties—those were the days," he sighed.

"Wonder if she would remember me," he mused. "Could you get a little message to her if I wrote on a card?" I assured him that I could. He went away quietly by himself for some time and then came back to me.

"What shall I call her? Do I have to write that Princess stuff or what is it, Your Serene Highness? No . . . to me she was Grace and Grace it will be." There and then, perched on the arm of an overturned chair, he wrote his little message which I duly sent to the Princess in her palace at Monte Carlo.

When asked later about Grace Kelly and his part in the film, Cary Grant was to tell Margaret Panton, "It was a delight, the whole film. From an actor's point of view she knew her business. She learned quickly, if there was something new to learn, and she didn't slow things down by temper fits. She saved the studio money.

"We had a scene in the film where I had to grab her arms hard while she was fighting me, and push her against a wall. We went through that scene eight or nine times, but Hitchcock still wanted it again. Grace went back behind the door where the scene took place and just by chance I happened to catch a glimpse of her massaging her wrists and grimacing in pain. But a moment later she came out and did the scene again—she never complained to me or to 'Hitch' about how much her arms were hurting.

"She isn't one of those girls who wastes time by being angry. She was always patient on the set, even when hairdressers and make-up men were fussing over her between takes of a difficult scene. If a dress didn't fit, well it just didn't fit, and that was that, with no hysterics. So, of course, they got the dress fixed faster for her than for a girl who was screaming about it. No wonder she was popular with the wardrobe and make-up people, even if she didn't go around slapping them on the back."

Sharing Grace's evenings after the day's filming was Oleg Cassini, who stayed two months with her during the making of the film. They lived in the same hotel, the Carlton at Cannes, and their evenings together had almost a subliminal domestic air about them.

Being the complete disciplinarian that she is, Grace divided her day into two parts. There was the professional day life on the set and her private evening world with Oleg Cassini. For each night after a hard day's shooting he planned a new gastronomic adventure.

An endearing thing about this then waif-of-a-girl was that she was the born *fourchette*, which, translated from the French means "a good fork." She was willing to try anything, and though she was still an inexperienced gourmet, with method and determination she set about to rectify this.

Every evening, sometimes alone, or occasionally with the Hitchcocks or Cary Grants, Grace and Oleg would try out a new restau-

105

rant. He knew every inch of the Riviera, from Saint Tropez to Portofino, and wherever they went, from five-star restaurants to small bistros, he was known. It was a period of good food, superb wines and lots of laughter—just what the overworked, overwrought Grace Kelly needed. They would hear that *mousse des poissons* were good at a certain restaurant or the bouillabaisse sensational a little further along the coast. Hitchcock was a renowned gourmand; and Cassini was not only an amusing raconteur, but also had a cosmopolitan knowledge of good living. The dinners were leisurely and gay as only the evening hours can be on the fun-seeking Mediterranean coastline.

Some nights they went to the Casino, where invariably the Kelly Irish luck held; some were spent dancing at the Palm Beach Casino or Maxim's in Juan les Pins; and others were spent driving through the hills which overlooked Monaco and watching the Principality in the pinkish haze of the setting sun as the night lights turned it into a gigantic jewel casket.

To everyone who saw Grace Kelly and Oleg Cassini, they seemed to behave like two people very much in love. They were totally isolated in a world of their own, in an unreal atmosphere guaranteed to nurture any romantic feelings.

One evening after dinner at a small harbor restaurant in Cannes, they went on to the Casino and later, dancing. In her direct way Grace asked Cassini what his plans were for the future and for her.

He explained that his plans for her included anything that would make her happy, including marriage. They had now known each other for over a year and were undoubtedly fond of each other. But if Grace had doubts she carefully put them out of her mind that night and let her heart rule her head. She and Oleg ordered a bottle of champagne and drank to the new life ahead of them. Her family's possible protests and Cassini's two marriages—formidable obstacles for any conscientious Catholic girl to overcome—were all carefully blocked out. They were just two people caught up in the euphoric glamor of the Riviera. If Grace had any further doubts she conveniently forgot them the next morning at church, where she went every Sunday. From the religious point of view the differences were not so insurmountable. Born of Russian parents, Cassini was of the Greek Orthodox faith, which was not too distant from the teachings of Roman Catholicism.

Where the heart had a reason Grace was even able to convince herself that his two previous marriages would not present a very serious problem because, as he had not been married in church, through Catholic eyes these marriages were not legal.

Her main concern, and a very deep one, was acquainting her family with the facts. Even with the Atlantic and Mediterranean between them, the influence of her parents was unmistakably present.

With all this in mind, Grace Kelly and Oleg Cassini agreed that the engagement was to be kept a secret until she had had time to discuss it with her family. In any case, it would never have entered her head to have had her engagement announced anywhere but from the Kelly home.

If there were any doubts about Mr. Kelly, Grace felt that at least her mother would understand her choice and condone it. She had always made it perfectly clear that she did not want her daughter to marry into the film industry.

"When I thought of her getting married at all I hoped that she would not choose someone from her own profession because it seemed to me that two stars in the family could put a real strain on family happiness," Mrs. Kelly was to say. "For those reasons I had hoped that she would marry someone of real distinction—not an actor, but perhaps a fine surgeon, a painter or a successful industrialist."

To keep up the deception so that nothing could leak to the press, they agreed that Grace would return to the States with the Cary Grants and the Hitchcocks on a boat as planned and that Oleg Cassini would fly ahead to await their arrival.

Grace arrived back in New York for a twenty-four-hour stopover before proceeding to Hollywood for the interior shots of the film. Already the pressures of fame had begun to catch up with her. Her family wanted to repossess her, her agents and the press were clamoring for interviews, the studio had things to discuss with her. Added to this, her fiancé was waiting for her outside her apartment house.

I asked him in New York about that fatal meeting with Mrs. Kelly which was, perhaps, the crux of the finale of the short-lived romance.

"It was all very difficult because of the pressures that were taking place, but Grace telephoned her mother and arranged that we would meet for lunch. I attempted some sort of humorous quips, but I immediately sensed that Mrs. Kelly was in no mood. It was a cold, almost bitter, reception possibly because she had been totally unprepared for the fact that we wanted to marry.''

Mrs. Kelly, in fact, came straight to the point, ''Look here, Oleg. You're a charming escort, but in my opinion you are a very poor risk for a marriage,'' she told him.

''I tried to tell her that time had elapsed since we had become involved, and in the decision-making process alone on the Riviera we had made up our minds. The essence of the matter was either Grace loved me or she didn't love me.''

It was not a very cheering lunch, and for Grace it must have been a distinctly chilling time. She had always thought her mother would support her in the engagement.

From then on it was open war. The Kellys brought in their friends and supporters, who all painted a lurid picture of Cassini, the womanizer.

''I don't know if it's commonly believed, but I have never considered myself to be a womanizer. I certainly have always liked the company of beautiful women. I never denied it. I tried to explain to Grace, and I think she believed me, that if you are a perfectionist you go out and look until you find the right person. I sincerely believed that for me, at least, that time had come.''

By now Cassini had been a constant companion of Grace's for nearly four months, a long enough period for two people to come to a decision simply because it had been so concentrated.

The press had begun to fan up the whole situation while the atmosphere with the family deteriorated. After a while, Cassini issued Grace a kind of ultimatum with a time limit attached. ''I am not marrying your family, I am marrying you. I want a final answer.''

In looking back over the whole period, Cassini has this to say today, ''It became a contest—the prize being Grace—between me, the studio and all the organized resistance that the family could bring to bear. It shouldn't have been like that.'' But Cassini's keen sense of competition committed him to the match.

Hedda Hopper pitched in with the family and wrote an article in which she said, ''With all the attractive men around town, I do not understand what Grace Kelly sees in Oleg Cassini. It must be his moustache.''

With Grace in on the conspiracy, Cassini answered with the

telegram, "Dear Hedda, I give up. I'll shave mine if you shave yours."

At one point in his courtship, Cassini had sought the advice of an old friend of his, Mr. Joseph P. Kennedy, who was father of the President. Cassini thought it would weigh in heavily to have the President's father—a senior citizen of some standing and a staunch Catholic—on his side.

Kennedy suggested that Cassini bring Grace over for lunch. "Don't worry, don't worry at all. Leave it all to me. I'll have a good talk with her," he had promised.

"We all went to a little French restaurant," Cassini remembers, "and no sooner had we sat down than old Kennedy started in on Grace. I sat spellbound as I listened.

" 'Now listen, Grace, you are a good Catholic girl,' he said. 'You represent a good Catholic family and you must not get involved with Oleg. He's a wonderful guy, but it wouldn't work.'

"I looked on in amazement. I said to him, 'What are you double-crossing me about in this way when your own daughter Pat married an actor [Peter Lawford]? Grace and I were completely taken aback. This is not what we had expected to hear."

Although their clandestine engagement had never been publicly confirmed, Grace Kelly and Oleg Cassini continued to see each other all through the following year. However, their relationship was to finish dramatically in December, 1955, when Grace telephoned him from New York to Florida, where he was then living.

"I want you to be the first to know because I don't want you to read it in the papers, but I have accepted to become the bride of Prince Rainier," she told him.

They agreed to meet two days later in New York. These two extraordinarily different people went for a boat ride on the Hudson so that they could talk in privacy and end their romance.

She explained that though she had cared a great deal for him during their time together, there were too many pressures against the marriage and for this reason it would never have worked out.

"That's how it ended," Oleg Cassini said quietly. "I was absolutely desolate because what could have been a very beautiful love story between two people had become some kind of international situation.

"I am a competitive person and I was bitter—very bitter. It took me a long time to get over it. It was not easy because apart from naturally being in love with her, I was sincerely fond of her and I really thought we could have made a life together.''

It is obvious that Oleg Cassini still has tender, poignant memories of Grace Kelly, and enjoyed recalling their times together.

''It is a nice feeling and in the final analysis I think she made a good choice. I honestly, truthfully say that she did the right thing and I think, in the long run, the life she has now is probably more enjoyable for her.''

When Grace Kelly's engagement to Prince Rainier was announced, Cholly Knickerbocker, loyal to his brother and in a rash moment of anger, wrote two stinging items in his gossip column which would certainly have been better left unwritten.

Today Oleg Cassini is a distinguished, silver-haired, sixty-two-year-old charmer. He has remained a bachelor, and I suspect that his romance with Grace Kelly is a fond memory.

Cassini last saw Princess Grace several years ago in Cannes. He was in a bathing suit rushing to catch a boat and she was accompanied by her close friend Vera Maxwell, the dress designer from New York.

''Hello, Grace.''

''Hello, Oleg.''

Only four words were spoken.

Sixteen

In 1955 the one star from Hollywood whom the French Government wanted at the Cannes Film Festival was Grace Kelly. Although she had not been seen in Europe in *The Country Girl*, she had made an astonishing impact there for her role in *Mogambo*. The cinema audiences liked what they saw. Her classical beauty and elegance were just as intriguing outside America as within. Rumors of her personal charisma had also seeped through from her stay on the Riviera the previous summer where she filmed *To Catch a Thief*.

Now once more she had gone back to New York and in her quiet, tenacious way had left her lawyers and agent to sort out the question of her suspension by M.G.M. She had intended to fill her time changing apartments, always a traumatic experience for her, and looking for a replacement for her secretary-companion, who was leaving New York to live elsewhere.

Then came one of those absurd anomalies that could only happen in Hollywood. Even though Grace Kelly was considered one of M.G.M.'s most prestigious assets, technically they could not ask her to go to Cannes because she was under suspension.

A telephone call was made to Rupert Allen, a former feature writer for *Look*, who had carved himself an annual niche as liaison at the Festival between the Hollywood contingent and the French Government.

Rupert Allen was educated at the University of Toulouse and is a man of culture and engaging charm—just what was required for such a delicate position. For instance, one American star and her husband decided that they had had enough of the Festival after two days and quietly took off with their driver and car, provided by the

Festival, for a trip to Italy. The French Government found such Hollywood behavior irritating and irrational. But Rupert Allen is the password for tact. He settled the matter.

When the problem of Grace Kelly impasse arose, the Festival organizers called in Rupert Allen. He recalled the incident, "I telephoned her and said something like, 'It is very easy for you to go and it's spring. You'll get a free trip to Europe and all your expenses paid in Cannes and you can stay as long as you like in Europe afterwards.

" 'Go and enjoy yourself over there instead of sitting around here and fretting about everything else. Your new secretary can wait. The Festival people will also be happy if you want to bring a chaperone.'

"Grace said that she would think about it. She does not make snap decisions. But she did call back and said that it was a marvelous idea and would I tell them that she wanted to bring with her Baroness Gladys de Segonzec, who had become a close friend during the filming of *To Catch a Thief*. They would arrive together from Paris."

She had earlier agreed to a request from Pierre Galante, one of the editors of *Paris Match* (and husband of Olivia de Havilland), that if she visited the Film Festival she would take part in a picture story for his magazine based on the not-too-original idea of Celluloid Princess meets Flesh and Blood Prince.

To the Prince it was just another day's job to publicize the principality and attract tourists. In addition he had always been agreeably amused with people from the entertainment world. For Grace Kelly it was part of a busy schedule, but also a point of honor in obliging a friend. She did not even know for certain that she would meet the Prince.

On arrival in Cannes from Paris she was slightly perturbed. The visit to the palace had been planned for her busiest day. Part of her amazing strength and ability in the management of her life and emotions is due to the fact that she likes everything to be properly organized and does not enjoy being caught off-guard.

When Pierre Galante explained to her that the audience was, in fact, with Prince Rainier and that it could not be canceled, she immediately agreed. But there were several practical problems still to be overcome.

The morning schedule included a press conference with swarms of gesticulating French and Italian journalists and photographers all shouting at her, "Thees way Gracee, that way Gracee." Furthermore, as there was no time for a hair dressing appointment, she washed it herself and dried it in the wind en route to Monte Carlo.

It is a two-hours' drive from Cannes to Monte Carlo. Elias Lapinere of the M.G.M. publicity department, who was designated chauffeur for the day, decided that there was only one way to get there and that was fast. He put his foot down on the accelerator and set off at Grand Prix speed. Following in a car behind were two *Paris Match* photographers.

For somebody like Grace, who does not like driving in cars, and positively loathes speed, the next half hour must have been traumatic. When Lapinere suddenly braked to avoid crashing into a motor truck, the *Paris Match* team behind accordioned into the back of the car in which Grace was traveling, smashing the rear end.

There was no time for remonstrances, so with the caved-in front and rear the cavalcade sped on. Near Nice they passed an Italian contingent of Festival stars, including Gina Lollobrigida. The photographers wanted to stop to take a picture of the two stars together, but Pierre Galante hustled them on.

The cars pulled into Monte Carlo at two fifty, and since Grace had not eaten all day, they all went to the Hotel de Paris for a quick lunch. With ham sandwich still in hand, Grace was driven across the city to the royal palace, which sat smiling in the sun with the royal standard floating in the breeze.

The standard, which normally indicated that the Prince was in residence, was, in fact, a false alarm.

The Prince was still lunching at his villa at Beaulieu where he shared much of his time with French film actress Gisèle Pascal. He sent his apologies and instructed an aide to show Miss Kelly and her party his palace, and promised to arrive as soon as possible.

To fill in time the *Paris Match* photographers took pictures of Grace wandering all over the palace. Just as she was about to leave to catch up with her minute-by-minute schedule at the Festival, the Prince arrived.

If she was nervous, Grace Kelly certainly did not show it. "She looked lovely, just lovely," commented Pierre Galante.

When they met, the American girl offered her hand elegantly to the Prince, who bowed. It was a moment of history. The Prince then turned on his incredible charm and took her round his private zoo, explaining how his animals all loved him and would not hurt him. He is known personally to each animal, who can almost sense his arrival before it sees him. The Prince showed Grace his chimpanzee, but what impressed her the most was that he put his arm into the lion's cage.

Together Prince Rainier and Grace Kelly made a decorative couple as they strolled around the grounds and posed for photographs inside and outside the palace.

Before agreeing to the picture session, the Prince had already talked the matter over with Father Tucker, rector of St. Charles' Church in Monte Carlo and his personal chaplain, spiritual adviser, and confidant. Both agreed that there could be nothing harmful in the pictures.

Later the Prince was to say to Father Tucker, "I granted permission for the visit, but I did not include in it that I would meet Miss Kelly."

Hand over heart, the loquacious Father Tucker, for evermore to be called the Cupid Priest, wrote his unofficial viewpoint for the *Philadelphia Bulletin* after the event.

"I sensed that the Prince was being half-apologetic, fearing that I might have some objection to his meeting a screen actress. I said to him, 'My Lord Prince, please get me straight on this. Grace Kelly is exactly the type of Catholic girl I want you to meet.' "

The same evening the Prince went over to the rectory to talk to Father Tucker about the day's events. Quite obviously that brief meeting had made a lasting impression.

"I found the palace all aglow," is how Father Tucker was to describe the next few days. "The Prince couldn't wait to talk to me about Grace. There would be all these little exuberances every time I met him and it seemed that on every possible occasion, he would drop me a note always mentioning something about Grace.

"I noticed, too, (over the next week) that the Prince betrayed signs of seriousness whenever a new item appeared about Grace Kelly, especially if she had been seen in the company of someone else."

For Grace Kelly, meeting Prince Rainier had been a pleasant interlude in the day. When the last photographs had been taken, there was a frantic dash back to Cannes where the American representatives to the Film Festival were holding a party and she was to be in the receiving line shaking hands with 1,500 guests. She herself was giving a dinner party for ten of her friends, to be followed by the screening of Paramount's entry, *The Country Girl*. This was topped off by an evening party given by the studio which finished at 4 A.M.

There was little time to speculate about the attractive man she had met that morning. On hindsight it is interesting to recall that she did not mention the Prince to either Galante or the photographer on the drive back.

Father Tucker, who had not been present at the meeting, with a twinkle in his Irish eyes, quickly followed up his hunch that this was to be a significant event by sending Grace Kelly a letter which read, "I want to thank you for showing the Prince what an American Catholic girl can be and for the very deep impression this has left on him."

One can sense the deliberation and delicacy with which the puckish little friar couched such a letter.

Grace Kelly replied in a conventional little note, saying that she was sorry to have missed Father Tucker but that she hoped that she would return to France soon and that they could meet then.

There was no exchange of any correspondence between the Prince and Grace Kelly nor any meeting until he arrived on the evening of Christmas Day that year for dinner at her parents' house.

The link between Grace Kelly and Prince Rainier was "Aunt" Eddie and "Uncle" Russie Austin, from Margate, New Jersey. The Austins had been friends of Margaret and Jack Kelly's for years since spending many summers together at Ocean City.

When the Austins arrived for the summer season at Monte Carlo, Russell Austin was told that there was not a table available at the Sporting Club, where one of the season's most colorful galas was taking place.

Impetuously he placed a call to the palace and asked to speak to Prince Rainier, saying that he was a friend of Grace Kelly's. It is most unlikely that the Prince would, under normal circumstances, have taken such a call. However, he not only took it, but sent the Austins ringside seats for the gala that night and invited them to tea at the palace next day.

They talked about America and the Kelly family in general.

"If ever you come to our country," Russ Austin said when saying good-bye to the Prince, "do be sure and let us know ahead of time so that you can visit with us."

115

The Prince assured him that he had no intentions at the moment of visiting the States. But just three months later this was exactly what he did.

Father Tucker claimed that he was the matchmaker. "Perfect matches are made in heaven, but safety matches are made by men" was one of his favorite axioms.

Russell Austin also takes the credit. "I was the Dan Cupid and directly responsible for the initial matchmaking between Grace and the Prince," he told friends.

But it is a pleasing thought that, on that spring afternoon in Monaco in 1955 when Grace Kelly first met Prince Rainier, there was a little magic in the air.

Seventeen

Since early in her film career, Princess Grace has always been interested in the occult. She herself is an intelligent amateur graphologist and reads the *Tarot* cards, but prefers to cast horoscopes for people she has just met—rather than for her friends—and then compare her predictions with her observations afterwards to see whether she was right or not.

Prince Rainier sometimes gives her a piece of writing from one of his official letters to hear her comments. Invariably she hits the nail on the head with her quizzical appraisal. She has had her own writing analyzed by Britain's Jeanne Heal, who has written a book on graphology for which Princess Grace has penned the foreword.

In all her homes in New York and on the West Coast stacks of horoscope magazines and the latest books on astrology were scattered round. Two books which she consulted frequently were *The Pursuit of Destiny* and *Astrology for Everyone.*

At her parties she was at her happiest sitting on the floor with her feet tucked up under her giving a guest a reading. She herself is a Scorpio. And as Vivien Leigh, another Scorpio, said, "Scorpions burn themselves out and eat themselves up and they are careless about themselves—like me."

But this appears to be patently untrue of Princess Grace. She prefers to waft through life at her own—often procrastinating—pace, but there is one similarity. Like Vivien Leigh she also revels in that enchanting occupation of serendipity. The Concise Oxford Dictionary defines serendipity as "the faculty of making happy and unexpected discoveries by accident." It was coined by Horace

117

Walpole after *The Three Princes of Serendip*, a Ceylonese fairy tale.

Most of Princess Grace's friends, it seems, were born under Leo—John Foreman, Carolyn Reybold, Bettina Gray, Maree Rambo, Gant Gaither and Alfred Hitchcock. Both Princess Caroline and Princess Stephanie are Aquarians and Prince Albert is a Pisces. The exact opposite in character to Scorpions is the Gemini with his double-sided character of dark and sunshine moods.

Prince Rainier is a true Gemini, which, together with his Mediterranean culture and nature, added the surprise element to their first years of marriage. While still single Princess Grace told friends that in her marriage she wanted to be dominated by a man in the important issues and not just in the choice of a restaurant.

Being married to an interesting and complicated man like Prince Rainier cannot always have been easy, but life with a Gemini is never dull. And the Prince is no exception.

Through the years her interest in the occult has diminished, although she is still fascinated by astrology. She has been interested in Dr. J. B. Rhine's theories of extrasensory perception, in Buddhist theories of reincarnation (of which she believes that the Bridie Murphy experiments were interesting evidence), in table rapping, the Ouija board and spiritualism. During her Hollywood days she enjoyed a good séance with a gifted medium, and when she was in New York often consulted her favorite gypsy fortuneteller at the Russian tea shops.

In August of 1955 before returning to Hollywood to begin work on a new film, she gave a Leo party for all her friends. The large cake was decorated with a lion.

When she turned forty in 1969, she revived the idea in Monaco and gave a party for all of her Scorpion friends who could make the journey.

In September, 1955, Grace Kelly flew to California to begin work on *The Swan,* the screen adaptation of the Ferenc Molnar play. It is a beguiling story of a girl who rejects the love of her young tutor in order to marry the crown prince. The cast was a formidable one, including Alec Guinness, on his first visit to Hollywood, and the French actor Louis Jourdan; it was directed by that veteran Charles Vidor.

It was a part made for Grace: romantic, enchanting, beautifully dressed and needing an extra dimension of acting to turn it from candy floss into charming sophistication. Helen Rose, who was later to design Grace's wedding gown, came up with some exquisite designs for the clothes. Fragile, beguilingly feminine, they suited Grace Kelly's porcelain beauty.

The trip to the West Coast was hazardous, as the plane was twice struck by lightning. This must be a contributing factor to the Princess's dislike of flying even today.

She settled into a house which she rented from the food reformer Gaylord Hauser. It was a small, charming white Regency-style house with a garden and pint-sized swimming pool for Oliver. Oliver was a smoky poodle given to Grace by the Cary Grants when her parakeet died. By now Oliver had become so much a part of her life that he was accepted by her friends as a personality in the Kelly household. Where Grace went, Oliver went, traveling curled up on her lap wherever and whenever she flew.

Two weeks after her arrival in California, the entire cast and crew took off in two DC-7's hired by M.G.M. for the trip. Their destination was North Carolina, for location shots at Biltmore, where they had leased the Renaissance-style chateau which George Vanderbilt had created.

Everyone was slightly overwhelmed at its grandeur, everyone but Grace. She told Jay Kanter, "It's like a beautiful palace. I love it."

Grace Kelly's public image was a hodgepodge of fact, fantasy and circumstances. Around her had grown a whole world of clichés —white gloves, frosty beauty, steel insides. She herself laughed at them; and although it upset her at the beginning, she was to say later, "I thought that I had dispelled that cool business after *Rear Window*, but I guess it's something I'm stuck with."

The truth is that she is far from cool with her friends. She is a fun-loving, warm-hearted woman who takes a delight in playing practical jokes on her friends. It is, in fact, one of the joys of her marriage to Prince Rainier—she totally understands and joins in his often schoolboyish humor.

In the script of *The Swan,* the prince admonishes his future princess, "Remember what it means to be a swan . . . to glide like a dream . . . silent, white, majestic . . . there you must stay, Alexandra, head high, cool, indifferent to the staring crowds."

Out of camera range, it was a completely different Grace. "I found her delightful and fun to work with, very professional and also full of giggles," Alec Guinness told me when recalling the film.

Jessie Royce Landis, who had played Grace's mother in *To Catch a Thief*, was once again playing her mother and aiding and abetting Grace in her pranks.

When they heard that Alec Guinness had received one of those fatuous, star-struck letters from a fan signed "Alice," they laid their plans. They had him constantly paged in his hotel by "Alice" (no one can remember the lady's last name). It was done with great consistency every few hours. When they heard that he was going to dine at Antonine's, he was paged again. They plagued him with loving telegrams all signed "Alice."

Alec Guinness was almost hysterical, wondering whether this madwoman did, in fact, exist, and became fearful that he might bump into her. It was a long time before he finally caught on to the joke. When he told Grace about his Alice nightmares, she laughed so much that she fell off the sofa she was sitting on.

"Roycie," as Jessie Royce Landis was called by her friends, also had a delicious sense of fun.

Film crews on location, living and working together in a confined space, tend to make their own fun. The clever practical joker who can lighten the off-set moments becomes like the queen in a beehive—indispensable.

New York is a city that evokes passion in people. For Grace Kelly it was home—the city she loved most in the world. Often when she would finish filming in Hollywood on a Friday evening, she would get on a plane for New York just to spend the weekend there.

Sitting around one evening after a day's shooting in the octagonal grey stone pump room at Asheville's Manor Hotel, where the cast of *The Swan* was staying, the conversation turned to New York.

"It's awful! Just like a bombed city these days," cried Jessie Royce Landis.

"I'm told they're tearing down Carnegie Hall next year," put in Louis Jourdan.

"The Plaza Hotel is going one day soon," Jay Kanter added, "and you know, they are even going to tear down the Met."

All this time Grace had been sitting very quietly with her hands folded, becoming sadder and sadder. Finally she burst out, "I can't stand it! I'm going to quit the movies, go back to New York, run for mayor and stop all this destruction!''

The film was finally completed on December 23. Grace packed her bags and set off for New York and a Christmas party at the Jay Kanters'.

Next day, still tired from jet lag, the completion of the film and the Kanter party, she left for Philadelphia and a typical Kelly family reunion.

Only this year there was one difference.

Eighteen

For some time the question of Prince Rainier's marrying and producing an heir had become a matter of urgency in his principality. Should he have failed to do this, on his death Monaco would have been taken over by France once again—a thought totally abhorrent to its 30,000 tax-free citizens.

To understand the immediacy of the problem, it is necessary to search back into the Grimaldi family history, which dates back to the twelfth century. This powerful family, wishing to expand their territory, set up a trading post at the foot of the Maritime Alps. They have been called merchant adventurers by some, brigands by others.

They flew their flag over Monaco for nearly five centuries until 1793, when the French revolutionaries annexed the area to France. This was short-lived as Monaco was restored to the Grimaldis by the victorious allies following their defeat of Napoleon.

It was not until the end of World War I that the French concluded an astonishing treaty with Prince Rainier's great-grandfather, Prince Albert. Because of a mysterious claim to Monaco by a truculent German family called the d'Urach's (a hideous thought), the French granted Prince Albert a treaty recognizing Monaco as an independent principality whose sovereignty could not be ceded to any foreign power except France.

There was a clause in the treaty that if the throne of Monaco ever became vacant for one day, it would immediately be returned to the protectorate of France.

Prince Rainier had succeeded to the throne from his grandfather, Prince Louis II, in a complicated way.

In 1869 Prince Rainier's great-grandfather, Prince Albert I, in a bid to curry favor with Great Britain, took an English bride—Lady Mary Douglas Hamilton, daughter of the 11th Duke of Hamilton and of Brandon. Shortly after giving birth to a son, Prince Louis II, she was so unhappy in the vast palace that she decided to flee the country, taking the boy with her. It took eight years of litigation before the marriage was declared void.

For a second bride Prince Albert looked to the New World and took an American girl, New Orleans-born Alice Heine. This marriage lasted several years and it was through the efforts of this first American Princess of Monaco that Monte Carlo became a cultural center.

After his disastrous marriages, Prince Albert returned to his constant love, the sea. When he served in the Spanish Navy, he was known as Albert the Navigator, and it is due to his efforts that the Oceanographic Museum in Monaco was founded at the turn of the century.

Lady Mary was the chief influence in Prince Louis's life, as he spent much of his youth in her care before he joined the French Army. There he fell in love with Juliette Louvet who, it is said, was an enchanting laundress.

One faction of Monegasques stoutly maintains that he did, in fact, marry the girl; but the more conservative historians say that, though it was an *affaire de coeur*, it was never officially acknowledged.

From this romantic union in 1898 was born a girl, Charlotte Louise Juliette, the mother of Prince Rainier.

The child was brought up in Paris until her teens, when her grandfather summoned her back to Monaco to be instructed in court procedure and in the role that she was destined to play as heiress to the throne.

Just one year later she married the dashing Duke Pierre de Polignac—who was named Prince Pierre on their marriage—and bore him two children, Prince Rainier and Princess Antoinette.

Even this marriage, which began so hopefully, fell apart a few years later and ended in divorce in 1933. Prince Pierre was banished from Monaco, and it was not until after the war that he returned to live in Monte Carlo. He is extremely fond of his American daughter-in-law and was to become one of Princess Grace's leading champions during the first perplexing years of her marriage.

After the breakup of her marriage, Princess Charlotte renounced her rights to the throne and left the principality to live in a large country house outside Paris. Princess Charlotte has not returned to the Monaco she loved so much since her son's wedding.

Prince Rainier, a handsome and virile twenty-six-year-old, was crowned *Son Altesse Serenissime* ("His Serence Highness") in 1949.

The title of *His Serene Highness* perhaps needs explaining. In a kingdom such as Great Britain, Holland, Denmark, Sweden or Belgium, where the king or queen is ruler, he or she is known as *Your Majesty*. In a principality such as Monaco, which is ruled by a prince—a title created for themselves by the Grimaldis in the fourteenth century—the sovereign is known as *Your Serene Highness* despite the fact that he is an absolute monarch.

For the early years of his reign Prince Rainier showed no signs of settling down, much to the consternation of his subjects. There had been his four-year friendship with Gisèle Pascal: As head of State, marriage to a divorced woman would not have been acceptable.

As the King of Sweden and Prince Charles know only too well, it is almost impossible for a prominent male member of any leading royal family to court a girl without the whole world looking over his shoulder. Prince Rainier was no exception. As he was to say in an interview in *Collier's* magazine to David Schoenbrun, before his fate-sealing trip to America, "You see, my greatest difficulty is knowing a girl long enough and intimately enough to find out if we are really soul mates as well as lovers.

"I consider a duty to my people to get married, but there is a higher duty above politics, the duty of a man to be true to himself, to fulfill himself as a human being, by taking a wife he loves and consummating that love. I will not marry except for love. I will not agree to a loveless marriage of convenience."

It is for this reason, also, that he refused to take part in the Adriatic matchmaking cruise organized by Queen Frederica of Greece in anticipation of finding suitable partners for her own children.

Just before he left for his Philadelphia rendezvous, Prince Rainier was asked to describe his ideal woman. It is no coincidence that it was a blueprint of Grace Kelly.

"I'd like a girl who is fair-haired, the sort of subtle beauty that grows on you. She has long flowing hair and her eyes are blue or hazel flicked with gold."

He also said that she must be charitable and unspoilt, as he particularly disliked the glossy smart-set type of international beauty.

"I want my wife to be a normal human being with her own personal likes and dislikes.

"I want an intelligent girl but not an intellectual. There is nothing more disagreeable to a man than to have a wife who knows more than he does on every subject. It is even worse than being beaten at tennis.

"I cannot bear intellectual snobs, or snobs of any kind.

"I must be the boss, or else I am not a man but, at the same time, I am not a dictator. It takes two to start a fight and two to make a marriage."

Financially, too, Grace Kelly slotted into the description of the Prince's ideal bride. He neither wanted to marry a woman who might covet not only prestige but also his money, nor did he wish to be embarrassed with a capricious heiress as a bride.

Through her film earnings, and later an inheritance from her father, Princess Grace has her own private income which helps her to maintain the financial independence she is accustomed to.

Meantime the citizens of Monaco sat and waited . . . and prayed.

It was against this intricate background that the news of the Prince's engagement was hailed with sheer delight in Monaco. It is difficult to assess how much the head ruled the heart among Monaco's tax-free subjects, but the outward burst of excitement—and relief—was real enough. They were soon to have their own princess—and a possible heir.

During the autumn of 1955, when Prince Rainier was quietly planning a trip to America, the puckish Father Tucker was positively bursting with conspiracy. And while Grace Kelly was to be seen every morning walking her poodle, Oliver, along Sixty-third Street, three of the world's most astute business brains had been conspiring in a most eccentric plot—a plot so bizarre, so daring and so improbable that it would have stunned the world. Had it come to fruition, the entire history of Monaco might have been altered and a love story as provocative as that of King Edward VII and Wallis Simpson been enacted.

I had first heard fragments of the story from Norman Mailer, but

125

was so disinclined to believe its veracity that I took the elevator up to the penthouse office of Gardner Cowles in the old *Look* building on Fifth Avenue.

Mr. Cowles, now a venerable figure in the history of American journalism, looked at me with clear twinkling eyes.

"Yes, it is true, but Norman does not have all the titillating details."

Spellbound I listened as he told me how Aristotle Onassis, George Schlee and he planned to save the finances of Monaco.

I tell the story in full simply because it seems incredible that three such formidable minds could have conjured up anything so audacious without even consulting the central figure, Prince Rainier.

"I had been a close friend of George Schlee for quite a number of years. Every summer Schlee used to leave his wife, the dress designer Valentina, behind in New York and go off with Greta Garbo for a month or two on Onassis' yacht in the Mediterranean.

"This particular year, in 1955, when Schlee came back, he and Valentina came up to stay with me at my house in western Connecticut. He told me that Onassis had just bought a tremendous portion of Monaco and that he wanted Schlee to help him promote it. Monte Carlo was no longer *the* chic place to visit on the Riviera as others had supplanted it. To maximize the return on his investment, Onassis wanted to do anything he could to bring Monte Carlo back as the smartest place to go.

"I asked George to tell me a little bit about Monte Carlo and Prince Rainier, whom I had never met. How attractive was he and so on.

" 'Well, he is a plump young man, but he is attractive enough,' he answered.

" 'Why don't you marry him off to an American celebrity and that would give Monte Carlo worldwide publicity and get the Americans going back again,' I told him.

" 'What kind of a woman have you in mind?' he asked.

" 'Well, what about a movie star?'

" 'That's not a bad idea, but which one?'

"I said, 'Why not start at the top—Marilyn Monroe.'

Marilyn was at the peak of her popularity at the time. Schlee got very excited about it, but cautiously said how could anyone persuade Marilyn to marry the Prince?

126

"I was publishing *Look* magazine at the time and we had done many stories on Marilyn and I knew her pretty well. She trusted me.

" 'That's great,' Schlee said, by now highly enthusiastic. 'I know Ari would do anything to promote this. Will you put it up to Marilyn?'

"It just happened that she was staying that month with Milton Green the photographer, who had a house three or four miles from mine. He was a close friend and adviser to Marilyn, so I phoned him that Saturday night and said I couldn't invite them to dinner, as we already had too many guests, but would they come along afterwards for drinks.

"They did, and George and I managed to get Marilyn to walk with us round the pool so that we could talk alone. We put the idea to her. She listened very carefully and said, 'Is he rich? Is he handsome?' Those were the only questions she asked. I don't think she even knew where Monaco was. But she agreed that we were to go ahead and arrange a meeting.

"As an afterthought I said to her, 'Do you think that the Prince will want to marry you?'

"Her eyes were full of light. 'Give me two days alone with him and of course he'll want to marry me.'

"I promised to be in touch with her the following week.

"Imagine my surprise when, on the following Monday morning, on the front page of the *New York Times* was the story that this high-ranking priest [Father Tucker] was being sent by the Vatican to reach an agreement with the Kelly family in Philadelphia.

"I called up Schlee, who wouldn't believe it and went out and got his copy of the *Times*. He just couldn't believe it. The reason that the story has stuck in my mind all these years is that the Kellys had the big advantage. They are among the high-ranking Catholics in the United States, and Marilyn Monroe, as far as I know, had no religious affiliation and anyway it would probably never have come off. But it was worth a try."

Gardner Cowles paused for breath and a chuckle. "It was quite an idea."

It was.

When one watches the painstaking dedication that Princess Grace puts into her work as a royal patroness, the calm and efficient way she handles people, the discipline that she imposes on herself, the effort she makes to be punctual, the genuine love she has for Monaco, "Her Serene Highness Princess Marilyn" would not have stood a chance.

Poor tragic, vulnerable, child-woman Marilyn. How irresponsible of these cold-blooded money tycoons to meddle in affairs of the heart. And how fortunate for Monaco that they did not succeed.

Nineteen

Prince Rainier and Father Tucker had arrived in New York on December 15. Also included in the entourage was Dr. Maurice Donat, the Prince's personal physician. It had been stated in the press that the Prince was in America for his annual medical checkup and a visit to the Johns Hopkins Hospital for a minor sinus operation.

As soon as the Prince arrived in New York, he got in touch with the Austins, the friends of the Kellys who had visited him during the summer. It was a masterpiece of strategy, and all part of the crafty plot of Father Tucker's to encounter Grace Kelly again.

It was felt that this would be the most diplomatic way of going about things, as the Prince wanted a certain protocol to be observed. Instead of having the Prince, Father Tucker and Dr. Donat to dinner as planned, the Austins telephoned Mrs. Kelly and asked if they might bring their guests along to dinner that night. As Christmas night is customarily a special one reserved for family gatherings, this in itself was a little unusual.

Peggy Conlan remembers the night vividly:

"It was Aunt Eddie and Uncle Russ who asked mother if they could bring over their guests to dinner on Christmas Day night. The Prince being a prince had to have an invitation from someone and he was always accompanied by Father Tucker and his doctor.

"When they arrived my father greeted them at the door. The Prince looked very handsome and rather shy. Father Tucker looked like a simply divinely cute parish priest with a twinkle in his eye. My father knew an Irish priest if ever he saw one and said, 'Father Tucker, sit down and I'll give you a cigar and let's go on from here.'

"It was a very gay and lovely dinner, and Prince Rainier and my sister sat and talked a lot. I think at first that Grace was a little shy and so was the Prince, but as the dinner progressed everyone seemed to warm up.

"Father Tucker left soon after dinner, as he was going to spend the night with the parish priest whom he knew. After all, he was a Philadelphian himself. My father offered to drive him there.

"Mother suggested that we young ones all go over to my place. So this we did. While the rest of us played the card game Thirty-one in one room, Grace and the Prince went into the other room to talk."

By the time Mr. Kelly returned from the train Father Tucker had already had a talk with him.

"Know what the good father told me?" he said to his wife on returning. "He said that the Prince wants to marry Grace and the Prince asked him to sound me out on the idea. What do you say to that?"

Mrs. Kelly is a realist, a woman with her head set firmly on those handsome Teutonic shoulders. "What will Grace say to that?" she answered.

Over at the Conlan house it was a homey family evening. When the party finally broke up, Prince Rainier's dark suit was covered with hairs from Peggy's dog and she had to get out the Scotch tape and clean him up before he left.

Once back at the Kelly household, it was already late when Mrs. Kelly asked Prince Rainier and Doctor Donat if they would like to stay the night. They both accepted.

The following day Grace and her sister took the Prince and doctor to Bucks County to see a hospital the doctor was interested in. Though the Prince and Grace were never alone, when they returned the second night to the Kelly home it was very much understood by the family that there was something in the air.

"It was the sweetest love story possible," Peggy continued. "You know, when you think of it, it was all rather strange as they both came from such different shores. But it must have been love at first, or at least second, sight."

During his two-day stay with the Kellys, Prince Rainier was to find his bed apple-pied one night and his pajamas sewn up at the legs and arms the other. It was his first intimation that he was becoming involved with a family that enjoyed practical jokes just as much as he did!

As there could be no question that Prince Rainier, one of the world's last absolute monarchs—even if his Principality is only three hundred seventy acres—would be accepted in his suit, Father Tucker became the intermediary.

Father Tucker was to write in *The Philadelphia Inquirer* at the time, "What pleased me most about my first contacts was the parents' hesitation about the romance of their daughter—even a sort of reluctance and concern about the whole thing. Mr. and Mrs. Kelly have shown the prudence and caution that can be inspired only by true parental love and attachment to the principles of their faith.

"Mr. Kelly's first question was that of any sensible man, 'What do the lad's parents think of all this?' "

Princess Charlotte, Prince Rainier's mother, who has an apartment in the Legation de Monaco in Paris, had stated her wishes previously to Father Tucker when she said, "All I want is that my son marries a Catholic and someone that he loves. And I hope she'll like her mother-in-law."

Mrs. Kelly, in particular, who had never been a mother to push her daughters into marriage, was not so much interested in Grace's immediate reaction as in the kind of life she would be required to lead in the future. Would it bring her the happiness that she deserved?

It could almost have been a scene from an updated *Little Women.* Peggy remembers whisking into the bathroom with Grace and each saying simultaneously and gravely, "He is very charming."

Grace Kelly went back to New York, and over the next few days saw the Prince constantly; but it was at a private party on New Year's Eve that he asked her to marry him. As there were several formalities to be observed, it was agreed that the date of the official announcement should be January 5, and that it would be made simultaneously in Philadelphia and Monaco.

On January 4 when the Prince and Grace appeared with their friends Carolyn and Malcolm Reybold in the Cub Room of the Stork Club, all heads turned towards them. Already there were ripples stirring among the gossip writers.

Jack O'Brien, a Broadway reporter for the New York *Journal American*, was also there, and boldly decided to send a note over to Grace Kelly.

He wrote, "Dear Grace, I understand you will announce your engagement on Thursday or Friday," adding two little boxes for "yes" or "no" and asking, "Answer one please."

131

The four conferred over the note and then picking up their fur jackets the girls made their way toward the table. Grace was peering through her pink-framed glasses to recognize the sender. When she saw that it was Jack O'Brien, she paused and said, "Hullo, Jack."

He stood and boldly said, "Are congratulations in order?"

"I'm sorry I can't possibly answer your note tonight, Jack," she parried.

"Can you answer it on Friday?" he dug deeper.

Astonishingly frank she replied, "Yes, Friday."

And that is how the first journalist got his scoop on the engagement facts.

Mr. Kelly had always had a great understanding and affinity for the press. He not only understood the power they had in presenting the Kellys' image, but respected them as people employed to do a good job.

"Grace, this is going to be a big thing," he told his daughter and then set about organizing it down to the last detail.

He arranged that Grace and the Prince would drive down from New York. They were to stop off briefly at the Kelly home at 3901 Henry Avenue before going on to the Philadelphia Country Club, where the news was to be officially announced at 1 P.M. at a luncheon party for twenty-nine guests.

Plans had been made that the engagement should be simultaneously announced in Monaco by the Minister of State. Everyone was so excited about the event that no one remembered that Monacan time is five hours ahead. So the news was, in fact, announced in Monte Carlo and back on the agency wires to New York before it was out in Philadelphia.

Father Tucker was in shining form as he chatted with the various guests, who not only included the close friends of the Kelly family but several dignitaries such as Governor and Mrs. George M. Leader, and Mayor and Mrs. Richardson Dilworth.

Prince Rainier and his fiancée arrived at one forty and entered the country club by a side door where the guests awaited them. There was champagne poured as Mr. Kelly tapped his glass and, standing tall and proud, said, "We are happy to announce the engagement of our daughter Grace to His Serene Highness Prince Rainier of Monaco. We drink a toast to them."

It was a simple, straightforward announcement as befitted the man himself. Grace looked happy and pretty in a simple gold brocaded shirtwaist dress with a blush-pink chiffon scarf tucked in at her neck. Her only jewelry was a pin on her right lapel and her engagement ring—a large twelve-carat solitaire diamond which the Prince had had specially brought over for him from Monte Carlo.

One photographer, Dominic Ligato of the *Bulletin*, and one TV cameraman were admitted to take pool photographs of the occasion. I am told that Prince Rainier looked very shy as he watched the way Grace faced the cameras—her usual cool, calm professional self.

After Ligato had taken four shots she told him, "Oh, won't you please take another? I think you got me cross-eyed on that last one."

Back at the Kelly home the place was swarming with nearly one hundred reporters and photographers. As there was only one telephone line, which was reserved for family calls, the press descended on neighbors, badgering them for telephones. Henry Avenue had never before known such excitement.

For a whole hour the cameramen moved in to take their pictures. They climbed over chairs, stood on antique tables, pushed and jostled, and even spilled into Mrs. Kelly's bedroom. Grace's sister Lizanne (Mrs. Donald C. LeVine), obviously very pregnant, had to stand on one side to be sure she wouldn't be pushed. Kell brought out his own camera and began taking a personal record of his sister's engagement.

At first Prince Rainier was acquiescent and patient as he listened to some of the inane questions being fired at him and his fiancée. When one woman journalist babbled about what plans they had for a family, Grace colored pink and Ma Kelly stepped in, smartly answering, "I should say they will have lots of children."

After a period Prince Rainier showed signs of restlessness and was overheard to say crisply to Father Tucker, "After all, I don't belong to M.G.M."

After the last photographs and interviews had been completed Mr. Kelly opened his basement bar and invited the press to celebrate with him. But there was little time for drinking as they swarmed out of the house back to their offices with first-hand accounts. For the *Philadelphia Bulletin* it was a field day to remember . . . they led all the way.

The following afternoon Grace held a small party in New York for two dozen of her friends. The Prince arrived wearing white tie and tails and his royal decorations, as they were both to go on to the

133

"Night in Monte Carlo" Charity Benefit later that evening. The fairy tale was now becoming a reality.

A touching moment at the party was when the Prince publicly thanked Mr. and Mrs. Austin for bringing Grace to him. "You have done more for me by this than anyone else has done for me in my life," he said.

At the gala at the Waldorf-Astoria that evening, Grace and her Prince were the center of attraction. It was as if satiated, jaded New York society wanted to gaze, or even physically touch, the fairy-tale couple in the hopes that some of their happiness would rub off.

Grace wore a Dior silk gown that showed off her slender shoulders, and had pinned a corsage of orchids on her bosom. This time her white gloves were of royal proportions and she had chosen to wear low-heeled shoes so as not to appear taller than Prince Rainier who stands 5 feet 7 inches in his bare feet, the reason he always referred to himself as Shorty.

They were suitably photographed with Grace folding her hands demurely in her lap and eyes beguilingly turned down. Standing behind her, Prince Rainier looked handsome, prosperous and pleased. There were other shots of them gazing rapturously into each other's eyes as they toasted each other with champagne.

According to *Time* magazine, which wrote lyrically of the event, "They sat uncomfortably in the royal box and nibbled crystalized violets while the Press howled at the door. Later at the Harwyn Club Grace nibbled Rainier's ear and danced with him until 4 A.M."

Both Prince Rainier and Princess Grace have made it very clear over the years that the timing of their meeting was just right.

Grace Kelly has a knack of always getting her timing right. As she was to say with disarming honesty to friends on board the *Constitution* as she sailed for Monaco and marriage, "If I had met the Prince six months previously, I doubt that it would have taken place."

Quotations taken out of context can be dangerous words. But two by Grace Kelly before she became engaged to Prince Rainier are relevant in that they indicate her shyness and uncertainty about life.

"Marriage is like life. You never reach a point where you can say, 'Now I have grown up' because you go on growing all the time. Love is a growing thing, too, because it takes on so many different aspects. I'm always falling in love with other places or other people."

"There are many people, many men I could love. I think it

depends on the man you want to devote yourself to spend your life with. This is the decision of marriage."

Prince Rainier said at the time, "It wasn't a sudden thought. . . . I think that we were both ready for marriage."

Mrs. Kelly had decided to shorten the Prince's name to Rai which she calls him to this day. Mr. Kelly was enjoying his new status.

In an interview with *Time* magazine during the week of the engagement, he was in an expansive mood as he spoke of his future royal son-in-law.

"I told him that I certainly hoped he wouldn't run around the way some princes do, and I told him if he did, he'd lose a mighty fine girl.

"The Prince solemnly promised that he would be an exemplary husband."

In a syndicated newspaper column at the time, Mrs. Kelly described the event in raturous words.

"Through it all Grace has remained calm. At the press conference she was her usual pleasant, retiring self. There was a difference in her behavior, however, that I believe I was the only one who noticed. . . . Whenever she looked at her Prince or her ring her feelings took possession of her face.

"She really looked like a girl who had found her prince!

" 'Mother, I never knew I could be so happy!' she said to me, time and again."

The "difference in her behavior" may, of course, have been one of three things: a fond mother's exuberance over her daughter's royal engagement; an inventive ghost writer from the paper; or perhaps, and this is what I believe, an astute mother commenting on a sensitive and fascinating facet of her daughter's character. The making of a princess had already begun.

When *Time* asked brother Kell what his reaction was, he replied, "I don't think we can make a sculler out of him. He's not tall enough. But I hear he is a terrific skin diver."

Carroll Righter, the well-known American astrologer who was writing at the time for the New York *Mirror*, pronounced that the romance could actually have been made in heaven.

"Comparison of the two charts finds eight out of ten points in common. Both Venus, the planet of romance, love, and concord, and the redoubtable Mars, the planet of energy, vitality, and consuming interest, play a very prominent part.

135

"Miss Kelly has planetary positions which are stated in text books as being 'a sign all by itself,' indicating she is such a personality in her own right that she will be imbued with a unique activity, career and viewpoint that set her a little apart from others. . . . Despite wealth, talent and what seems to be a quick and easy rise to fame, there is no question that many things have been done the hard way by her.

"The horoscope of the Prince of Monaco indicates he has a decided, restless urge to go places, see people and do things. This does not interfere at all, however, with his capacity to love deeply and sincerely.

"Any woman would be happy to have him around the house because he is a born problem solver. There will be no lack of love for Grace from him because he likes to show little attentions a woman craves.

"There will be considerable problems, however, to prevent the relationship from bogging down into too great contentment. . . ."

Covering himself for all eventualities, Righter continued, "There is one danger, and that is of unconventionality or confusion from different backgrounds. However, an understanding attitude on the part of both persons can provide an added respect and a deepening of the existing ties."

Twenty

Grace Kelly was to become the most married girl of the year. With her two weddings—civic and religious—to Prince Rainier all set for April 18, 1956, she first had to go through a wedding in the film *High Society*, which she had already contracted to make before the Prince's arrival and proposal.

The film was a remake of that classic *Philadelphia Story* starring Katharine Hepburn, James Stewart and Cary Grant; and though I find the original a much more stylish production, the Grace Kelly, Bing Crosby, Frank Sinatra, Celeste Holm version was opulent and had a starry quality due, no doubt, to the new ecstatic happiness of Grace Kelly.

On the first day when the cast met on the set there was a certain apprehension. It occurs on every first day—the same kind of feeling that children have when starting school. With cosseted, egotistical actors the atmosphere is often charged with tension.

Grace had made one film with Bing Crosby, and Celeste Holm had worked with Frank Sinatra before, but the combination of all four was as yet an unknown. The director was Chuck Walters, an ebullient extrovert. Grace was gracious on that first day, if a little shy, simply because while all the others were used to doing musicals, this was to be her first.

Even with a string of successes now behind her, Grace was still uncertain working with experienced stars. Writer Maurice Sollito explains this withdrawal. "An actor who worked closely with her said, 'She goes to incredible lengths to avoid any situation in which there is even a remote possibility that she might be rejected. She

137

doesn't trust people. She is afraid of looking stupid and that's why she doesn't talk very much.' ''

Celeste Holm, who remembers that first day, confirms this. Talking to me in New York she said, "She kept very much to herself. At the time she was dieting like mad. She would have grapefruit, honey and tea for lunch and nothing else. She was so slender that I thought it was a little odd, but she was so strong-minded, almost stubborn about it."

On the first day of shooting Grace had one request to make of the director. She asked if she could wear her own engagement ring in the film. Next day she arrived with her diamond ring.

"It was the most wonderful diamond I have ever seen. Most diamonds I think look just cold and icy but the thing about this one was the colors in it," Celeste Holm said.

When Bing Crosby says in the film, "Some stone, George. Did you mine it yourself?" the audience was able to get a close-up view in glamorous Eastman Technicolor plus VistaVision.

In most cases when two blondes are to share honors in a film, the bigger name demands that the other actress dye her hair to avoid confusion. When Betty Grable first co-starred with Alice Faye, she bleached her hair to platinum so as not to interfere with Alice's corn-color hair. Sheree North wore a black wig to contrast with Marilyn Monroe's blondeness. Agnes Moorehead, a lifetime redhead, had to switch to blonde to contrast with Jane Russell. But when Celeste Holm and Grace Kelly met there were no complications—they remained their own colors.

"No one gave it a thought that we were both blonde. Grace wastes no time on such banal matters. She was lovely to work with simply because there was not one trace of temperament even though these were harassing days for her."

Every day during the lunchtime breaks, Grace had to give an interview of some sort. The press were relentless and M.G.M. equally keen to squeeze the last drop of publicity out of the situation.

"Grace seemed to move without any consciousness of self," Celeste Holm continued. "She has remarkable self-composure. The publicity demands on her were overwhelming. With it all she retained absolute equanimity which she maintained at all times. I have worked with many actresses who would have collapsed under the strain."

Miss Holm happened to drop in on one such interview when

Grace was being interrogated by a dragon from Associated Press "with a voice of shattered glass."

" 'Tell me, Miss Kelly, how long do you think it will last?' the reporter asked.

" 'I beg your pardon,' Grace answered.

"The woman repeated the question.

" 'A Catholic marries for life,' came the answer.

" 'Do you plan on having any children?'

" 'I certainly hope so.'

" 'How many children are you going to have?'

" 'Well . . . that is out of my hands,' she replied without any hint of impatience.

"I would have punched the lady hard," Celeste Holm remarked. "But Grace was so courteous and gracious.

"Once after such a scene I asked Grace, 'How is all of this affecting you?'

"She replied, 'I'm tired. I'll catch up on my rest later—I guess!' She has a keen sense of humor and a human receptiveness."

In between the endless interviews Grace had to have numerous fittings for her trousseau and wedding gown, answer letters and invitations and take many personal calls from well-wishing friends. She never had a free minute to herself.

Grace was determined to sing her own songs and not have them dubbed as many other stars do.

"She had a very dear contralto voice—lovely and totally appropriate. She made no effort to sound like a professional singer. On the day she was to sing that lovely, lovely song "True Love" with Bing we all hung about to hear them."

During the making of the film, Prince Rainier and his father, the Duke de Polignac, visited Hollywood and were invited onto the set of *High Society*. A luncheon was given for them in the paneled executive dining room which at Metro was considered rather a joke simply because it was so small and could only seat eight.

There was Grace Kelly and Prince Rainier, Chuck Walters and Dore Schary, the Duke de Polignac and Celeste Holm. The lunch rippled along happily even though Grace seemed nervous. Chuck Walters, who had a tendency to be enchantingly obscene, could not have been more correct. Then suddenly it happened. Dore Schary asked Prince Rainier how large Monaco was. The figure of five square miles was mentioned.

"Five square miles," Schary answered. "That's not as big as our back lot."

Suddenly a cold wind went through the room. Celeste Holm was so perturbed that she stuck a knife into her steak, it skidded and the sauce spluttered all over the front of her dress.

"I knew that second that Grace Kelly would never make another picture," she recalled.

Grace and Celeste were both invited to the Red Book Party, an annual movie colony event, and planned to go together.

"Who are you going with?" Celeste asked.

"My Prince," Grace replied.

As it turned out the dinner was to be late, and with an early morning call the girls decided not to go.

When Prince Rainier returned to New York, Grace Kelly promised him that she would neither drink nor dance with anyone until they met again. And she kept her promise except at a party in her honor when Danny Kaye and Frank Sinatra telephoned the Prince and asked his permission.

Mr. and Mrs. Kelly also paid a visit to the Coast to see Grace. Mrs. Ben Lyon and her former husband were old friends of the Kellys' and gave a party for them.

"We made the arrangements for it at the Beverly Hills Hotel right after Grace's engagement was announced.

"We had calls from everyone wanting to come, but by that time our guest list was completed. It was a beautiful party and we had orchid corsages for both Grace and Margaret. Grace looked incredibly beautiful that night in a long white brocaded satin chongsam. Her hair was drawn back into a chignon, but she outshone everyone by her simplicity and beauty."

Members of the cast of *High Society* had a hard job trying to find the crooked roulette wheel which they gave to Grace as a wedding present.

Helen Rose of M.G.M., who was given the coveted job of designing Grace Kelly's real wedding gown, gave her a shower-party for eighteen. Among the gifts Grace received was a shower cap with ermine tails. Guests were asked to bring lingerie—"I have never in my life seen such beautiful things. They were all in white, blue and beige," Celeste Holm recalled.

A surprise guest was Annette Kellerman, the famous swimmer,

who brought a rosepoint handkerchief given her by Gatti. Nibbling dainty sandwiches with coffee and fruit, they were all speculating as to when Grace would return to making movies after her wedding.

Only the bride-to-be remained silent.

Grace was to be given three more bridal showers. Virginia Darcy, her hairdresser who was traveling to Monaco to make the French pleat hairstyle on the wedding day, organized yet another one in Los Angeles. The only shower given in New York was arranged by a bridesmaid, Sally Richardson; and in Philadelphia, Mrs. Jay Hamilton asked the guests to bring something suitable for a yacht. The Prince then owned the *Deo Juvante II*.

Celeste Holm still has the note that she received from Grace about her Central Park passion. It is typical of her that even at her busiest, she cared enough to find the time to write it. Celeste Holm is an official of the Friends of Central Park, a society which campaigned to get the park made into an historic landmark. The park was created in 1855 and designed in such a way that no buildings were visible when you were inside it—a piece of countryside within a city. This rural atmosphere is what its Friends are trying to preserve against the encroaching city skyline.

The note reads, "Dear Celeste, Thank you very much for doing all you are doing. Keep up the good work and be sure they keep the *bridal* path open."

Grace Kelly's last night in Hollywood as a working actress was to prove the sterner stuff that she is made of and why, with her polished façade, she is the born princess.

After completing *High Society*, she remained there to present an Oscar to the best actor at the Academy Awards ceremony.

Toward the end of the ceremony, she was called to the stage to present the Best Actor Award to Ernest Borgnine. Was it nervousness or calculated inverted snobbism that the M.C. Jerry Lewis introduced her as "Gracie" for the first time in Hollywood history? Miss Kelly blushed a deep rose shade.

Later the stars were hustled to the basement for a photographic session. For someone who hates crowds it was an ordeal for Grace as she was pulled, pushed and shoved from room to room. At one point an Academy official begged her to retreat to the interviewing room but she firmly replied, "They don't want to interview me. I haven't won anything."

Then came a voice from the crowd—the only spark of humor in this whole witless and tasteless evening—"Yes, you have. You've won a prince."

Now came one of those scenes which takes a thoroughbred like Grace Kelly to handle. When she was finally dragged into a newsroom full of reporters who were busy filing their Oscar stories there was a ghastly silence. She was as stunned to see them as they to see her.

"Please get me out of here," she pleaded to the M.G.M. publicity man, Morgan Hudgins. Once out in the corridor the frenzy began again and the only one to keep her head was our heroine. White-faced, white-gowned, she stood calmly like a neo-classic piece of sculpture.

"I will be delighted to pose with Mr. Borgnine for a picture," she said softly, "but I do have to get up at 5 A.M. to fly to New York."

The evening was over. Hollywood with all its brash phoneyness, its schmaltzy warmth, its hard-working, insincere gospelers; the Hollywood that had turned Grace Kelly into a household name throughout the world was now behind her. It would be interesting to know the thoughts that she had as the limousine slipped away, and looking every inch a princess, she waved farewell to the crowds . . . and Hollywood.

Twenty-one

There had been much discussion among East Falls residents, both privately and in the newspapers, when the engagement was announced. In a single vote the 20,000 citizens all wanted the wedding to take place there. To be specific, in St. Bridget's Roman Catholic church—the Kelly family's parish church—just a wave's lash from the Schuylkill River.

"The church is plenty old enough . . . it is one hundred two years . . . and Grace should be married in St. Bridget's like her folks before her. If Grace and her prince want to be married for a second time, then it can be Monaco but we want to be first," protested Mrs. Angelo Bellofatto of Stanton Street.

But as an absolute monarch and head of state as well as an astute businessman, Prince Rainier had explained that the wedding of the year belonged to Monte Carlo and his Monegasque subjects.

Monte Carlo businessmen were reported as overjoyed when they heard that the wedding would take place there. The timing in the late spring could not have been better in order to attract outpourings of tourists in the off-season.

Leaving her apartment and the New York she loved was a poignant experience for Grace. Intelligent and sensitive as she is, she was the first to realize that it was much more than that. She was not only leaving behind her family and country, but a way of life that she understood. Before her was the unknown.

In those last days Charlie Kelly, her cousin, came from Philadelphia, where he was a professor of Latin and Greek, to help her.

There were still two years left on the lease of the apartment, and Grace decided to keep it so that she could return and her family

143

could use it. It may even have been a subconscious reluctance to sever all ties with her past.

Packing was not without humor as Grace remembered the two trunks that she had sent ahead and wondered what the staff's reaction would be at the palace in Monaco when they unpacked them. Instead of a bridal trousseau fit for a princess, they were stuffed with old jeans, shirts, sneakers and sweaters. Everything dear and old and sentimental had been packed into them.

The furniture had been moved out of the dining room to make space for the trunks of clothes and wedding presents stacked around waiting for the professional packers. Grace herself is an erratically organized person and did most of her own personal packing. She even made a list of what to wear for every night on the ship and the week at the palace before her wedding. She was leaving nothing to chance.

In that last week she made an unexpected and sentimental journey to Central Park, where she went riding for the last time.

From a riding academy which has a school of livery horses she hired Daisy, a horse well known to American television audiences for its appearance in *Howdy Doody* and *Robert Montgomery Presents*. A charming animal, it made a pretty picture with Grace riding side-saddle, an accomplishment she had learned for her part in *The Swan*.

As every hour of those last days was dogged by newspapermen, her arrival in Central Park at 2 P.M. with dapper instructor Fred Birkner soon became known and the photographers began a feverish Grace-hunt around the park. To avoid the press, Mr. Birkner had arranged to meet her at a police exit at Ninetieth Street and Fifth Avenue, but the press caught up.

At the family holiday ranch house at Roc Agel in the hills above Monaco, where several horses are kept, Princess Grace still rides whenever she has time and prefers sidesaddle to astride. She has a natural seat and even the Empress Elizabeth of Austria could not fault her straight back.

Princess Grace's sidesaddle anachronism is very much in keeping with her character and points up the enigmatic and individual person that she is and always will be.

During the last week she also attended the wedding of Rita Gam, who was to be a bridesmaid at her own wedding in Monaco. Rita, who had previously been married to film producer Sidney Lumet, was now marrying Tom Guinzburg, the scion of The Viking Press publishing house. It was a charming ceremony held in the elegant drawing room of the Guinzburgs' family house in Sutton Square.

Rita and Grace, who had spent so many hours together when they shared a flat in Hollywood discussing their various beaux, were now both making highly desirable marriages. There were happy but sentimental tears amid the orange blossoms. Grace was, in fact, the last among her group of girl friends to marry.

All of Grace's trousseau shopping had to be sandwiched into one huge buying spree during a hectic week in New York between finishing *High Society* and leaving to spend Easter in Philadelphia with the family.

As time was so short she called in a friend, Eleanor Lambert, one of America's best-known fashion authorities. The final choice was always Grace's, but Eleanor Lambert helped in making it possible to see so many things in so short a time.

"It was a liberal education as well as a thrill to watch the world's most famous bride-to-be select her trousseau," Miss Lambert said at the time.

"Future brides who may not boast Miss Kelly's gift for looking divine in everything, her background of wealth or her personal earning power could still take lessons from her in thrift, discrimination and firm budget control," she added.

Grace Kelly chose middle of the road clothes in the colors of white, blue and her favorite honey beige, that would outlive current fashion fads. She just plumb did not go for fussy, hard to care for clothes either. As she says even today, "I am very easy with clothes."

Ben Zuckerman turned out to be her favorite designer and his clothes mainly created the Grace Kelly look which permeated American fashion that year, and which, after twenty years, has returned full cycle to fashion once again. The silhouette is a long-molded torso with a gently flared skirt, a fashion she loves to wear in blonde silk jerseys and crepes. The most patient of shoppers, she was fussy about only two things: that her clothes fitted snugly at the waistline and that the hems were immaculate.

The list of designers was formidable, and I give it here simply because it reflects how much she affected American fashion that year. Claire McCardell, Brigance, B.H. Wragge and Marquise designed her sports clothes, whereas her day clothes were designed by Adele Simpson, Mollie Parnis, Larry Aldrich, Christian Dior, Traina Norell, Branells and Suzy Perette. Cocktail dresses came from Pauline Trigère, Harvey Berin and James Galanos. The evening dresses, all so beautifully simple, were the work of Fira Benenson, Trigère, Galanos and Branells.

Grace confessed that she had gone wild over hats and bought far too many. All her shoes, in deference to the Prince's height, had low-curved Louis heels.

The precious wedding gown of ivory silk and 125-year-old Brussels lace embroidered with seed pearls had arrived from Hollywood, where it had been designed by Helen Rose, and was now packed for the voyage in a long steel wardrobe box from Metro. During the sea trip, Mr. Kelly was so alarmed that something might happen to it that he personally insisted on going down into the hold to inspect the trunk and cases of wedding presents. He found that the wedding box had tipped up on end and made sure it was firmly set down horizontally.

With all the grandeur of a pharaoh marrying off his favorite daughter, Mr. Kelly had organized the Kelly entourage of seventy-eight which was to sail on the S.S. *Constitution* from New York to Monaco. Family, friends and bridesmaids were all invited to travel together on a voyage that was to take eight days.

It is doubtful whether prosaic Jack Kelly thought in allegorical terms, but there was a touch of classical drama in the idea of the New World bringing its favorite daughter as a gift to the Old World.

As she left her apartment building that grey April morning, a small girl jumped forward and handed Grace a jaunty nosegay. She believed it to be an omen of good luck.

The rain tumbled down—sheeting New York rain—as she sped in a black limousine along the West Side Highway to Pier 84 at Forty-fourth Street where the S.S. *Constitution* was berthed. The rest of the party were already aboard. She had traveled on the ship before as part of an advertising campaign at its launching.

Metro Goldwyn Mayer, which to this day keep a watchful eye on Princess Grace whenever she visits America, had sent along Morgan Hudgins to accompany their brightest star. Newsmen swarmed all over the place, pressing around her as she was maneuvered to her stateroom where she made her first broadcast to the people of Monaco. It had been arranged through Radio Monte Carlo, which had linked up with the Voice of America. She said, "I am deeply

146

moved as I prepare to leave the United States, where I was born and spent my early years. But also I have the great joy today of bringing to the Monegasques the sincere affection of their American friends. All those who know the principality want to go back there; many would like to remain. I was there one year ago and I am going back again . . . to stay.

"I would like to tell my future compatriots that the Prince, my fiancé, has taught me to love them. I feel that I already know them well, thanks to what the Prince has told me, and my dearest wish today is to find a small place in their hearts . . . to share their joys and sorrows as well as their hopes and aspirations."

A press conference was immediately held in the observation lounge, where Grace answered yet another hundred questions with quiet and dignified patience.

Darting among the guests were her small nieces Meg and Marylee, who were to be flower girls. When they saw all the fuss being made they grabbed Grace by her skirt and demanded, "Aunt Grace, if you are going to be a princess, why aren't we?"

As the ship steamed down the Hudson River, Grace stood on the captain's bridge between her mother and father waving farewell to her sister Lizanne on the wharf, who could not go as she was expecting a baby any day, and to her sister-in-law Mary, who was to fly over later as she, too, was expecting a child.

When Grace at last arrived in her stateroom, S-5, there sitting on the bed was Oliver and beside him a gangling, temperamental Weimaraner puppy that turned out to be the surprise gift of Philadelphia friends Mr. and Mrs. Albert Greenfield, Jr., which ultimately grew to the size of a Great Dane. In the excitement he had already proved not to be ship-trained.

Oliver had also received a surprise gift from the Hitchcocks, who had sent him a chain leash deliriously decorated with white carnations and satin bows with an accompanying card which read, "You'll love Monte Carlo. Happy barking." It was signed "Philip," the name of the Hitchcocks' dog.

Grace's stateroom, which had been specially decorated in beige raw silk for the trip, was brimming with flowers and gifts and well-wishing telegrams.

Every night there were parties for the Kelly clan, beginning with the captain's Welcome Aboard Reception on the first night.

France Soir, Paris Match and *Life* as well as many American

147

newspapers all had teams of newsmen aboard to cover every hour of the day. During the voyage Grace made time to pose specially for every photographer aboard so that he could claim to his newspaper that his, indeed, were exclusive pictures. It was the kind of thoughtful gesture that had made her the darling of newsmen in her Hollywood days.

At night when everyone was still merrymaking Grace would slip on an old coat, collect the dogs and take a walk on the top deck all by herself. She had much to think about on those starlit nights.

During the day there was plenty to do: In an old tweed skirt, shirt and sweater, with dark glasses and a scarf round her head, she played shuffleboard with her nieces, answered all her letters, or lay chatting on deck chairs with her parents. During the voyage she always wore a pearl-studded charm bracelet with a large golden coin dangling from it. This was the medallion that the Prince had given her—on one side was his face in profile and on the other the royal crest of Monaco. Prince Rainier also cabled Princess Grace every day of the voyage.

One of the most memorable nights on the trip over was the impromptu sing-song when Judy Kanter and Grace gave impersonations of Judy Garland and Rosemary Clooney. Few people outside her own close circle of friends realize that Princess Grace is a brilliant mimic. Her impersonations of Garbo and Zsa Zsa Gabor have such sharp-edged detail that they must be among the best in show business. The evening ended with Grace singing some of the Cole Porter songs from *High Society*. As the New York *Daily Mirror* was to head their dispatch: "Grace and 60 on a Showboat to Monaco."

During one night when everyone was dancing, the *Constitution*'s sister ship, the S.S. *Independence*, passed close-by and blinked "Good luck, Gracie!"

When the message was announced on the public address system, Grace remarked to Gant Gaither, "You know, I never really cared anything about an engagement ring or the conventional wedding gown with all the trimmings. It never meant anything to me. Now, look. All this! Isn't it ironic?"

Everyone has his/her own private memories of this trip. When Mrs. Ben Lyon remarked to Mr. Kelly, "It must be very difficult for Grace to give up her career when she is just at the top," he replied, "When you get to the top, where else is there to go?"

The party had fallen into two groups—"The Seniors" and "The Juniors." Grace and her sister naturally spent much of their time with "The Juniors." One night they decided to play, for probably the last time, The Game, and everyone joined in with Grace heading one team and the family dentist, Dr. George Coleman, at the helm of the other. She had to act out "Beware of the Danger Line," which was a well-known toothpaste advertisement, and became so involved in acting out "danger" that the heels of both shoes broke off and she spent the rest of the night in her stocking feet.

The evening finished with a real Kelly family sing-song, ending with the old favorite "The End of a Perfect Day."

Instead of giving individual, irrelevant wedding presents, the *Constitution* friends had a splendid idea. They banded together and, under the advice of veteran film producer Mervyn Le Roy, bought $14,000 worth of equipment necessary for a cinema to be installed in the palace at Monaco so that Grace would not fall behind in seeing all the latest American movies. At the palace in Monaco, a part of the garage where the old carriages had been kept was converted into the cinema, which exists today and is used whenever they have a film evening. Small individual supper tables are set and guests eat while watching a movie.

Grace did not go down to dinner on the last night but spent it quietly in her own cabin, as she had to rise early in the morning. Peggy joined her after dinner and calmly set about manicuring Grace's nails. It was a typical gesture between sisters and illustrates the naturalness and closeness that exists in the Kelly family.

Normally the *Constitution* does not make a stopover at Cannes, but special arrangements had been made for this occasion. All the other passengers were delighted to have the chance of seeing the Princess's departure as she joined the Prince in the Bay of Hercules when his yacht *Deo Juvante II* met the liner.

The *Deo Juvante II* was an old English boat built by Camper Nicholson in 1928. She was a comfortable boat with an agreeable, spacious atmosphere and a cruising speed of eleven knots.

Just as the mayor of Monaco boarded the *Constitution*, the sun broke through the clouds, spotlighting the sun deck where the official presentations were to take place. With the blue sky above and shimmering blue sea all around the yacht, even Sam Goldwyn could not have planned a more impressive arrival scene.

Circling the ship was a helicopter dropping white and red carnations, a brilliant and fragrant welcome from Aristotle Onassis, who, during that period, was the majority stockholder in the company that controlled Monaco's gambling casinos and best hotels. His personal wedding present was a diamond bracelet and his company had given a diamond and ruby tiara. The carnations were an afterthought.

At 10 A.M. a gangway was lowered from the side of the *Constitution*, and Miss Kelly and her parents walked down to board the yacht. Grace was breath-taking in her navy blue faille coat topped with a huge white hat of organdie and Swiss lace. The picturesque but ill-chosen hat was the first lesson that Grace Kelly was to learn about the protocol of royal fashion. The Prince delicately pointed out to her that it would be difficult for the people of Monaco lining the streets to see her face, but by now the ceremonies were well under way and there was no chance to go and make a change, as all her luggage was being unloaded.

The whistle of the *Constitution* blatted a series of farewells as the passengers cheered and the yachts in the harbor all opened their voices to make a crescendo of happy noise.

Prince Rainier, dapper in navy blue, who had spent frantic weeks personally supervising all the arrangements for the wedding, now looked relaxed and smiled contentedly as he took his fiancée's arm and led her to an open car to drive through the streets of Monte Carlo and up the winding road to his castle on the rock. The people cheered as they watched this real-life fairy tale unfold before them.

Within three hours, having first been greeted by her future father-in-law, Prince Pierre, and sister-in-law, Princess Antoinette, who were to stay with the Kelly family in the palace during the pre-wedding festivities, there was a large family luncheon party.

Two servants in full livery with the Grimaldi royal crest stood behind each chair.

"The servants had so much gold braid that you couldn't tell them from the generals," Mr. Kelly remarked to a friend.

Prince Rainier had elected to stay at his villa farther along the coast until moving back into the palace on their return from their honeymoon.

Twenty-two

For a week before the wedding took place, all Monte Carlo was *en fête*. With the *Constitution* clan firmly entrenched at the Hermitage Hotel, there were parties and galas every night.

The Kelly family itself was something of a refreshing surprise to the old set of Monte Carlo, who looked on somewhat askance as Peggy sauntered through the hotel lounge in her neat Bermuda shorts followed by a gaggle of unselfconscious children.

There were parties every night. At the International Sporting Club the program included a ballet with Tamara Toumanova; and Eddie Constantine, the American singer who made his name in Paris, came specially for the occasion. The climax of the evening was a fireworks display with the initials *R* and *G* interlaced for the first time.

Mr. and Mrs. Kelly were hosts to one hundred guests at one of the most glamorous events of the week—a dinner and ball at the Monte Carlo Casino. It was a splendid dinner, consisting of game bird soup with quenelles, golden paillettes, parboiled Loire salmon, English saddle of lamb, iced gooseberries, early fruit pie, salad Caprice and surprise omelette. The wine served was Pommery Grenot Brut 1949.

The Prince and Grace were the first to step out on the dance floor as Aimé Barelli's orchestra struck up "A Woman in Love." They danced alone to everyone's delight. Grace, who is a beautiful dancer, seemed to glide around the ballroom with all eyes on her. Already looking the part of a princess, she wore champagne *peau de soie* with baby puff sleeves and fitted bodice. Apart from the change of place, time and man, it could almost have been a scene from *The Swan* in which she had starred just a few months before.

This was the first time their friends had seen Grace and Prince Rainier so relaxed.

"It was quite obvious that here were two people deliriously in love and they danced oblivious of everything around them," one of the bridesmaids told me. "It really was a fairy story come alive."

When the second number began "Love Is a Many Splendored Thing," Mrs. Kelly, looking every inch the one-time "cover girl," proudly took the floor on the arm of Prince Pierre. It was a night the Kelly family will never forget . . . and a long, long way from Philadelphia.

For a touch of their hometown, Stan Rubin and his Tiger Town Five from Princeton had been specially flown over, but the jazz sounded so discordant in this Cinderella-at-the-ball atmosphere that Mrs. Kelly quickly reverted to the Barelli music.

When the ball ended Grace said good-night to Prince Rainier on the steps of the Casino. They did not kiss but clasped hands and looked into each other's eyes.

Grace drove back to the palace with her parents and the Prince to his villa at Cap Ferrat.

And so the storybook romance continued, with daily delights for the bride-to-be. With superb planning the Prince saw that each day Grace received yet another piece of jewelry. One was in the form of a large pearl which the Prince had inherited from his mother, Princess Charlotte; two other handsome pieces were also from his mother.

Whenever possible Grace would slip along to the Hercules Gallery in the palace to see the wedding presents which continued to arrive hourly. There was a gold serving tray from Queen Elizabeth, a fragile antique desk from the Cary Grants, a small Steuben glass rabbit, treasures of gold and silver, paintings, a great many rosaries, and a length of cloth of gold from the Ambassador from Pakistan to the United Nations, the Nawab Mir Nawaz Jung.

All Grace's friends knew that she liked picture frames, which fascinate her even today. The assortment was enormous—silver from the Cornelius Vanderbilt Whitneys, white satin from playwright Lexford Richards.

There were also the "honkey ones," as Grace described them.

The hundreds of garters, a *Cookbook for Two*, numerous pot holders and a Shamrock-green double bed for Irish luck.

She insisted on entering each one in the white satin bride's book which she had brought from America. By the time she was through, she had used a dozen books.

One of the official presents became the center of an unpleasant incident which the Prince has described as "a sordid affair."

The National Council of Monaco decided to present the Princess with a wedding gift and selected one of their members to purchase it. Despite a handsome sum of $61,500 he chose an unattractive, old-fashioned necklace that was most unsuitable for the Princess.

When the Council decided to return the necklace and ask for their money back, the jeweler refused to return the deposit, which ultimately led to a lawsuit. It was altogether an upsetting incident, which Princess Grace took in her usual calm style. If she discussed it at all, it was in strictest privacy. It was her first taste of royal diplomacy.

The Princess's gift to her bridesmaids was an original idea and made by Cartier. It was a gold medallion engraved with the initials *R* and *G* surmounted by the crown of Monaco. At the time the bridesmaids wore the medallions on their gold bracelets, but today most have them on golden chains as is the present fashion. They gave her a silver dressing table set from Cartier, with a silver tray on which all their signatures were engraved.

Looking back on that week, Princess Grace says that so much went on it is difficult to remember everything. It was one glorious, exhausting whirl. Over the immediate weeks before the wedding she lost ten pounds and even her wedding gown, made in the Metro-Goldwyn-Mayer design studios, had to have last-minute adjustments.

One night she has not forgotten is the time Prince Rainier took her by car up onto the Grande Corniche, a ribbon of road that stretches through the sky way above the Riviera. They drove up in his sports car to watch the dawn break. At Super Eze they left the car and climbed up through the sleeping village to a small chapel at its apex.

They returned to Monte Carlo in the hot morning sun at 8 A.M. Before them was a day during which every hour was scheduled. There was the buffet luncheon for the palace staff, which Prince Rainier had arranged; and in the afternoon the acceptance of a Rolls-Royce, the gift of the people of Monaco.

153

That afternoon the children of Monaco gathered in la Place du Palais with a large plastic mailbag filled with letters addressed to "La Belle Princesse de Monaco," "Notre Princess Grace Patricia" and so on.

A special stage had been constructed in the Place de Palais where the Festival Ballet from London performed, as did acts from the London Palladium, the superb choir of Monte Carlo and many other entertainers.

The day ended with Prince Rainier and Grace standing hand in hand at the windows of the white and gold salon watching the fantastic fireworks display. Part of the precision planning had been the turning off of all the lights in Monte Carlo and on the boats in the harbor. Not a light remained as suddenly the whole sky over the bay burst into brilliance like ribbons of sapphires, emeralds and diamonds as the fireworks exploded in the sky.

Prince Rainier's civil marriage to Grace Kelly began at 11 A.M. on April 18 in the gold and crimson throne room of the royal palace. All in Monaco stopped work to watch the ceremony on their television sets.

Prince Rainier entered first, followed by Prince Pierre, Princess Charlotte and Princess Antoinette.

Grace, resembling a beautiful French porcelain doll in a short dress of tea-rose *mousseline de soie* over lace with a Juliet cap trimmed with matching silk roses, looked serene and calm. Small pink gloves had replaced her usual white ones. Though inwardly she was shaking, no one would have suspected it as she walked behind Count Ferdinand d'Allières, chief of protocol. He was to collapse a few minutes before the service began and was taken to the palace infirmary.

Seated in groups around Prince Rainier and Grace were the members of their families, the bridesmaids and their husbands, and a few close friends.

It was a simple, dignified service as the bride and groom remained seated. Judge Portanier read the civil marriage rites of the Napoleonic Code. As he looked down at this beautiful American girl, he said, "Mademoiselle Grace Patricia Kelly, do you take as your husband His Serene Highness, My Lord, Prince Rainier III, here present?"

In a low but firm voice she answered, "Oui."

Turning to the Prince, who was shifting nervously in his chair, he

154

asked, "May I respectfully ask Your Serene Highness if he agrees to take as his wife and legitimate spouse Mademoiselle Grace Patricia Kelly, here present?"

The Prince raised his head and said in a firm clear voice, "Oui."

It was all over in sixteen minutes.

Grace Kelly had now become Princess Grace de Monaco and the most titled woman in Europe—142 titles all told—albeit thanks to ancient titles referring mainly to villages that no longer existed.

It was a solemn occasion, and despite the intimacy there was a certain amount of tension. The Prince was the first to sign the register and after that, Grace. Prince Pierre followed, then Princess Charlotte, Mr. Kelly and Mrs. Kelly, Princess Antoinette, Grace's sister Peggy Davis (as she was then), who was a witness for Grace, and finally Kell.

The tension was at last broken when Grace turned and said smilingly, "At least I am half-married."

Immediately after the service Their Serene Highnesses Prince Rainier and Princess Grace stood and greeted 4,000 of their Monegasque subjects in the Court of Honor of the Palace. It was the first time in Grace's life that people had curtsied to her in her new role as Princess.

After the last guest had gone, in a very tender and private ceremony the Prince invested his wife with the Order of Saint Charles, the highest honor given by his country.

While dressing Princess Grace's hair that night for the Opera Gala, two women who had been so close over the last years met in the privacy of a bedroom. Virginia Darcy, who had been Grace Kelly's hairdresser for many of her films and had come over specially to take care of her during the wedding week, was placing a diamond coronet on Princess Grace's hair when suddenly she burst into tears and cried, "I have always called you Princess, but this time it isn't a paste prop. It is for real."

Just after 9 P.M. Princess Grace of Monaco took her place beside Prince Rainier in the Royal Box, which now had the initials *R* and *G* on the frosted glass sides. She seemed to glide into the box wearing a beaded bell-shaped dress by Lanvin and her new order, a family coronet of diamonds and the diamond necklace given her by the people of Monaco.

Slowly she turned her head from right to left, inclining it with a tiny motion just as she does today. It was not a smile, just the corners of her mouth turned up. No one could possibly have guessed that without her glasses the auditorium was a blurry haze. She stood still, indestructibly beautiful and unbelievably regal.

The celluloid had dissolved into reality.

Twenty-three

Today on the first floor of the Philadelphia Museum of Art on a wax model resembling Philadelphia's famous daughter is the wedding gown of Princess Grace of Monaco.

As they shuffle past, the tourists stand and stare and one hears the odd remark, "Look, Martha, doesn't that have a small waist. . . . I'm not so sure I'd have had those bows . . . I liked her best in *The Country Girl.*"

Twenty years ago on April 19 this wedding gown was worn by Grace Kelly when she went through her second wedding ceremony and became the bride of Prince Rainier in the eyes of the Holy Roman Empire.

It was the most enchanting royal wedding of the century. No bride could have looked more fragile, more beautiful.

"My God, to see Grace was like seeing a statue of alabaster marble. I have never seen anything so exquisite in my life," Earl Blackwell, New York's social lion, told me.

If she was tired—and she must have been desperately tired—the Kelly discipline prevented her from showing it. It was the picture that all the cameramen had waited for as she glided down the staircase of the ecru-pink royal palace at Monaco on the arm of her father and walked down the cobblestoned courtyard path to the Cathedral of St. Nicholas.

Father and daughter passed slowly through an honor guard of sailors and marines from visiting American, British, French and Italian warships. Grace's eyes under her veil were demure and shy. Mr. Kelly was tall and proud.

The Cathedral of St. Nicholas, the beautitul old church which

157

dominates the town of Monte Carlo, was filled with six hundred international celebrities and minor royalty. It was reported that King Farouk almost skipped the wedding of his friend Prince Rainier as he could not get four extra tickets for his bodyguards. Instead he sat and sulked alone. When the Egyptian Minister arrived and saw Farouk, he promptly left the Cathedral.

Aristotle Onassis's silver head was noticeable. He had been taking playful bets among friends that he would be "bumped off" in the Cathedral. But there he sat, delighted to be among the elite.

Another famous figure was Somerset Maugham, who once coined the quip, "Monaco is a sunny place for shady characters."

Two of the most elegant women in the Cathedral were the Begum Aga Khan, sitting next to the aged Aga Khan, and Ava Gardner, who had come out of hibernation to be present at her friend's wedding.

The religious ceremony which followed the civil service the day before was to be three hours in length. Prince Rainier had already arrived at the Cathedral.

It is said that he himself designed his uniform, whlch was based on that worn by the palace guard. The trousers were blue with a gold stripe at the sides and the tunic navy blue with gold epaulettes and shoulder cord. His left breast was covered with twelve impressive medals that glinted in the morning sun.

The Bishop of Monaco, Monseigneur Gille Barthe, performed the wedding ceremony, which was followed by high nuptial mass. The bride's parish priest from Philadelphia, Father John Cartin, delivered a message of good wishes to the royal couple.

The service was marred only by the technical apparatus necessary for the use of television and motion picture coverage.

There were the ordinary minor mishaps of any wedding which I recall only to emphasize that despite all the grandeur these were only two human beings taking part in an age-old ceremony. This was a real wedding and not a rehearsed spectacle.

A page boy dropped one of the rings used in the double ceremony; at one point Prince Rainier seemed to get tangled up with his sword; the Princess's ten-foot-long train caught on a chair, and the bridegroom seemed strained as he had trouble getting the ring on the bride's finger.

But never once did Princess Grace show the slightest signs of nervousness or hesitation. Of all the parts she had ever played her own wedding was her finest performance.

The Prince and Princess over the years have had only one regret about their glorious wedding. It is a regret that every royal bride in the world would understand. They wished that they had not been so involved and could only see the immediate things around them. As the Prince was to tell Peter Hawkins:

"There was such a lack of intimacy, it was the disappointing culmination of all that had gone before. For a man, perhaps, this is less important, but for the Princess it meant a great deal. It is difficult for a girl, for her wedding, if she can't be alone with herself for a moment. And the Princess did not have a minute to herself from the moment she set foot in the Principality.

"Another thing that astonished me when we actually stood together in the Cathedral was the fact that during this wedding in front of the altar there were cameras and microphones everywhere. Such lack of solitude and dignity. Reflecting on this afterwards, we both agreed that we should really have got married somewhere in a little chapel in the mountains. That is the sort of impossible desire one has after these things."

In their family film library, collected and mostly made by the Princess, is a souvenir film of their wedding.

After the ceremony Prince Rainier and Princess Grace left by open car to drive round the old town of Monaco waving to their subjects who packed the narrow streets.

They stopped at a small peach-colored shrine under the railroad bridge of Monte Carlo where Princess Grace knelt in the dust and prayed that St. Dévote, the patron saint of Monaco, would bless her marriage.

She then kissed the relics proferred to her by the robed priests and placed her bridal bouquet of lily of the valley at the feet of the virgin saint who had brought Christianity to Monaco.

Once the royal car had left, the wedding guests were allowed out of the Cathedral and began the walk across the cobbled forecourt. Many of the men and women were frantically looking for the *Dames* and *Hommes*. Suddenly someone found a gardeners' *cabinet de toilette* and the word spread. In a matter of minutes a long queue of elegantly dressed women, and men in their white ties, tails and top hats, had formed outside the little door.

As soon as someone from the palace saw what was going on, staff were quickly sent to direct the guests to special cloakrooms; but it was a sight so human that it could have been snipped from a Cartier Bresson album.

A royal enclosure had been made at the foot of the staircase where the wedding party sat at small tables. The rest of the guests mingled in the sun-filled courtyard, eating a buffet lunch.

With his hand over his bride's Prince Rainier cut the five-tiered wedding cake with his sword.

Just before she left the palace, Princess Grace took her private farewell of her bridesmaids—her sister Peggy, Judy Kanter, Maree Pamp, Rita Gam, Sally Richardson, Carolyn Reybold and Bettina Gray—girls whose friendship stretched back to Grace's early modeling days. Virginia Darcy, always the wag, had lined them up and said, "Now let's all curtsey to the new Princess, girls."

Peggy's good-bye to Princess Grace was in the Kelly tradition. In a fun moment so desperately needed to prevent the tears that were near she quipped, "See you later, alligator."

To which Prince Rainier, who had just come into the room, replied, "In a while, crocodile."

There was laughter and a desperate moment had been saved.

While the wedding party had been in progress, outside in the streets tourists were lining up to obtain the first release of the new postage stamps which bore the head of Princess Grace. The photograph had been specially taken in New York, and the denominations ranged from 1 franc to 500 francs. And so Grace Kelly from Philadelphia, now Princess Grace of Monaco, had become the first film star to have her face on a postage stamp.

By 5 P.M. the *Deo Juvante II* set sail as two rockets dropped the American and Monegasque flags in the sky. The bridal couple and Oliver stood for a moment by the ship's rail until the coastline faded. By this time the sea was terribly rough and the yacht began to rock.

Down in the stateroom the crew had prepared a supper of snacks, caviar, foie gras and champagne, and left the Prince and Princess alone. Instead of eating they collapsed into chairs, completely exhausted by the day's events, and slept for a couple of hours.

At the advice of the captain, the yacht pulled into a small cove only a few hundred yards from the Prince's villa and they dropped anchor till morning.

That night Oliver took up his usual position at the foot of his mistress's bed and did so every night until his death some years later.

As long as they were at sea the Prince and his bride had all the privacy they craved for. The Prince had always loved the freedom that sailing gives, which he has compared to the sensation that one has in the mountains.

"You are really at peace with nature and existence," he has said many times when discussing the subject.

The honeymoon took them first to Spain, where Princess Grace caught such a severe cold that she had to see a doctor. From there they went on to Corsica, Napoleon's birthplace and a spot of immense interest to Prince Rainier, whose Napoleonic collection, begun by Prince Louis II, is regarded as one of the finest in the world. It is now installed in a new museum which Prince Rainier designed and arranged himself.

Some of the honeymooners' happiest days were spent picnicking on the white sandy beaches of Corsica, totally alone. Knowing Princess Grace's dislike of the hot sun, the Prince would construct small Robinson Crusoe shelters for her and Oliver from bits of wood he had collected and canvas he had brought along. Puttering along the beach together, sunbathing, talking, sleeping, collecting shells: two contented people far from the responsibilities that lay ahead of them.

On the return from their honeymoon and after a quick trip to Paris to check with her doctor, Princess Grace calmly told the Prince that it was now definite—she was pregnant. The Prince joyfully announced the news to his subjects.

All Monaco was dizzy with delight and celebrated the news for days. Princess Grace had given them hope for the one thing they wanted most of all—an heir to the principality.

Twenty-four

"When I married Prince Rainier, I married the man and not what he was or who he was. I fell in love with him no matter how it might all turn out."

These words were spoken by Princess Grace after she had been married ten years. They remain as unimpaired today as when she first thought of them.

What kind of a man is Prince Rainier, who was now to become such a dominant factor in her life? Trustingly, gratefully and hopefully, she had placed her life and happiness in his hands.

No two people could have outwardly been more different: she with her reserved strength, reserved intelligence, reserved emotion; and he with his inherited Latin temperament, Mediterranean upbringing and authority that being an absolute monarch creates.

No husband and wife either could have had a more different family background: the Kellys with their boisterous family life filled with fun and caring; Prince Rainier with his disturbed and lonely childhood.

In an interview with English journalist Douglas Keay several years ago, Prince Rainier said, "I think the experience of my parents' separation when I was only six has subconsciously made me very much want my own marriage to succeed. So the Princess and I have always tried to minimize any sort of incident or little disagreement between us in the interest of keeping the family together—so that the children should not suffer."

Prince Rainier was born on May 31, 1923, the son of Princess Charlotte of Monaco and the Count Pierre de Polignac. Six years later his parents separated, and this tubby little boy who seldom smiled was then shuttled between his grandfather, Prince Louis II, and a nanny. With no real parental anchor of his own, he was apparently not a particularly attractive child. No one recognized that the tantrums and sulks were a desperate cry for affection.

At eight years of age, speaking little English, he was suddenly sent, on his father's wish, to a preparatory school at St. Leonards-on-Sea—a fearsome experience for any small French boy, let alone a cosseted prince.

He has never forgotten what loneliness means, and far from curing his shyness it only increased it.

Speaking of his childhood to Peter Hawkins in his biography *Prince Rainier of Monaco* (William Kimber), Prince Rainier said, "When you are twelve years old, you feel that the Channel is terribly wide. The plane services weren't so regular in those days, either.

"I suppose I enjoyed it—but, like most little boys who go to prep school, I was caned. This shocked me in the fact that it was a physical punishment, but no more. The attitude of all English youngsters at that age is that being caned is more of an occasion to have a good laugh, and fun, so there was nothing dramatic about it."

He then passed on to Stowe, that stern, laudable seat of learning high up in the beautiful, cold Cotswolds. For a child from the sun, it must have been a chastening experience. He was totally friend-less—the only foreigner among five hundred and sixty English boys.

Soon after his arrival, in sheer desperation, he did the only sensible thing a small boy could do: He ran away. He was picked up by the police in Buckingham and taken back to school, where an understanding housemaster, a retired army major, gave him a cozy tea of hot muffins and jam.

One of the first shocks that the Prince experienced at Stowe was the English system of fagging from which no one is exempt. He was astonished at this feudal custom, in which a younger boy is expected to get up early in the morning and do the drudge work for a senior boy before getting himself ready for the day.

From Stowe he went to the Ecole du Rosay in Switzerland, which in itself must have been a traumatic experience. Not only was he back to speaking French all day, but his mathematical studies had to be switched into the metric.

He enjoyed Rosay and preferred its more liberal approach to

education to the in-bred ambiance of an English public school. This was short-lived as he was removed to Monaco for safety when the Germans began their bombardment of Lyons. It was only after some time had passed that he went to Paris to continue for his French baccalaureat. A year at l'Ecole des Sciences Politiques in Paris completed his scholastic career.

After a period again in Monaco, during which time he found it very difficult to live with Germans around him, he volunteered for the French Army, where he served under the name of Lieutenant Grimaldi. With his chums he answered to the name of Shorty. During a campaign in Alsace, he won the Croix de Guerre, but at the time of the Armistice was transferred to the economic section of the French Military Mission in Berlin.

During Father Tucker's "reign" in Monaco as spiritual adviser and confidant of the Prince, they had a standing joke which never failed. In the First World War Father Tucker had served as a chaplain with the 103rd Field Artillery, which had seen action at Verdun. Whenever he began with his oft repeated remark, "Now when I was at Verdun . . ." Prince Rainier used to jump to attention and begin singing "The Star-Spangled Banner."

In April, 1949, Prince Rainier was recalled to Monaco, where his grandfather was suffering a long illness. A few months before he died he delegated his powers to Prince Rainier.

At age twenty-six Prince Rainier was now sovereign over 2,000 Monegasques and 20,000 other inhabitants of the principality.

His first task was to find a completely new staff of his own, including a Cabinet, in an effort to bring new thinking and modernization to the principality. And this he did with firmness and clarity.

Prince Rainier quickly developed from an awkward princeling into a man of immense personal strength who later in his reign had the courage to stand firm against two of the world's most powerful men—General de Gaulle and Aristotle Onassis.

When de Gaulle criticized his "grandeur," Prince Rainier remarked, "My grandeur only comes up to his ankles."

Pinpointing Monaco on the map, one is tempted to make a wisecrack about this tiny principality. From the windows in his study Prince Rainier can take in in one glance all five hundred acres of his principality.

Before the marriage, Monaco had been going through a period of economic instability. Tourism had fallen off by 1955; the famous

Casino was in disrepair and urgently needed refurbishing; and there were rumors of a planned attempt to replace Prince Rainier by Princess Antoinette, who at least had the children necessary to give the country an heir.

Through the vision, determination and hard work of both the Prince and Princess today skyscrapers jostle together like stacked cards; new factories have been built that, by law, have dispensed with ugly chimneys and have roof gardens instead; and flowers tumble down the steep cliff of the roads etched from the hillside. It is dazzlingly beautiful in the brilliant sunshine.

Two promontories enclose the new harbor. On one is the Casino and those dowager hotels, L'Hermitage and Hotel de Paris; and on the other the Prince's palace, which changes color through the day from pale apricot at dawn to Pompeian pink in the sunset, and is set on a tiny medieval town.

For many Monaco is still a kind of Ruritania, a set from *The Student Prince* or *Perchance to Dream*. To others, escaping from the cold climes of Scandinavia, Germany and England, it is a tax-haven paradise.

To its ruler, Monte Carlo is Big Business. Through his influence its gambling image has diminished. Today Monaco's budget depends hardly at all on gambling. More than 80 percent of revenue comes from such unromantic items as V.A.T., state monopolies (including postage stamps) and industrial development.

During the last seven years, fifty-three acres have been won from the sea—an area set aside for Monaco to expand its light industries which, in turn, will attract foreign capital.

There are still the old ladies in the park; still the chalk-faced beauties of indeterminate age who emerge in the evening from their one-room "homes" to try their luck on the wheel yet again; still the picture-postcard gardens, planted with red and white cyclamen, a floral carpet in the Place du Casino.

But there are also many more hotels bustling with scientists who have gathered for international conventions on the disposal of radioactive waste, pollution in urban life, destruction of chemical refuse and other such world problems.

Given sufficient hotel accommodations Monte Carlo could well become one of the leading conference countries in the world—a role which the Prince would find agreeable as much for its moral as its commercial values.

Prince Rainier also sees Monaco as a kind of headquarters for a few base companies—English, American and Canadian—from which they could direct their European operations.

One of Prince Rainier's earliest schemes in the modernization of Monaco was to run the railway through the principality underground, which afforded acres more land not only *in situ* but by using the excavated rock for reclamation. Here he ran up against the old-fashioned conservatism of the National Council, which challenged him. "Why waste that money in making a tunnel when the railroad has been running as it is for forty-five years?" they said.

He won his point and today it is one of the triumphs of Monte Carlo.

Prince Rainier is an absolute monarch. He rules his kingdom seriously, conscientiously and lovingly by "le Droit Divine."

He is deeply sensitive about any comparison of Monaco with what the French call a *pays d'opérette*—musical comedy country. "I cannot understand, for instance, why Monaco has more jokes about it than Liechtenstein or Luxemburg," he once remarked.

"It is a small country. It is a serious country. The more I go out, the more I think small countries are useful. They have no eagerness to possess what their neighbors have. They should be given more latitude. They have a place in the world as peaceful mediators."

Not everything new that has mushroomed in Monte Carlo over the last ten exciting years has pleased its ruler, however. Not all modern architecture enthuses him; but when his business advisers persuade him that it is good for Monaco, he acquiesces.

The most convincing testimony to Prince Rainier's statecraft is that he remains an absolute monarch, yet by temperament he is the least autocratic or pretentious of rulers.

Peasants in the hills behind Monaco who bring their vegetables, fruits and cheeses down to the Monte Carlo market are all familiar with the Prince in jeans and sweater who sometimes walks round their stalls in the early morning, buying from here and there. He knows them by name and remembers the details of their family life.

Though the changing of the guard outside the palace does have a toy-box quality about it, the object of the exercise, in addition to security, is that it attracts thousands and thousands of tourists every year, which is a much healthier situation for Monaco than is the Casino.

In his private life Prince Rainier is a charming man. He is 5 feet 7 inches tall, but looks shorter due to a weight problem with which he continually struggles. A year-round suntan gives his face a youthful appearance and the hair, black at the time of his wedding, is now a distinguished grey. Women find him appealing once they have broken through his reserve.

Much has been written about the Prince's "wild oats" days before his marriage. It would be untrue to say that he was ever a playboy. His chances of ever becoming one, should he have wished, were slender compared with those of the Duke of Windsor when he was Prince of Wales, or the late Aly Khan. The principality is a tight little fortress of gossip and he would scarcely have escaped it. The one romance of his life worth recording was a four-year friendship with the French actress Gisèle Pascal, sometimes termed by the gossips as "the uncrowned queen of Monaco."

Although the Prince once explained in an interview, "It was never intended to be serious and was good training for later on in life but never more than that," it is unlike him to have kept up a friendship so long if it had not been meaningful to him at the time.

Miss Pascal, who was heart-broken at the time of their breakup, has been quoted as saying, "People resented the fact that I was not of royal blood. They gossiped when they saw the Prince spending so much of his time at my home. I waited, hoping that everything would work out, but it didn't. It is only in fairy tales that the prince and princess live happily ever after."

The more plausible explanation is that as Miss Pascal was a divorced woman, a permanent relationship would have been impossible.

Prince Rainier would be the first to agree that he is not an intellectual, but rather a man of varied and amusing interests. He has a schoolboy's love of practical jokes and gadgets. American friends pander to his unabashed delight in the latter. One that misfired was the chicken dissector that he brought back from America. The French chef's comments are unprintable.

The Prince is also easy to talk to and and has an infectious sense of humor. When he was once asked what he would like to have been had he not been a ruling prince, he answered, "I would have liked something to do with the sea or farming, an activity close to nature. Or a circus clown. . . ."

Above all, Prince Rainier is a man of simple tastes. His happiest moments are spent with his family or alone with one of his many hobbies.

As a young man, he was keenly interested in underwater diving and photography, and became an expert at them. Among his friends he counts Jacques Yves Cousteau, who helped him in the preparation of the new Oceanographic Museum in Monte Carlo, of which he is a director, and whose exploits around the world the Prince supports.

The Prince also used to hunt, but his love of animals made the sport of killing unbearable, and he does it less and less today. Instead, he is preoccupied with the animals in his private zoo, as the Princess was to discover. This was something that no American bride could have possibly foreseen.

Basically a sporting man, the Prince skis, water-skis, and plays golf and tennis. Before his marriage, he had a lightning career as a competition motorist in the Monte Carlo Rally, which he and his co-driver, a mechanic from the palace garage, entered with a D.B. Bonnett. Both of them exhausted, Prince Rainier gave his partner the wheel while he had a catnap; unfortunately, they ended up against a telegraph pole. Neither of them was injured, but the car was a write-off.

In the royal garages are, perhaps, twenty cars, ten of them pre-1923, which are kept in pristine condition. In the early evening the Prince likes to go round the garage and chat with the mechanics. He admits to a fanaticism about his cars.

Prince Rainier's passionate interest in football has been passed on to his daughter, Princess Caroline. Whenever the Monaco team plays, father and daughter are to be seen cheering their team on to victory.

The Prince has an enormous collection of jazz records. His Napoleonic collection is also extremely fine, with the select bits scattered around the palace. One of the treasures that Princess Grace enjoys most is the little wooden cradle of Napoleon's son, L'Aiglon. From time to time, the Prince adds to the collection, whenever the dealers show him something that appeals to him.

In addition to photography and metal sculpting, the Prince has two secret hobbies at which he truly excels: writing poetry and drawing. His sketches of the children are excellent likenesses, and he has also made several studies of Princess Grace.

This, then, is the man whom Grace Kelly married. In private he is more complex—as she was to find out. He is the true Gemini: a twin-sided being. He is also a Mediterranean who can explode with anger, but in a minute all is forgotten and the recipient of the wrath is bathed in unconditional *bonhomie*. And, like all Mediterranean men, the Prince can become unreasonably jealous. He likes Princess Grace to wear only the jewelry he has given her or that has come from the family. In fact, on her wedding day, she gave several attractive pieces from unnamed donors away to her girl friends.

There were many facets of Prince Rainier about which Princess Grace had not even begun to know as the *Deo Juvante II* sailed back into Monte Carlo harbor.

Twenty-five

Princess Grace, the real woman, is much more intriguing than her fairy-tale image. As she herself has said, "I am not complicated but full of contradictions. I am easily influenced by climate, by moods and by the people round me."

Taken in that order, the first obstacle she confronted upon returning from her honeymoon in June was a Mediterranean summer. According to the tourist brochure, "In Monaco there are more than 300 days of the year that have sun, with an average of 10 hours a day in summer and 5 hours a day in winter, except February with 4.5 hours of sun per day."

Princess Grace is a heliophobe—a moon creature. The sun saps her strength like a flower without water. Consequently, she dislikes intense bright light and heat, avoids the sun if possible and wears dark glasses to shade the glare from her near-sighted eyes. She is happiest on dull, wintry days and does not feel the cold. She loves the gentle misty days of autumn in the New York State countryside, the soft moist atmosphere of early winter in London, the crisp embracing air of Switzerland in the winter.

When the nostril-drying, eye-stinging Mistral season begins in Monaco, she stays indoors to avoid the hot irritating wind. She is said to become depressed and quiet. During the hottest month, August, the family always moves to the *mas* at Roc Agel, where the night air is cool and the days more bearable than down by the coast.

Throughout that first summer in Monte Carlo, when she was pregnant, she found the heat exhausting, almost intolerable. She went out as little as possible and clung to the shade of the palace garden.

In California she had disliked the summers, too, but there was always the knowledge that it was only for a few more weeks, a few more months, and then the film would be finished and she would be back in New York where the heat was sticky but less glaring.

Princess Grace's favorite sports are swimming and walking. The palace pool—around which the family practically lives now in the summers—had not yet been built and the large palace gardens lack privacy as they are open to the public every afternoon.

"I never went out anywhere," she remembered. She did not shop, go to restaurants or walk freely in the streets. Her only public appearances were at the Red Cross Gala and a short trip to Paris to buy maternity clothes.

Apart from the heat, Princess Grace said that the biggest adjustment she had to make that first year was to the Latin temperament. It was entirely different from the American temperament to which she was accustomed. She not only had to adapt to the disposition of her husband and the staff of the palace, but to conform to the Mediterranean attitude toward marriage, which was entirely different from that of America or England.

There was also the court protocol to observe in this most royal of principalities.

"There were 15 footmen to wait at table during a recent palace dinner for only 10 people," the *Sunday Express* reported on June 17, 1956.

"Before entering the drawing room to be received, lady guests were told by an equerry, 'Will you please remember to curtsey to both the Prince *and* the Princess.' . . . Friends say that Grace appears rather awed by the imposing formality insisted upon by her husband's courtiers."

Actually Princess Grace was not in the least embarrassed when people curtsied to her. "They are honoring my husband's position and not me," she explained pragmatically to American friends.

Even within the family, Princess Grace had to face the delicate problems of protocol. Before Prince Rainier married, his sister, Princess Antoinette, had acted as the First Lady of the land. Although on her marriage to Alec Noghes, the Davis Cup tennis player, she had relinquished all rights to the throne, she had gathered around her her own private court, many of whom would have resented the intrusion of any other woman—especially an American.

Apart from acting as Prince Rainier's hostess on official occasions, Princess Antoinette was also vice president of the Red Cross, of which the Prince was president.

"I must say I have great respect and admiration for the Princess, because I think she came back from her honeymoon to what must have looked rather a grim situation and faced up to it marvelously," the Prince said some years later.

Among a coterie of the Monegasque aristocracy, Princess Grace had a great deal of prejudice to overcome. They had enjoyed the pomp and importance of the royal wedding, but now the gossiping began.

"We had read all these reports about a bricklayer's daughter," one countess explained to me. "It is very hard for us to understand the American way of life and, of course, she did come from Hollywood. But once she arrived and we finally began to see her, it was quite different. She was cultured and charming and, of course, quite different from what we had expected."

This remark came from a well-traveled, highly educated, cultured woman. But for many years she had lived within the ivory towers of Monaco, which she proudly described to me as "the last outpost of elegance."

"C'est une Américaine" was a phrase that was to be repeated in the *vieux rose* salons. Its translation into English does not carry the derogatory undertones of the original French.

"It was very strange. That big wedding and then we never saw her. She should have shown herself more," the proprietress of a small hotel told me. "As far as we were concerned, there was no difference from before the Prince was married."

It did not help the situation, either, when it was erroneously reported that the Prince had banned all Grace Kelly films from the principality. What were these films? "There must be some good reason that he has done this. Pourquoi . . . pourquoi . . . pourquoi?"

The facts are that the Prince did not ban the showing of the films, but what he was afraid of was cinemas cashing in on Grace Kelly festivals and turning her image into vulgar commercialism.

It is doubtful that Princess Grace would have been told of these outpost rumblings, although there is every reason to believe that Prince Rainier knew of them. But her sensitive—almost oversensitive—feelings made her painfully aware of the situation. Had she been another kind of person, she might have stretched out to meet the people sooner. Any lingering suspicion could have been overcome by her charismatic personality. As it was, Princess Grace behaved according to her ''act''—the only way she knew she could cope sincerely. She went slowly, shyly, cautiously.

Within the principality Prince Rainier has his own intelligence antennae which enable him to be in touch with the thoughts of the true Monegasques who are the ''grass roots'' of this small country. Many of these local people have lived in Monaco's five square miles all their lives, and there are senior citizens there today who have never ventured farther afield than Nice or Roquebrune-Cap-Martin. They are a heady mixture of Italian and French blood, and many have names as Italian-sounding as Grimaldi. To them the people of Grasse or Cannes are as suspicious as the Sassenachs are to the Scots.

Beneath the surface lies an uneasy contempt for all strangers. Tourists are different. They come and go like the Mistral. They are also business and are therefore necessary for the economy. But foreigners who have chosen to make their home in Monaco say that they are no more accepted by the Monegasques after ten years than the day they arrived. For this reason they tend to stick together in cliques—the Scandinavians, the Germans, the Americans and so on—with their own clubs and interests.

Prince Rainier was the first to appreciate Princess Grace's fey qualities. ''A woman's intuition is much more acute than a man's, and in those early days I found that the Princess was asking questions about people I'd worked with and taken for granted for years— people whose motives I had never thought to question,'' Prince Rainier said in an interview some years later.

In those first months in Monaco, the Princess was very homesick. Although a thriving American colony existed in the principality and it would have been natural for her to gravitate toward it, this she did with considerable caution. In the hot-house society in which she lived, she was a Monegasque Princess and no longer an ordinary American citizen.

According to Prince Rainier, although she has retained her American citizenship, she has a Monegasque passport and is now more Monegasque than American.

Her homesickness also stemmed from the fact that for five years she had been treated like a queen in her own right as one of

America's most adored women. Now she was the wife of an indulged royal prince in a country where she did not even speak the language.

Although she had a smattering of French and could speak it slowly, all through that summer she took regular French lessons and continued until she became fluent. She found reading French plays and poetry more amusing than text books, and was so thorough in her studies that she even bought a book on French slang. Today her French is grammatically perfect. She has not so much an American accent as intonation, which her French friends find fascinating.

Between themselves and within the family, the Prince and Princess always speak English, although the children speak French among themselves. The Prince now has a more pronounced American accent than the Princess, and all the children use American colloquial slang as if it were their native tongue.

The Princess's homesickness was probably made more acute by her pregnancy and self-imposed seclusion. Her hay fever often gave her an excuse for the red eyes which the staff were quick to notice.

"I don't think people understood how hard it was for her to be cut off from her family and friends in America. She was very homesick for a long time and even now finds it difficult to make friends," said the Prince.

"If she was homesick she never complained. Never once," her sister Peggy explained to me. "Her letters were always filled with fun and the pleasures of making her own home. Grace is not one to complain . . . it is not in her character. Besides, she could always see something funny in even the dreariest situations."

Right from the start, Princess Grace found allies in Prince Rainier's father, Prince Pierre, and in Madame Banac, a grand old lady of Monaco and mother of Mr. Vane Ivanovic, the consul general for Monaco in London. They both loved and admired her and were conscious of the difficulties she had to overcome.

Prince Rainier's mother, Princess Charlotte, lived outside Paris in a beautiful house at Marchais and had removed herself many years earlier from the Monaco scene. A lively and original woman, she has devoted herself to the rehabilitation of prisoners. Her naïve kindness caused her to employ as her chauffeur one such ex-criminal, who was euphemistically known to the French underworld as "René the Swagger Cane." His term came to a sticky end when

Princess Charlotte applied to a French court to have him evicted from a villa on her estate. This made a piquant story in the French press.

The palace, with its two-hundred-odd rooms, was in a forlorn state. For years it had lacked the touch of a woman. Its vast rooms were lifeless, soulless—even the roof needed urgent attention. The Prince had lived in his thirty-room villa at St. Jean Cap Ferrat, about twenty miles from Monaco; and it was here that he did his private entertaining. He entertained in the palace only for official functions.

Most of the palace's official rooms had been furnished in the unyielding, traditional French style. These included the main reception and dining rooms, the grand salon in white and gold, the blue room, red room, throne room and Duke of York room, the hall of mirrors and two rooms containing the Prince's collection of Napoleonic relics.

For several months the Princess did nothing to the furnishings. She just sat and looked and made mental notes. She did not even move a chair. The arrival of her own furniture from her flat in New York began her first positive attempt to render the family living quarters in the palace more homey, more livable. These included practically new damask drapes; deep grey carpets; comfortable easy chairs in light, attractive colors; and a charming little sofa covered with deep blue brocade through which is woven "I love you . . . I love you."

The box in which the wedding dress was packed and sent to Philadelphia made the return trip. This time it had been filled by Mrs. Kelly and the family with gossamer-soft American toilet paper and cake mixes of all sorts, including pancakes and scrapple, a breakfast delicacy as dear to the hearts of Pennsylvanians as maple syrup is to Vermonters. Scrapple is a cross between salami and luncheon meat, and is served fried with eggs instead of bacon. It had always been a favorite of Princess Grace's, and even Prince Rainier has succumbed to its obscure charm.

Princess Grace had a special cupboard where she kept the cake mixes and used to delight in making chocolate cakes, angel cakes, waffles and other American specialities especially for the Prince and Father Tucker.

It was all one big joke and no one, least of all the staff, who saw these miracles appear in no time at all, knew that it was all due to those magic cake mixes. Even the Prince was in awe of his wife's culinary skill. But it was her secret and she kept it.

Slowly, and with great delicacy, the family quarters began to come to life. The Princess filled the palace with flowers, but this was not always an unqualified success. Once, to brighten up one of the state rooms as a surprise for the Prince, she had boxes planted with white chrysanthemums arranged along one wall. When Prince Rainier saw this, he was horrified and exclaimed, "Not chrysanthemums! These are the flowers of the tomb!"

The chrysanthemums were immediately removed, as in France they are always associated with death and burials.

Neither the Prince nor Princess was very satisified with their efforts to turn the palace into a livable home. It continued to retain the impersonal air of a museum.

Princess Grace was also to discover that her life now was anything but private. Throughout that first summer, tourists stood in the cobbled palace courtyard, which looks like a setting from a Donizetti opera, hoping to catch a glimpse of her.

"Everyone's marriage is a series of concessions," the Prince said at the time. "Whatever force of love there is between two newly married people, however strong the bonds, it would be very difficult for any young bride trying to adapt herself in circumstances like these. Plus the problem of dealing with the horrible old bachelor and getting him rid of his bad habits."

And so the year slipped by until Christmas, her first in Monaco. A memorable year. A difficult year. A developing year in the life of Princess Grace.

Though her baby was due very soon, the Princess insisted upon helping arrange a series of parties for the Monegasque children at the palace, a custom she and the Prince have continued ever since.

Rooms that had been bare and friendless for many Christmases suddenly came to life as she personally arranged the candles and elaborate Christmas decorations she had made.

Five hundred children in all were invited and left the palace clutching small presents. In those early days, the children were given a large tea at the palace before the Punch and Judy or conjuring shows which followed. It was the Princess who noticed that they wanted to take home something for their mothers. At the Christmas parties now, each child also gets a small bag of cakes and biscuits, as well as his or her present, to take home. "They absolutely love it as they go off clutching their paper bags," the Princess explained to friends.

When the New Year dawned, everything was ready for the arrival of the baby. George Stacey, a New York decorator, who at the time was working in France for a client, was called in to hurry up the endless delay in the creation of the new nursery, which was next door to the private apartments of the Prince and Princess.

The Princess had chosen to decorate the nursery in yellow—one of her favorite colors—and white, and Stacey installed an ingenious shelving unit for the baby's wardrobe.

At first it was planned that, like most American mothers, the Princess would have her baby in a hospital; but with the arrival of the world's press as well as for security reasons, the Prince asked her if she would have the baby at home. Ma Kelly flew over a week ahead of schedule to be with her daughter. This was due to the fact that because Princess Grace had been too active over the holidays, the baby might arrive early.

It was reported that Princess Grace had been extremely angry when her mother wrote a series of intimate articles about her for a Philadelphia paper before the marriage—the proceeds of which went to Women's Medical—naturally. The Kellys are a family, a very united family, and clearly all this had now been forgotten in the excitement and anticipation.

The library was transformed into a delivery room and the Princess's obstetrician, Dr. Emile Hervet, stood by.

Monaco went about its business with hushed voices and there were more than the usual glances up at the palace on the hill which flew the national flag. All Monaco was awaiting the birth of this baby—this very exceptional heir to the throne.

Twenty-six

Nine months and four days after her wedding, in the library of the palace at 9:27 A.M. on January 23, 1957, Princess Grace gave birth to a baby daughter—Caroline Louise Marguerite. The birth had been normal, if a little long, and the Princess had her baby naturally as she wished without twilight sleep or any other form of anesthetic.

The Prince and Princess had chosen Dr. Hervet to follow the pregnancy through delivery. The doctor has the eminent status of Professeur Agrégé à la Faculté de Médecine de Paris, Gynécologue Accoucheur des Hôpitaux et Chef du Service de Gynécologue Obstétrique du Groupe Hospitalier Pitié-Saltpétrière.

Dr. Hervet arrived from Paris with a nurse and moved into the palace two weeks before the actual birth.

The baby was charming and because of her weight—8 pounds 11 ounces—was a complete little human being with a fuzz of peach-colored hair and large blue eyes.

As Prince Rainier was to remark at the time, ''Apart from Caroline, I had seen other people's new-born children whilst making official visits to the maternity home and they had always appeared to me as being rather ugly little red creatures. Probably I was biased, but my own babies never seemed that way at all. They weren't red and they weren't ugly—in fact they have all been rather big babies, large children already when they were born and not all wrinkled and old-looking.''

Hungry for any snippet of news, the reporters latched onto the talkative Father Tucker, who gave his own unofficial daily bulletin. His pride and joy were not to be contained.

"Prince Rainier told me with tears in his eyes, 'It's a beautiful baby girl,' " he announced solemnly.

Princess Grace was extremely well after the birth and sat up in bed to drink a glass of champagne. Unlike most royal mothers anxious to preserve their figures, she had insisted that she would nurse the baby herself. To this day she is a strong advocate of breast feeding, which she considers "wholly normal and right."

In those first days were formed the thoughts which she was to express five years later when she delivered a paper on the subject of breast feeding at a convention organized by the LaLeche League in Chicago. In words very dear to her heart she gave this imaginative message to the mothers of the world:

"It would seem to me that the closeness to the child resulting from breast feeding is somehow an extension and affirmation of that very love that has resulted in its being there. A man and a woman have united to create this little being that one is holding to oneself and nurturing. And this nurturing is to be treasured for it is a relationship that is to end all too soon, the very first of many partings.

"If one but realized it, with the onset of the first pangs of birth pains, one begins to say farewell to one's baby. For no sooner has it entered the world when others begin to demand their share. With the child at one's breast, one keeps the warmth of possession a little longer."

At the same time, she not only urged mothers to breast feed their babies, but to allow other children in the family to watch and teach them "the wholesomeness of sex and the naturalness of it." And this she subsequently did with her own family.

On Friday, January 25, Prince Rainier officially certified the birth of an heiress apparent before Judge Marcel Portanier and three witnesses.

One would like to think that there was genuine delight in Monaco for these attractive royal parents on the arrival of their baby; but the cynical pragmatists were relieved at the birth as they quickly noted that for at least another generation, the people of the principality would have no taxation or military draft under French rule which would have been their fate had the royal line not produced an heir.

For whatever reasons all Monaco went wild with joy. Flags flew, cannons boomed and the boats and yachts in the harbor hooted a nonstop lullabye. Everyone was happy and the wine flowed.

During the week after the baby's birth, seven thousand messages of congratulations arrived at the palace, including those from Queen Elizabeth and Queen Juliana. Gifts began to pour in as well, from homey knitted baby clothes to the pearl ring and diamond clasp that Prince Rainier gave the Princess to mark this splendid occasion.

For Princess Grace one of the first tasks was to get her figure back, as she had put on a great deal of weight during the pregnancy. Once again she approached this with her usual thoroughness. She did exercises daily and took long walks with Oliver whenever she could.

Her female friends were amused when she told them where she did some of her exercises. "I do isometrics in church, so while I'm doing my soul some good, I'm doing my body some good, too."

A Swiss-German nanny had been engaged to look after Princess Caroline although Princess Grace herself spent a great deal of time in the nursery and has always been actively involved in bringing up her children.

Right from the start there was a strict rule that was always kept in the palace. No one except Prince Rainier, Princess Grace and the immediate staff concerned was allowed to visit the nursery. In this way the Princess thought that she could keep her children's infancy as normal as possible.

As is customary in court circles in France, the baby was referred to as "Madame Caroline" by the official palace staff, but by the Princess's personal staff she was simply called "Caroline." It was not, in fact, until she was several years of age that she was aware of the fact that she was any different from other children. She believed that everyone lived in a palace and had special parents called Their Serene Highnesses.

The Prince and Princess had naturally discussed having children before their marriage. They had both been anxious to commence a family as soon as possible and to have their children within a limited time period. This they felt was better for the family itself and would allow the Princess to more quickly resume a normal life and take up her own interests again.

It was to become an all absorbing occupation. Within fourteen months Princess Grace was to give birth to her second child—a prince for Monaco.

Prince Rainier described the birth as one of the most wonderful experiences of his life. It also changed the historic outlook in the

(Above) It takes a clever woman
to steal the hero and the picture
but this is just what Grace Kelly
did in Mogambo. She is pictured
here with Ava Gardner and
Clark Gable. She called him "Ba"
(Swahili for "father") and he
called her Kelly.
Photo: The Kobal Collection

(Below) Tea for Two:
Grace Kelly and Danny
Kaye share a cup on the set
of High Society.

(*Above*) *Grace Kelly meets
a fan while making* Green
Fire *in South America.*

(*Below*) *Mr. and Mrs. Alfred
Hitchcock relax between
scenes with Grace Kelly on
the set of* To Catch a Thief.

(*Above*) *"There's hills in them thar gold," cracked Alfred Hitchcock when he saw Grace Kelly in the spectacular dress Edith Head designed for her in* To Catch a Thief.

(*Below*) The Country Girl *was the film that raised Grace Kelly from just another pretty film star to an Academy Award winner. She is pictured here with Bing Crosby.*
Photo: The Kobal Collection

*Field day for photographers as Grace Kelly waves
good-bye to America from the deck of the
S.S.* Independence *before sailing for Monaco and
a new life as a princess.*

Grace Kelly and Oliver are welcomed aboard
Deo Juvante II *by Prince Rainier in the harbor at
Cannes and watched by fellow passengers lining the
deck of the* Independence.
Photo: Fausto Picedi

*Princess Grace and Prince Rainier share a toast
after the civil wedding service in Monte Carlo.*

Princess Grace and Prince Rainier exchange a
tender glance during their second wedding service
in the Cathedral of St. Nicholas.

*"God give me strength. . . ." Princess Grace
during the wedding.*

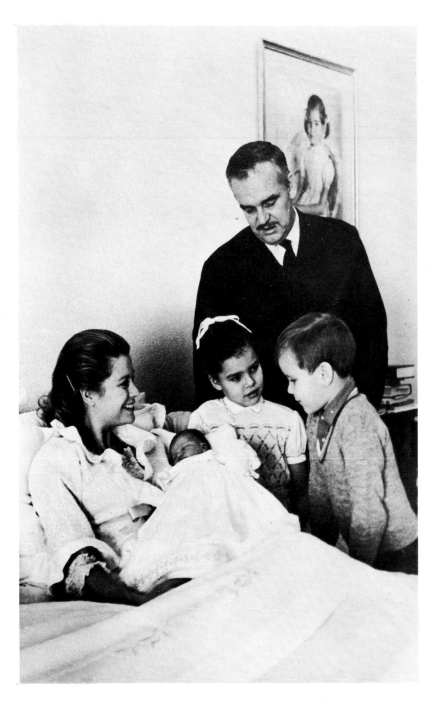

"Can we have a boy next time?" Prince Albert asks
Princess Grace when she shows him Princess
Stephanie. Prince Rainier and Princess Caroline
complete this family snapshot.
Photo: John Hillelson Agency Ltd.

*(Above, left) Air vents are
fascinating: Princess Grace lifts
Princess Caroline for a better
view on board Prince Rainier's
yacht.*
Photo: John Hillelson Agency Ltd.

*(Above, right) A family party:
Princess Caroline and Prince
Albert claim Princess Grace's
attention.*
Photo: Cliché Archives du Palais

*(Below) Prince Rainier at the
helm with Princess Grace,
Prince Albert and Princess
Caroline in the* Albecaro *named
after the children.*

(Above) The growing Grimaldi
family in their first formal
photograph, taken in the gold salon.
It carries Princess Grace's signature.
Photo: Collection Archives du
Palais Princier

(Below) An informal
photograph of the family
relaxing with the new poodle
who has replaced Oliver.
Photo: René Maestri

(Above) Three for a ride: Princess Grace loads up while on winter holiday in Switzerland.
Photo: Jean-Pierre Rey

(Below) The family out walking during a holiday visit to Princess Charlotte's castle "le Château de Marchais" in the Ardennes.
Photo: John Hillelson Agency Ltd.

(*Above*) *Princess Grace and Princess Stephanie wear Monegasque national dress. Their dashing escort is Prince Albert.*

(*Below*) *Flanked by their grown-up children Prince Albert and Princess Caroline, Prince Rainier and Princess Grace attend a Soirée de Gala in 1974.*

*All Monaco turned out to greet the Grimaldi family during the
celebrations to mark the twenty-fifth anniversary of Prince
Rainier's reign in May 1974. Princess Grace wore
honey-colored chiffon for the cathedral service.
Photo: John Hillelson Agency Ltd.*

*The proud parents Princess Grace and Prince Rainier
escort Princess Caroline at her first Red Cross Gala.
Father and daughter had the first waltz alone on the
ballroom floor.
Photo: John Hillelson Agency Ltd.*

*Princess Grace and Prince Rainier leaving the Royal
Opera House with Princess Margaret and Lord
Snowdon during their official visit to Monte Carlo.
Photo: John Hillelson Agency Ltd.*

*Seated with Lord Mountbatten at a charity dinner, the
Princess has a warm regard for the former Admiral of
the Fleet.
Photo: John Hillelson Agency Ltd.*

*Scorpios hold hands: Princess Grace and
Richard Burton at her fortieth birthday party,
the Fête des Scorpions, on November 15, 1969.
Photo: René Maestri*

Princess Grace with Margot Fonteyn and Rudolph
Nureyev at the Festival des Ballets, Monte Carlo,
in 1968.
Photo: John Hillelson Agency Ltd.

Princess Grace arrives with Prince Rainier for a 1900s
ball in Monte Carlo. Note the Prince's Dali moustache.
Photo: John Hillelson Agency Ltd.

As Texas saw Princess Grace during her visit there for
the Neiman-Marcus Fête des Fleurs. The Princess
wore one of her fantasy hair styles.
Photo: Zintgraff

Princess Grace in gypsy mood dances
at a gala in Monte Carlo.
Photo: John Hillelson Agency Ltd.

*The Belle of the Ball at a fancy dress gala in
Monte Carlo.*
Photo: John Hillelson Agency Ltd.

The happy married couple stroll
arm in arm.
Photo: René Maestri

*(Above) The Prince and
Princess sharing wine at an inn
in Switzerland.
Photo: Ardopress*

*(Below) The ruling couple
dance, oblivious of the room
around them.*

*(Above) The kiss that tells
everything.
Photo: John Hillelson
Agency Ltd.*

*(Below) Just another chic
Parisian walking her dog in
Avenue Foch.
Photo: John Hillelson
Agency Ltd.*

*(Above) Christmas again at the
royal palace. When Prince
Rainier saw the Princess's new
short hair, he was so dismayed
that she quickly grew it long
again.*
Photo: John Hillelson Agency Ltd.

*(Below) Princess Grace talks to
two small ballerinas at the
inauguration of the Sergei
Diaghilev Exhibition at the
Winter Sporting Club in Monaco
in 1973.*
Photo: Robert de Hoé

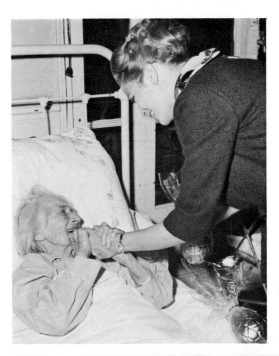

*Princess Grace has always been
concerned with the elderly, and
arranged for a new Old People's
Home in Monaco.
Photo: Lukomski*

*(Below) A small citizen of
Monaco receives his Christmas
parcel from Princess Grace at
the annual party at the palace.
Photo: Detaille*

(Above) Prince Rainier and his
elegant passenger Princess Grace
set off for the Brighton run in
their De Dion Bouton vintage
car in 1968.
Photo: Syndication International

(Below) The late Graham Hill of
Great Britain recounts to Princess
Grace an episode during his
winning race at the Monte Carlo
Rally.
Photo: John Hillelson Agency Ltd.

(Above) The Grimaldi
family photographer.
Photo: John Hillelson
Agency Ltd.

(Below) As does all the Kelly
family, Princess Grace enjoys
and participates in all sports.
She is pictured here skiing
in Gstaad.
Photo: Keystone Press Agency

(Above) Swimming has always
been part of Princess Grace's
keep-fit program.
Photo: John Hillelson Agency Ltd.

(Below) Fishing tackle can be
flummoxing: Princess Grace
opens the fishing festival at
County Mayo in Ireland in 1961.
Photo: C. Kindahl-Dalmas

principality. Although there was a Constitution Law which said that the first-born of the Prince should succeed, this only applied until a male child was born who would take precedence.

Again the confinement took place in the library, which had been converted into a delivery room with Dr. Hervet in attendance. Prince Rainier was given the news of his son's birth by a midwife who stuck her head round the corner of the room adjoining the library and shouted ecstatically, "It's a boy!"

Both parents had been wishing for a boy, but as Prince Rainier was to say, "Had it been a girl, I would not have been upset."

The baby boy was christened in the Cathedral of St. Nicholas and given the names Albert Alexandre Louis Pierre. He also weighed 8 pounds 11 ounces, and was promptly nicknamed Albie, which has stuck with him ever since.

Among the galaxy of celebrities invited to the christening were two from England, Sir Bernard and Lady Docker, whose behavior gave cause for more inches of space in the British press than the event itself.

To understand the incident, one must also know about the English and the Dockers. England is a land where eccentrics are encouraged to flourish. It is part of their national character.

During the 1950s Sir Bernard and Lady Docker brightened English breakfast table reading every morning with their social antics. Though one did not always condone the behavior of the pretty loquacious Norah, perceived in an English context it was more acceptable than in Monte Carlo, where the couple frequently visited in their yacht, *The Shemara.*

Norah Docker, a former milliner, had been one of the prettiest and most graceful hostesses in the Café Royal in London. With her blonde bubbling looks, stylish figure and extraordinarily acute assessment of men, she had married three millionaires, who all adored her. Two of them died and left her their fortunes while the third, Sir Bernard Docker, the successful head of Birmingham Small Arms, was at the time one of Britain's most successful industrialists.

They were rich, happily married and unconcerned with the storms that invariably broke around them.

My experience with them is illuminating, and illustrates their amused status in the British press. We thrived on them. It was the year after Lady Docker had startled the motor show at Earls Court by appearing in a gold-starred dress to match the body work of a new Daimler which her husband's firm was exhibiting.

The following year, as woman's editor of the *London Evening News*, I was again sent to cover the motor show from a woman's angle. I reported what I thought to be correct—that Lady Docker was once again there in a slate blue dress to match the new slate blue Daimler. It made the front page.

The next morning I received a telephone call from a voice identifying itself as Lady Docker's press agent.

"You've got it all wrong. You've made a boob and Lady Docker is very angry with you. It was the Daimler that was painted to match her favorite dress and not the other way round."

The editor was only too pleased to print an apology—on the front page.

This, then, was Norah Docker: lovable, irascible, amusing, outrageous.

You never knew what she would do next. She played in the English marbles championship at Tinsley Green; she stood on her head in public; she was pictured dancing a sailor's hornpipe with the crew of *The Shemara*. She was never dull. Her only crime was that under certain circumstances, when the pink champagne flowed, she tended to be remarkably outspoken.

When Sir Bernard and Lady Docker were invited to the christening of Prince Albert, they asked that their own nineteen-year-old son be included in the invitation as his birthday was the same day.

"It seemed a natural enough request to make," says Lady Docker today.

Their request was denied them for the simple reason that everything had already been planned and the number of guests allocated. The Dockers were hurt and perhaps confused.

Their first mistake was to refuse to attend the christening and instead to hold an impromptu press reception in Cannes at the Hotel Majestic. The next day they returned to Monte Carlo, where a regrettable fracas occurred in the restaurant of the Hotel de Paris.

The restaurant staff reported at the time that Lady Docker not only said some insulting things about Their Serene Highnesses but, snatching the flag of Monaco from the table in full view of everybody, broke it in two and flung it to the floor.

Later, from his flat in Claridge House in London, Sir Bernard told the British press his version of the story.

"As we rose to leave, Norah's hand knocked a tiny Monaco flag out of the bowl of flowers in the center of the table. In her disgust with the way they treated us, she picked it up and threw it on the floor.

" 'Well, we shan't be needing any of those,' she said.

"I can't think anyone saw us except one or two waiters. Norah was pretty cross. I don't blame her."

The story exploded all over the world. It was the kind of irreverent piece of gossip that every tired news editor jumps at, and was blown up into proportions far beyond its merit.

When rumors of the Dockers' proposed expulsion from the Riviera reached her, the indestructible Norah retaliated in the *Daily Express* in true fighting form.

"As far as I am concerned, Prince Rainier can go and jump in the sea. I am signing my own decree that I will never set foot in that Hyde Park Principality again. I never went to the reception. I would be glad if they sent their presents back. I will not take my yacht within shooting distance of the place. Well, one thing is certain. They will miss us more than we will miss them."

What should have been a forgettable incident rankled both sides and to this day the quarrel has never been settled. According to Prince Rainier, although he has been approached several times by the Dockers' lawyer—the christening incident was only a part of an accumulation of distressing incidents—his reply has always been, "Will Lady Docker retract what she said, and the attitude she had at that time, and will she freely engage herself not to do this sort of thing any more?" And this Norah Docker will never do.

A new addition to the royal household in Monaco that year was an English nanny, who was to stay with the family for seven years. Her engagement was purely by chance but is indicative of the unconventional attitude of Prince Rainier and Princess Grace toward their staff.

She was no traditional English nanny bristling with diplomas and nursery clichés but a plump, jolly, apple-cheeked, cherry-lipped girl from Rugby in the Midlands of England.

Maureen King had been employed by the celebrated French playwright Jean Anouilh to look after his two children in Paris. This was subsequent to a similar position she had held in Belgium. Her mother read in a magazine that Princess Grace was expecting a second child; and, unbeknownst to Maureen, her sister wrote a letter to Princess Grace asking if there was a vacancy for a nanny. The letter began, ''Dear Madam, It occurred to me . . .'' and was signed ''Maureen King.''

Two months later when Maureen was home on leave, a letter with the royal cipher was delivered by the postman, and it was only then that the family confessed to writing the original correspondence. The letter invited Maureen to fly to Monaco for an interview with Princess Grace.

In telling the story to me, Mrs. Maureen Wood, now a slender mother of two, recalled, ''I said to my mother, 'I can't go. I did not even write the letter.'

'' 'Go. You can always say that you slept a night in a palace,' my mother said.

''And I went completely with this attitude. I was quite sure that I simply couldn't land the job. For one thing I had had no formal training at all. It was a chance in a million that I landed the job.''

Some years later when the royal family was on holiday in Switzerland, Princess Grace asked Nanny King to invite Jean Anouilh, who had a home nearby, to drinks before dinner. Grace had played in *Ring Round the Moon* when she had been a young actress in New York. ''It was fascinating to see how they were both obviously delighted to meet each other,'' Maureen Wood remembered.

She was later to meet another young member of the palace staff, American Phyllis Blum (who is now married to Somerset Maugham's nephew, Julian Earl, and lives in London). At that time she was personal secretary to the Princess.

These two lively girls were to become fast friends and brighten up Princess Grace's life in many enjoyable and rollicksome ways over the next few years. They were always filled with fun.

After a few months, ''Big Fat Nanna,'' as Princess Caroline aptly called her nurse, was in sole charge of the two children.

Speaking of those early years of her marriage, Princess Grace was to say, ''During the first years of my marriage I lost my identity because I didn't have the ways of recharging my batteries that I had depended on before. I tended to let my husband and his life and work absorb my personality. This was wrong. I had to find ways of finding myself in this life.''

Twenty-seven

By 1958, with her two babies growing up, palace life running reasonably efficiently and smoothly, and her French much more fluent, Princess Grace was ready to take up some activities outside her family life.

"I don't think it was because she was bored with family life, but merely that she could see so much to be done and with her American efficiency was longing to get started," a Monaco friend told me. "While most of us take up charity work when our children are grown up, she had to do it right at the beginning."

On May 23, 1958, Prince Rainier named as his successor as president of the Red Cross his wife, Princess Grace.

The Monegasque Red Cross was founded in 1948 by Prince Louis II, who entrusted its presidency to his grandson. Today under Princess Grace's guidance, it is one of the most active societies with the International Red Cross. Princess Grace is what the French in their picturesque language would call a "participant president." She is not just a nominal head, but is involved with some aspect of Red Cross work almost every day of her life. Whether she is in residence at the palace in Monaco, at their apartment in Paris or abroad, she is in constant communication wtih the secretary, and all decisions of policy are referred to her. Although there are heads of the various services, the Princess reviews nearly every case herself, often personally seeing the people concerned.

Because Monaco is such a small country to operate under the umbrella of the Red Cross, all kinds of programs came to life despite the fact that it was not always easy and there were some misunderstandings along the way.

Princess Grace's main problem in the beginning was that she tried to bring a kind of American efficiency and know-how to this essentially Mediterranean atmosphere. She would arrive at meetings complete with her notes and businesslike glasses, totally briefed and ready to get on with the business at hand.

"Good morning," she would say and then expect the meeting to be dispensed with as quickly as possible. It seemed the most polite way to save people's time.

The Monegasque members of the committee were completely confused. They felt she was abrupt, cool and impatient. Gradually she learned that in Monte Carlo one begins the conversation with "How is your mother? . . . Is your sister back from England yet? . . . Is your husband's asthma better?" Only after these pleasantries are exchanged can one then begin to get down to the business on hand. The people need to be coerced into the mood, and this can take two or three times as long as in America.

As the Princess herself explained, "One misses that fine American custom of saying, 'Of course it can be done. Why not?' "

Every year the Red Cross Gala, which raises many thousands of francs for the society, is one of the most important events of the summer social season.

This is a labor of love for the Princess, who not only chooses the elaborate decorations and color scheme, but is also responsible for persuading some of the world's top names in entertainment, who are also her personal friends, to come and perform gratis. Their expenses are met, but few people could entice such a galaxy of talent to give up their time and fly in from all parts of the world. Princess Grace can and does.

In an interview with American journalist Nancy Schraffenberger, the Princess was asked if she would have chosen to take on civic involvements had she not been married to a man whose station in life required it. She replied, "Perhaps. We were brought up to participate and enter into things—they don't happen automatically. My father didn't care what interests we had, but we had to be interested in something. He couldn't stand anyone who didn't have enthusiasm."

Princess Grace, as well as Prince Rainier, also took an active part in the reconstruction and development of Monaco's new hospital, which opened in 1958 and now carries the name Hôpital Centre Princess Grace. Through her reading and visits to the States and whenever she saw or heard of something that might be useful, she would gather up all the information. At her instigation, an Assistance Center, again composed of volunteers, now operates in the hospital.

Three years after she was married, Princess Grace went to see the Monaco Old People's Home and was desperately depressed by what she saw. "Can't we put some flowers here? . . . Can't we do something there?" she asked the matron.

The matron replied, "There is no use doing anything because the old people won't even come downstairs. We have movies for them, but they won't even come and see them."

The Princess then called in her Red Cross helpers and suggested that they make a schedule of volunteers to visit the aged persons, talk to them and take them for outings—"to get them out of themselves." She also arranged that the Girl Guides went so that the old people would have some contact with the young.

It worked like a charm. The atmosphere of the home completely changed and the old ladies came downstairs to enjoy not only the movies, but also the special birthday parties that were given for each person.

Prince Rainier and Princess Grace next planned to have a new building for them constructed, and personally supervised the selection of building materials, decorations and furnishings. It is now an extremely attractive home with a completely different atmosphere.

Every Christmas there is a special tea for the old folk of Monaco, and the Princess distributes both a food parcel and something new to wear to each person.

As one old lady summed up, "She brought us heart."

It is natural that children are Princess Grace's major concern. She is not only devoted to her own children but is concerned with the children of other people and other nations—particularly suffering, needy, handicapped children or those whose mental health is in danger.

In 1963 she became the honorary president as well as one of the most active founding members of the Association Mondiale des Amis de L'Enfance (World Association of Friends of Children). During the ceremonies to mark the founding of the Italian branch, the Princess spoke these words:

"The A.M.A.D.E. was born of this anguish, born with no strength except its founders' will to succeed. Its cradle lies within the smallest nation in the world. But, from frontier to frontier, we fully intend to spread over the earth a network of childhood's true friends."

On her doorstep there were many problems that she personally took a hand in solving. When she heard that there was no day nursery for working mothers, the Red Cross acquired a dignified house in Boulevarde de Suisse in Monte Carlo and turned it into a nursery which is called Garderie Notre Dame de Fatima, named after a beloved saint.

Princess Grace personally chose the color schemes and much of the equipment right down to the cheerful yellow and white kitchen, with the latest gadgets for preparing meals for the children.

In the playrooms and sleeping quarters the walls are decorated with animal cut-outs which she bought in America. In the entrance hall under a ceramic plaque of Our Lady of Fatima is a huge teddy bear which once belonged to one of her own children. She raided their nursery and sent most of the toys which are still in use there today.

The Princess not only discusses the children's menus with a dietician, when they are planned for the various seasons, but it was her idea that a daily menu should be put up on the wall at child-level in the entrance hall.

As the mothers deposit the children on the doorstep on their way to work, there is a rush over to the wall to see what is for lunch today.

Every Christmas the Princess sends them her Christmas cards so that the staff can decorate the nursery to make it look gay.

There is also a music academy in Monaco where any child can have music education without having to pay a franc.

Another project dear to her heart is the multi-racial family of the late singer Josephine Baker. Princess Grace's admiration and friendship for Josephine Baker was immense. When in 1969 she read that the black singer, through blissful ignorance of the reality of money, had gone bankrupt and lost the chateau in the Dordogne Valley where she had made a home for her family, she got in touch with her.

With the aid of an initial loan from the Prince and Princess, and afterwards, with the help of the Monegasque Red Cross, Josephine Baker was able to install her family in a comfortable villa at Roquebrune-Cap-Martin. She was given an opportunity to appear at the Red Cross Gala in 1969; and because of this and other engagements, she was able, and made it a point of honor, to repay the Prince and Princess and the Red Cross for all their support.

Roquebrune-Cap-Martin is a charming villa filled with sunshine and furnished in the mood of the twenties, with aquamarine and white sofa and chairs, and poignantly nostalgic with mementoes of this remarkable woman's career.

She was so cold in the ghetto of St. Louis when she was a child that she decided to become a dancer to keep warm. Here in this villa, where the blue sky meets the blue of the Mediterranean, she was able to find peace and pleasure with her "rainbow children."

One of her greatest triumphs had been at the Folies Bergère, where she would slink onto a mirrored platform clad in a bunch of bananas. Nothing else. "I wasn't really naked," she liked to say in later years. "I simply didn't have any clothes on."

When I called one brilliant sunny day last June, I found some of the children there—still bewildered and confused as to what the future held in store for them.

Marianne, who is French and nineteen years of age, invited me in for a cool crème de menthe drink as we talked of their future. Akio, a Korean, is twenty-three and works in an office; Luis, a twenty-two-year-old Brazilian, lives in Brazil; Jarri, a Finn, and Jeannot, a Japanese, both twenty-two, are students; Moise, an Israeli, is nineteen and works; Marianne and Brahima Berber are nineteen and students; Koffi, an African, is eighteen and learning to be a pastry cook; Mara, an Indian, is seventeen and a student; Noel is French, sixteen years of age, and a student; and Stellina, an Arab, is at school in England and is only eleven years old.

Miss Baker's husband lives in Brazil most of the time, but her sister, Mrs. Wallace, lives in Monte Carlo. "Tante Tante," as the children call her, will keep a family eye on them; but all the papers and official problems in their lives will be taken care of by the Red Cross.

Princess Grace is adamant that the family will remain together as long as possible or as they wish.

There was a healthy respect for each other between these two

189

women—Princess Grace and Josephine Baker—both professionals in their spheres: the art of giving people pleasure through entertainment and the art of giving love to children.

When Sammy Davis, Jr., outrageously snubbed Princess Grace and her 1,200 glittering guests at the grand opening of Monte Carlo's Sporting Club Casino, Josephine Baker—the Black Venus —then aged sixty-seven—joined black comedian Bill Cosby, Desi Arnaz, Jr., and pianist Burt Bacharach to give an impromptu performance at less than an hour's notice.

She not only slayed the sophisticated audience with her devastating talent and charm, but it was also to prove to be an encouraging point in the rejuvenation of her career. From then on she was offered cabaret contracts all over the world.

On the night before Josephine Baker died in Paris, Princess Grace went to say good-bye to her. Though Miss Baker was unconscious from a stroke and it was known that she would never recover, Princess Grace asked if she might visit her in the hospital. She arrived at the back entrance of the hospital so as not to attract attention and the eyes of the newsmen lurking around the front door.

In the cool twilight of a Paris spring evening, she sat alone with her friend.

In 1965 the Princess Grace Foundation was created which was primarily used to encourage local artists and craftsmen of all ages. This was originally inspired by the Elder Craftsmen Shop in Philadelphia, although the Monaco version is not strictly for older people.

The Princess bought a shop in the old part of Monaco near the palace and gave it to the Foundation for the sale of their goods. A branch has now opened in the city of Monte Carlo. Along with the knitted hats and scarves and pretties made from Provençal prints there are pottery, ceramics and paintings. But one of the most successful sales to tourists is a scarf designed by Princess Grace.

It is charming in thick white silk with a rouleau edge in pink. There are pastel-colored flowers, drawn in the style of Picasso or one of her children, and around the edge a stylish border that, upon close inspection, proves to be composed of the words "Monte Carlo" repeated in an entrancing pattern.

The Foundation has now extended its perimeter to help people in need who do not qualify under other charities. For instance, the Red

Cross cannot give money directly to people, but through the Foundation Princess Grace was able to send a young man to New York University.

Every now and then Princess Grace adds money to her Foundation in the most unusual ways. When she twice read extracts from the Bible on *Stars on Sunday*, Britain's popular Sunday night program—on which the Archbishop of Canterbury, Yehudi Menuhin and hosts of other world celebrities have performed—she was offered a handsome fee. This money went directly into the Foundation funds.

When an American magazine asked her to write an article about the merits of breast feeding, the Princess agreed simply because it is a subject dear to her heart. But upon publication of the article the magazine offered to pay her a fee, which she graciously accepted and placed directly into the Princess Grace Foundation. The Princess has a great respect and understanding for all mothers—not only for what they have achieved but for the difficult task they face in bringing up their children.

Twenty-eight

It is generally known that Princess Grace loves flowers. She loves living with them, giving them to friends, arranging them, and drying them and making them into enchanting collages. Her life is surrounded with flowers.

In 1968 she decided that Monaco should have a garden club to develop its members' artistic sense through a knowledge of flowers, plants and decorative floral arrangement. At one of the early meetings Princess Grace gave a lecture, accompanied by slides, about the trees of America and the development of the great forests there.

"It was absolutely fascinating," an American who was there said.

From this club, she then wanted to expand to an international flower arranging competition. One of the judges in the first occasion was Julia Clements (widow of Sir Alexander Seton, the 10th Baron of Abercorn), author of fourteen best-selling books on flower arrangements and an international judge and lecturer. With two roses named after her—Julia Clements and Lady Seton—she was once described as the "arch priestess of flowers who had led more than 5,000,000 women into the grip of flower arrangement."

The first show was a brave little venture but, being the perfectionist that she is, after the show when the officials and judges were walking around the palace garden, Princess Grace sent her lady-in-waiting across to Julia Clements and asked her not to leave when the others did but to go to the Princess's bureau.

"I noticed a delicate-looking dry flower arrangement on the desk; then shortly afterwards the Princess walked in with a note pad and pencil in her hand saying, 'Now do tell me how to improve this show.' "

They discussed staging, schedule making, judges and various

192

definitions. The Princess took down many notes and asked pertinent questions which resulted in Miss Clements' returning to Monaco to give lessons to the founder members of the new garden club.

"I find that Princess Grace does not like too many principles or technicalities, even when teaching. I will make arrangements one way emphasizing principles, but when working she will do it her way, which not only displays her originality but the results are often much better," said Miss Clements.

"After one lesson, when she had made a very original arrangement, with striking strelitzias and fruit, she was so pleased with the result that she said, 'Oh, do help me take it back to the palace. I want my husband to see what I've done.'"

The Princess became the president of the garden club and the flower show, and is always thinking of different methods of presentation or ideas to make the show more appealing.

One of her bright ideas was to have a "Men Only" class. But her problem was how to get the husbands to enter. She invited several husbands and wives—including writers, film stars and artists—to the palace for drinks one evening. They all wondered why they had been asked, but after a few drinks she told them of the flower show and said, "I want all the ladies to stay with me and the men to go into another room."

The men thought the women were going to have flower-talk while they continued their drinking. They were wrong. A long table was laid out with flowers, dishes, pinholders and scissors. The Princess told them that as she wanted each one of them to enter her show, now was the time to practice. And this was how the most amusing class held in the competition every year was created. It has become the "Men Only" class with titles which vary each year. Some years it is sport, others a proverb and last year the theme was astrology.

On a May morning last year, a blue-jeaned competitor carried in his equipment and jocularly greeted the other husbands. Then he seriously set about creating a Scorpio motif with his little bags of sand, tin tray of pebbles, tiny red-tipped cacti (like fat little candles) and a plastic crab—or was it a scorpion? After he had finished, he meticulously cleaned up like the other men around him.

At the awards ceremony, held the following day at the Hotel de Paris, a happy and bashful Prince Rainier acknowledged the clapping when it was disclosed that his arrangement had been highly recommended by the judges.

No one knows quite how Princess Grace persuades Prince Rainier and their male friends to enter the competition year after year. But she does. And so sincere is Prince Rainier's interest that he gives up two whole days to her gardening club events. The Prince varies his name for entering each year, usually choosing one of his other titles; but in any case, the judging is done quite anonymously.

The two-day event now attracts visitors from all over the world. Last year for the first time the South Africans, who had arrived with boxes of marvelous flowers from their own gardens, reaped most of the prizes. I was sitting with them during the luncheon at the beach club when Julia Clements came over to our table and said, "Princess Grace would like to meet the ladies from South Africa."

Cameras were whisked out, lipstick applied and smiles adjusted as they went over to the Princess's table where she was sitting with Prince Rainier, Princess Stephanie and Prince Albert. The Princess could have been any pretty girl in a red cotton skirt, white lawn shirt, navy cardigan, her hair pulled back into a ponytail with a strand of heavy red wool, and huge trendy sunglasses. She carried a floppy navy-blue and white beach hat. Nothing could have been simpler.

But for these housewives who had come from half a world away, first winning many of the prizes at the Ghent Flower Arranging Show in Belgium and then being persuaded to come on to Monaco, meeting Princess Grace was the highlight of their trip.

"It was worth all the expense and all the traveling. Everything. Just to go home and say I have talked to her. And she was so lovely. . . ."

The Princess is filled with fun on these occasions when she sees that all are enjoying themselves. During a children's flower parade, when the royal family was throwing flower heads at the children as the floats passed by, she suddenly became tired of this and turned to the next box and threw flowers at the people in that.

Princess Grace has become so advanced in the art of flower arranging that she has been made an international judge, and last year judged in the great Ghent Floralies. The other judges were impressed with her wealth of knowledge when discussing composition, color and interpretation. Had she entered herself, she probably would have walked off with many of the first prizes.

In 1970 Princess Grace was invited by the Flower Arranging Society of Solihull in the Midlands of England to be their guest of honor. She exhausted and enchanted her hostesses. After a tiring afternoon of looking at all the exhibits, she remembered that there was something else to see.

It was past 9 P.M. when the Princess asked, "And what about the church?" The parish church, St. Alphege, had been specially decorated for the occasion.

Someone quickly rang through to a church official to open up the church, which had been locked up, and the Princess spent an hour there before leaving for the drive back to London.

Although Princess Grace does not always have time to arrange the flowers in the palace, when she does, guests always recognize her touch. At one luncheon party, she had all the children helping her make fantastic concoctions of flowers and fruits and vegetables for each of the small tables around the pool.

In the new living room in the palace extension there was a large twisted and gnarled root out of which a cascade of cymbidium orchids tumbled. They looked just right. Princess Grace had pulled up the root from a barren part of the mountain at Roc Agel when she had been out for a walk. Some of the Princess's happiest private hours are spent in the large flower room she has made on the ground floor of the palace, which is stacked with bases, containers, wire, pinholders and everything needed for flower arrangement.

Dried flower pictures, which began as a Kelly family hobby, has now been developed into a high art by the Princess. This year in Paris she will hold her first public exhibition of about fifty of her creations.

The finished product, mounted in a deep, recessed frame, is a work of art. The most spectacular are the fantasy flowers which she creates herself with stamens from one flower and petals from another. They are wildly exotic and extremely beautiful. Her wild flower pictures are delicate and exquisite. No telephone book in the palace is ever thrown away. Princess Grace keeps them all and fills them with flowers she finds out walking in the mountains behind Monaco or those grown in the palace gardens. She presses them for a month before using them.

"I walk behind the gardeners and pick up the clippings," she said.

When a Monegasque woman said to me, "She has brought life to Monaco," she meant it. From a beautiful faded city, forecourt to the crematorium, Monte Carlo is now bursting with tourists, exhibitions and everything to do with the arts. All this comes mainly from the Princess's enthusiasm.

Grouped in 1970 as the International Arts Festival, concerts, ballets and theater performances, cabaret and literary events succeed each other from June to September. The Festival was created in 1966 at the Princess's initiative upon the occasion of the Monte Carlo Centennial.

The best ballet companies in the world have danced within a specially conceived set in the Place du Palais: the Paris Opera Ballet, the National Hungarian, the Soviet Ballet of the Novosibirsk Opera, the Harkness from New York, the Slask Polish ballet, the London Royal Festival Ballet, the New York City Ballet and the Mexican Folk Ballet.

The Comédie Française regularly performs there, and the concerts given by the Monte Carlo Opera National Orchestra in the main courtyard of the palace have attracted some of the world's most prestigious names: Igor Markevitch, Mstislav Rostropovitch, Georges Prêtre, Paul Klecki, Zubin Mehta, Lovo von Matacic, Elisabeth Schwarzkopf, Tamas Vassary, Yehudi Menuhin, Rudolf Firkusny, Galina Vashnewskaya, Emil Gilels.

During their rehearsals few of them ever recognize a small figure sitting intently behind her glasses in the back of the theater, listening and watching. Her body is in the audience, but her mind is right there with the performers. She will be back there at night as the glamorous Princess Grace of Monaco but now, sitting in her skirt and cardigan or simple shirt-waist dress, she is Grace Kelly, the professional artist.

While Prince Rainier concentrates on the developing of the business interests, in reclaiming land and watching real estate and small industries becoming big business, Princess Grace is the tourist attraction. They queue for hours just to catch a glimpse of her—not the grand tour regulars at the Hotel de Paris but the £10-a-day trippers who flood in from St. Remo in Italy or French resorts along the coast.

On gala nights Princess Grace is always there, just as breathtakingly beautiful as they imagined. As Prince Rainier has explained, "Often when we have to go to a gala she has a stinking headache, but it doesn't show because she has this ability to put on a mask for the required time. I suppose it is something to do with her dramatic art training."

196

Although Princess Grace enjoys wearing simple clothes in her private life, for galas she dresses up as she fully understands that people want to see a princess. However, her elaborate preparations once backfired.

In 1968 for the re-opening of the Monte Carlo Casino which had just been redecorated, there was a grand ball with everyone wearing spectacular headdresses. Among the guests was Sophia Loren, who had flown in from Rome.

Alexandre, Princess Grace's hairdresser, came from Paris to create many of the fantasies worn that night. She was to be his last client and, as usual, he arrived late. Finally her elaborate headdress was finished as the Prince, a wily mandarin in pigtails, chafed at being late.

There is an autocratic rule in the principality that no one is allowed to dance or have a drink before the arrival of the Prince. The Princess went out to leave in the car only to find that her headdress just would not go in . . . it was staggeringly beautiful but too high. Everyone offered advice and every suggestion was tried, but it was impossible. At last one of the palace service vans was brought round, a carpet hastily placed in the back with a chair for the Princess. She arrived at the Casino—extremely late—via the back-door entrance.

Sadly, to this day in Monte Carlo, everyone only talks about how late the royal party was in arriving and how hot it was without a .drink. Few people know the real reason. Perhaps now they will understand why she was late.

Every summer through one or another of the Princess's enterprises, Monte Carlo is once again packed with celebrities from all over the world. It is doubtful whether tourists would have recognized Queen Victoria Eugenia of Spain, King Umberto of Portugal or Princess Sophia of Greece, but they will stand for hours just to catch a glimpse of Elizabeth Taylor, Richard Burton, Sophia Loren, Gina Lollobrigida, Danny Kaye or Cary Grant.

It is not just the sun that brings these busy, sophisticated people to Monaco, but the charm of taking part in some of the last of the fabulous social occasions left in this weary world.

Princess Grace is one of the best public relations officers in the game. It is a business that she understands and works at tirelessly— for Monaco.

Twenty-nine

"The most exciting day of my life wasn't the day I got the Oscar. No, it was the day when Caroline, for the first time, began to walk and she took seven small steps by herself, one after the other, before reaching me and throwing herself into my arms."

These are words spoken by Princess Grace when reminiscing about her days as a movie star. And anyone who knows the Princess intimately recognizes the truth in them. Some of her happiest days have been those early ones in the nursery at the palace in Monaco with her children when they were small.

With the birth of her second daughter and third child on February 1, 1965, the Princess's family was complete. Once again it was an incredibly pretty baby and she was christened Stephanie Marie Elisabeth.

"This is the most beautiful day of my life," Caroline announced when she saw the baby for the first time. Caroline's only disappointment was that she could not look after the baby all by herself and she longed for the day when she could take her to school!

Albert looked for some time and then said quietly, "Next time, could it be a boy?"

Once again the library had been turned into a delivery room. Princess Grace now preferred to have her children at home. As she told an American magazine, "Perhaps it is less hygienic to have one's baby at home rather than in the hospital, but it's much more pleasant. Even if one has a baby in the hospital, the husband and other members of the family can only see it and not hold it. That practice of keeping the baby away from the father behind a sheet of glass is so impersonal. As for the baby, to come straight from the mother's womb and almost immediately be placed in a room full of screaming infants—I'm not at all sure that that is a good practice. I feel that the system here of having babies at home if you can is much better than in America.''

And as before, to the magazines which were quick to note that Princess Grace had put on weight, the truthful answer to *Look* could not have been more appealing, ''I always have a weight problem after the birth of a baby because I breast feed my babies for at least two months. I feel it gives them a good start and would continue longer, only my many obligations do not permit. In order to feed a baby properly, a nursing mother should not diet. And I am too concerned about the well-being of my children to worry about my own line. It is not that important at this time.''

The centuries-old christening ceremony took place in the Cathedrale de Monaco, the same cathedral in which the marriage had taken place. Eugene Cardinal Tisserant, a prince of the Roman Catholic Church and a senior member of the Sacred College, came from Rome to officiate at the baptism.

After the ceremony, from the flower-decked palace balcony Princess Grace showed her baby to the people of Monaco and Prince Rainier gave this message:

''She comes to us in all her innocence and purity, bringing us once more as did her sister and brother joy, happiness and pride. Yes, indeed, pride! For she, like them, is a symbol and the bond of a family and patriotic union of which we can justly be proud. And these three children, who certainly belong to the present, also represent for us all the future.''

There would have been another child in 1967 had the Princess not had a miscarriage when attending Expo '67 in Montreal. She became ill after a reception and dinner for two hundred Canadian artists and government leaders who had been invited by Prince Rainier and Princess Grace to the new Chateau Champlain Hotel.

The dinner had followed a grueling day during which 10,000 visitors jammed the Place des Nations in hot, muggy weather to celebrate Monaco's National Day and get a good look at Princess Grace. Despite the heat she weathered a press conference, but looked drawn and distracted during dinner. The Princess was later rushed to the Montreal Royal Victory Hospital, but the doctors were unable to save her baby.

People in France were at first quite confounded about the way Prince Rainier and Princess Grace decided to raise their children. To begin with it is not customary for children to address their parents in the familiar *tu* (thou) instead of *vous* (you). Even in these enlightened days among the aristocracy of France, children still use the formal form of address.

"We have deliberately not brought up our children in a princely manner," Prince Rainier has said on many occasions. Both parents right from the start made it clear that they were opposed to the manner in which children are brought up in many aristocratic homes in Europe even today. They are often shuttled off to their own quarters with a nanny and only see their parents at set periods. There until the age of five they are practically invisible. This is followed by a brief period in the nursery before once again being banished— this time to preparatory school.

The Prince has too many sorrowful memories of his own childhood, when exactly this happened.

Right from the children's babyhood the day began with breakfast with their parents in the library. At 8:30 A.M., while the Prince and Princess were still in their dressing gowns, a trolleyed table would be wheeled in with breakfast on it, and the children would come tumbling in from their nursery, which adjoined their parents' private apartment.

In the small private kitchen the Princess usually prepared the breakfast, which consisted of a grapefruit popped under the grill and boiled egg. The Princess likes tea for breakfast and the Prince coffee. She would tempt the children to eat with slices of hot, buttered toast.

In many French families where the mother of the family is rarely seen until lunchtime, these American-style family breakfasts were quite an innovation. Thursdays and Sundays were always kept free so that Prince Rainier and Princess Grace could join the children for lunch, and when the children became older, on any other day when they were free of schoolwork.

All through their school days in Monaco and even today, the Princess has breakfast with her children. In Paris, instead of allowing any members of the staff to take Princess Stephanie to school, she prefers to do it herself at 8:30 A.M. before settling down to her desk and the day's work. In the afternoons, whenever possible, she is at the gate with the other mothers to meet Princess Stephanie after school.

The children were never spanked if they were naughty. Instead, their parents and their nana punished them by refusing privileges. For instance, on one occasion when Prince Albert had needed chastising, Nana King had said quite firmly, "No television for you tonight." Sometime later she entered the library and found the little boy sitting with Prince Rainier glued to a Western.

"I thought I said to you that there was no television tonight," she admonished.

Prince Rainier asked why and then on hearing the reason promptly turned off the set.

The Princess invariably bathed the children herself, and when she discovered teeth marks on Prince Albert's body she inquired of Princess Caroline if she knew anything about it. It appeared that she had, in fact, been biting her brother at play. Princess Grace immediately bit her daughter on the arm and remonstrated, "You must not bite your brother. You see it hurts."

Even when the children were irritating as only normal lively children can be, Princess Grace never raised her voice to them. Once when they were about four and five she went into her dressing room and found a mess of lipstick and powder. Calling Princess Caroline and Prince Albert to the room, she said, "Now I want the truth. Who has done this naughty little job?"

One of them said, "I didn't do it," and then the other, "I didn't do it."

As thousands of mothers before have said, Princess Grace remarked, "Well, somebody must have done it."

In the same breath they both answered, "I did it."

Far from being cross, Princess Grace was delighted that they had not told on each other and the incident was forgotten.

The children are extremely kind and considerate, and have been brought up to respect other people. Right from the beginning, the Princess was determined that her children would have good manners.

"People who are overly indulgent with babies are inclined to say, 'Oh he is just a baby,' " she once said in an interview. "But how a teenager behaves depends very much on how he behaved before he was a teenager."

A typical example of this was one occasion when Prince Albert was young. The story comes from Nana King.

"Albert was getting ideas one evening. You know, the butlers were standing around and he was late finishing his dinner and so when he did finish, he said, 'I'm ready' in a very imperious tone of voice. The Princess quietly said, 'Just a minute. Just a minute. That is no way to speak to anybody. You get down and take your own plate out.'

"The humiliation of having to get down from his chair and walk past them all with his own plate was punishment enough. Little things like that. They weren't allowed to get away with anything as children by either the Prince or Princess.''

The high priority which Princess Grace gives to discipline is best explained in her own words as told to John Bainbridge of *The Philadelphia Inquirer Magazine.*

"In Monaco there still exists a respect for authority. This is so important, particularly for young people. On television, in pictures, and in books, there is so much effort expended in trying to be funny or clever, which often has the effect of actually tearing down the important qualities that young people should hang on to. It seems to be the case that young people who are in search of truth and reality are afraid to admit that something old can be something of value.

"I was just reading an article in which Margaret Chase Smith said that the word 'square' has become outmoded. It used to be one of the most respected words in our vocabulary. We talked about the 'square deal' and the 'square shooter,' and they were honored words. She said that nowadays the person who seems to get the attention and applause is the one who plays the angles. 'What we need today,' she said, 'are more square people, more people who are dependable in the old-fashioned way. . . .'

"I'm always appalled when I see parents intimidated by their children and I must say that I see that quite often when I go to the United States. If I say something about the discipline in our household, they say, 'Can you do that?' Now, really, parents do have to take a stand. So far we've been very fortunate with our children. So far, so good.''

When she was young Princess Caroline was touchingly so-licitous—and still is—to the people around her. Whenever she saw someone at the palace with a cut finger or injury, she amusingly offered them advice or wanted to bandage them up from her own first-aid kit.

Usually on birthdays the children had a few of their friends to celebrate with them. On her fourth birthday Princess Caroline went to Princess Grace and said, "This year, Mummy, I want to invite all the children in the palace [the palace staff]. You see, I didn't invite them last year. They must have been very upset." So they were all invited to a glorious ice-cream and balloons party.

All the children have been brought up not to have expectancy of any privileges because of their royal parentage. Prince Albert is a particularly kind boy. When he won a swimming competition and received a medal, he noticed a little girl crying because she had not won one. Without any ado, he went straight over to her and gave her his medal.

When Princess Stephanie won a prize in a flower-arranging competition for a bouquet she had made, she was so surprised and so overcome with emotion that she promptly burst into tears and ran to her nana. Although Princess Grace was present, the child knew that it simply was not done to embarrass her mother with her tears.

On evenings when he was present the Prince would always have a bedtime game with the children. The old apartments were especially well laid out for this and he would romp around with the children. One hilarious game they all enjoyed consisted of the children running after Nana and calling her "fat." They would continue to do so as she would grab them and tickle them, and the more she tickled them, the more they said it. This went on until they could not breathe and she would stop when they finally admitted, "You are not fat—you are thin."

"Of course, the Prince would egg them on and then he would chase them around in a glorious game of hide-and-seek. Typical father, of course, getting them all excited before they went to bed," Mrs. Wood recalled.

"Princess Grace was particularly good at story telling. I have never heard anyone better. I couldn't help but listen myself," she remembered. "She put such feeling into her stories."

One night when Prince Albert was still very young, Princess Grace decided to read a story to him. She was just about to sit down and read when he said to her, "Are we going to do it in French or English, because your French sure needs improving."

As the children at that time did not get any pocket money, they invariably made their parents' presents. They did paintings or cut-outs, made up bouquets of flowers and learned little poems to say to Princess Grace on her birthday. Prince Albert's gift to the Princess on one birthday was reciting "The Land of Counterpane" from Robert Louis Stevenson's *A Child's Garden of Verse*.

There was always lots of laughter with a completely free atmosphere. One day Prince Albert and Princess Caroline were watching the *Sound of Music* Trapp family on television. There is a part where the mother has to go for an audition and she does not come out of it very well. She is told to go away and practice sex-appeal.

A few days later the Princess was in the library walking up and down and cooing to Princess Stephanie who was a small baby at the time. Princess Caroline was watching and asked, "Are you practicing your sex-appeal, Mummy?" Princess Grace nearly dropped the baby in surprise.

One of the children's great delights was to help choose their mother's clothes when she was getting dressed. Even as a child, Princess Caroline was typically feminine and would love trying on her mother's hats. She also enjoyed offering her advice, "I like this dress best, Mummy. Won't you wear this one tonight?"

Both Prince Rainier and Princess Grace were determined that their children should grow up with healthy bodies and an enjoyment of sports. Today Prince Albert is a fine swimmer and has inherited his father's enjoyment of underwater swimming. Princess Caroline lives in the water during the summer at Monaco and Princess Stephanie is catching up fast.

To the rich mothers of Monte Carlo it was a shock when they saw Princess Grace at the Monte Carlo Beach Club teaching her children to dog paddle. In these circles it is usual for a professional to take complete charge.

The Princess taught the children not only to swim but also to dive without any self-consciousness along with the other children. During the children's early swimming days, she frequently presided over the children's swim-meet, which was a regular occurrence at the select Beach Club.

"I've loved every age of the children. We try to include them in everything we do," the Princess once said. Wherever they went or whatever they did, the Prince and Princess included their children, and still do.

204

Princess Grace maintains that her children are able to have a much more normal and natural life than people think.

"Perhaps they are isolated in certain ways, but during the winter term at school they are all exposed to various social and economic levels and meet children of all languages and cultures," she said.

During the Vietnam war in order to make their children conscious of the suffering there, all the family wore copper bracelets on which were engraved the names of American prisoners-of-war. These bracelets were sponsored by an organization which also forwarded the letters the family wrote to their adoptives.

Princess Grace had two cousins fighting in Vietnam, and one Christmas Prince Rainier invited ten boys who were recovering from wounds received in the war to Monaco as the family's guests.

It was the irrepressible Father Tucker who finally summed up the early years of the marriage of Prince Rainier and Princess Grace.

"Since their marriage I've gotten this impression. Both of them take much more stock in being married, man and wife, father and mother, than in being Prince and Princess."

Thirty

At this stage, after twenty years of marriage, it is time to explode some of the myths that have surrounded Princess Grace during her years in Monaco.

These myths were bound to be created simply because there are some sections of the European press which thrive on destructive, sensational stories about royal personages. It could be subconscious envy, as they invariably appear in the republican Italian, German and American presses.

Last year Prince Rainier had a legal suit with a German newspaper which wrote a story that Princess Grace was seeing a well-known doctor in Paris who specializes in cancer. Not only is the story wickedly untrue, but the sequel is that it was ricocheted around the world through the medium of the popular press.

There are certain elements in France who have made a point of saying that Princess Grace abhors gambling and wishes to see it stamped out in Monte Carlo. Nothing could be further from the truth. She is not out to reform Monaco, as it needs no reforming. The element of gambling, once a mainstay of the principality's revenue, is no longer so important. Of Monaco's revenue, which fluctuates round $51,250,000, the Société des Bains de Mer, the quaintly named company, is obliged to contribute no more than 4.5 percent of Monaco's annual budget; often it is far less.

As a member of the ruling family of Monaco, Princess Grace is by law not allowed to set foot inside the Casino gambling rooms. Neither can any other Monegasque, except as an employee.

One of the most frequently circulated stories in the European press in those early years of her marriage was that the Princess was responsible for the Americanizing of the traditional Casino by the introduction of one-armed bandits at the entrance and crap tables.

As one who remembers the Casino in the faded but elegant days just after the war, I would say that the intrusion of these ugly, vulgar reflections of modern-day living seemed undesirable. But neither the Prince nor the Princess had any say in the matter. The Casino is owned and operated by a private corporation, the Société Anonyme des Bains de Mer et du Cercle des Strangers de Monaco. (This is the same society of which, at one time, Aristotle Onassis owned 35 percent of the shares and was the largest single minority shareholder.) The Prince did advise, however, that if these slot machines had to be there, they should be installed in a room in the basement and not in the elegant period foyer.

In 1958 it was decided to close the Casino on Good Fridays, and in Monaco one hears that it was in fact a wish of Princess Grace's. But she has never privately or publicly conceded this. The nearest one gets to the possible truth is that when she was once asked by an American journalist, instead of one of her usual noncommittal silences, she did reply, "I would rather not say."

There was also the episode of the pigeon shooting for which she was blamed and actually had nothing at all to do with. According to that esteemed *New York Herald Tribune* journalist, Art Buchwald, whose word I would never doubt, it was Prince Rainier who wrote to Aristotle Onassis and said, "The best wedding gift you can give me is to stop the sport of pigeon shooting in Monte Carlo."

Mr. Onassis then told Mr. Buchwald, "All right, I'm going to give the Prince his wedding present. . . . Frankly, I did not know until I came down here that they shoot live pigeons. I thought they used clay ones."

International pigeon-shooting matches had been held for a long time in Monaco and it is an old European custom. The birds, which were a special breed from Spain, had their tails and one wing clipped so that they flew on an erratic course. This not only made them harder to shoot, but the gunsman also had to shoot into the sun. The birds were released from boxes on the terrace outside the Casino, and the marksmen did not know from which box they would fly. There was a tremendously unattractive element in that many of the birds were wounded and fell into the sea or onto the terrace. The pigeons which were retrieved were sold to restaurants and hotels, and presumably eaten.

207

In many ways it was no more disagreeable than some of the low flying pheasant shooting that is done in the name of sportsmanship by affluent businessmen the world over.

The story that was reported was the Princess Grace was walking on the terrace and saw the "sad spectacle" of pigeon shooting. She is said to have gone straight to Prince Rainier in his "office" and demanded that this bird slaughter be stopped. The result was that many of the hotels and restaurants were unable to serve pigeons, and the spring of 1960 was known in Monaco as the "Grace Kelly Recession."

The truth behind this story is that, like Prince Rainier, she did not enjoy the sight of the pigeon shooting. She loves all animals and birds and, if anything, is a conservationist. But it was something in which she could not, and would not, interfere. It was the patrons of the Hotel de Paris who complained as the birds began to drop on the terrace and it was the management of the Casino which finally abolished the sport.

Another legend that must be disavowed is that Princess Grace effected the healing of the breach that occurred between Prince Rainier and Onassis over the Greek's interference in the policy of the Société des Bains de Mer (S.B.M.), the holding company which owns not only the Casino but the sporting club, seventeen hotels, restaurants, night clubs and many other tourist attractions in Monte Carlo.

It is true that the two men differed over the future of Monaco. Prince Rainier wanted a much more healthy approach—"democratizing" Monaco so that it was less dependent on the fickleness of the big gamblers and more dependent on middle-spending tourists. Prince Rainier visualized 2,000 beds in new hotels for middle-class tourists. The "Golden Greek," as Onassis was dubbed by the columnists, preferred to create his own little domain where he could be "king" over the two to three hundred extremely wealthy patrons who were making the Casino pay. All that Onassis wanted was a base for his business interests, which he was then operating in Paris, and the social cachet that being the uncrowned king of Monaco would bring him. In the international world of finance, he was still a minnow in a large pond; but in Monte Carlo, he was the big fish who desired to control his own pond.

Onassis's final decision to break with Monte Carlo was, in fact, a business deal, and the Princess would have had nothing at all to do with this. It was a matter among Prince Rainier, the S.B.M. and the National Council. Additional help was supplied by some shrewd outside advisers whom the Prince brought in.

What Princess Grace *did* do was to keep the social doors open throughout the difficult period when Aristotle Onassis and his beautiful wife Tina were separated. She reportedly tried to bring about a face-saving reconciliation, but this proved unsuccessful.

It has also been said that Princess Grace strongly disapproved of Onassis's relationship with Maria Callas on the grounds of the Princess's devout Catholic approach to divorce. False again. Princess Grace is far too sophisticated to have been shocked by this extraordinary romance. The Prince and Princess joined a large party as guests of Onassis and his beautiful diva in 1961 for a four-day cruise on the *Christina* to Majorca. What people did in their private life, Princess Grace felt, was no concern of hers. She has always admired Maria Callas as a supreme artist.

One of the highlights of the trip was attending the opening of the newly decorated Hotel Son Vida. The talent that night was immense, with Elsa Maxwell bashing the piano, Prince Rainier pounding the drums, Maria Callas shaking the maracas and Princess Grace clapping to the beat. The next day they all went on to the bull-fights in Plaza de Toros.

Although Princess Grace did not visit Mr. Onassis during his illness in a Paris hospital, she was kept informed of his condition. After he died she was to say, ''He was very tough because that is the way he was. But he was also a man of great sensitivity and was thoughtful and interesting. I also believe that he was a deeply religious man with a sense of family and responsibility.''

The clear, impassionate newspaper image of Princess Grace receives a jolt every so often when, unlike any other European royalty, she rushes into print to vindicate any injustice that she feels has been made to herself or her family.

It has long been speculated that Princess Grace and Jacqueline Onassis are not on good terms. When President Kennedy was suffering from a back injury in a New York hospital, his wife brought Grace Kelly to see him, knowing how enchanted he was with her films. Both Prince Rainier and Princess Grace were later to be luncheon guests of the President and Mrs. Kennedy at the White House.

When President John F. Kennedy was assassinated in November,

1963, neither Prince Rainier nor Princess Grace attended the funeral. This was thought to be unusual in many American circles. But it was that sharp-tongued columnist John M. Cummings of the *Philadelphia Inquirer* who drew public attention to the fact.

With Mr. Cummings's permission I quote:

"If you want to know why Prince Rainier and his Philadelphia princess, the former Grace Kelly, were not among the notables at the funeral of President John F. Kennedy, you may be satisfied with the explanation of the State Department.

"It seems that Monaco, the tiny principality ruled by Rainier, has no diplomatic representative at Washington. So Rainier and his Princess, because they could not, under protocol, be considered heads of State, were not eligible for recognition in the cortege.

"For a pair that manages to horn in on a lot of functions, diplomatic and otherwise, it seems strange that, in effect, they gave the funeral the brushoff. They displayed no such reluctance when they attended a luncheon in the White House as guests of President and Mrs. Kennedy. Of course, the Kennedys were gracious enough to extend an invitation at the time the Monacoans were here as guests of the city, and honor guests at a great wingding in Convention Hall.

"It would be difficult to estimate the number of people who attended the President's funeral without invitation. By the tens of thousands they lined the streets over which the President's body was borne to his last resting place in Arlington cemetery.

"As reigning heads of a dice table, it would appear natural enough for the Rainiers to establish diplomatic relations with Las Vegas to qualify for protocol in this country.

"It has been suggested by an expert in protocol that before sulking in their mansion on the Mediterranean, they should have consulted with their 'prime minister' and 'Ambassador at large,' Aristotle Onassis.

"Perhaps the Prince and his Princess could have received some advice from Maria Callas, one of their 'ladies-in-waiting,' who knows her way around.

"The late, free-loading Elsa Maxwell, had she been around, would have been of inestimable value to the royal and regal pair. Elsa would know how to duck a funeral gracefully and leave a stream of speculation behind. Elsa, who spent her rent-free summers in Monaco, did have a reputation for telling upper crustaceans how to deport themselves in public, and how to drink their soup from silver service.

"The Rainiers couldn't get over here to pay their respects to a man who befriended them. But Eamon De Valera, well past 80 and nearly blind, could come in from Ireland, where the Kelly clan as well as the Kennedy had their origin.

"Rainier has the proper raiment for a State funeral conducted with military precision. When on the go here, which is frequently, he plasters his manly chest with more medals and ribbons than you'd find on the prize bull at a county fair.

"While her native land was in deep mourning for the slain President, Princess Grace was on an outing in a Monaco park. A photograph shows her in a shooting event on that tragic weekend. She is taking aim at the imitation ducks found in a shooting gallery.

"It was on Sunday that the great of the world were arriving in Washington for the funeral of the President the following day. Anybody who wondered why the Rainiers didn't come over to join in the last sad tribute to the martyred President might have been shocked to know that in Monaco it was pleasure as usual and never mind the expressions of sorrow."

Princess Grace was quick to retaliate with the following letter which was published the following week in the *Philadelphia Inquirer*.

"Dear Mr. Cummings:

"Your article of Friday, November 29th, was brought to my attention this morning. I cannot tell you how shocked and deeply hurt I was by the things you had to say, particularly as you have always treated me with fairness in the past.

"As a responsible journalist, I should think the first step in attacking someone would be to make sure that you have the correct facts. You obviously have not taken the time nor the trouble to do so in this instance.

"I have ignored many newspaper criticisms against my person, family and life as I consider that everyone has a right to his own opinion, but this unfounded and cruel attack on my loyalty to the country of my birth and my sentiments regarding the atrocious assassination of the late President cannot be passed without a strong protest.

"To begin with I am as grieved and heartbroken as any American over this tragic loss to the country and to the world and I am very

211

sorry not to have been at the funeral. You say that my husband and I 'manage to horn in' on many occasions—that is exactly what I tried to avoid doing in Washington last week.

"My relationship with President and Mrs. Kennedy has been more on a personal basis rather than an official one and I preferred to express my condolences and grief also in a personal and private way.

"For your information, the photograph published with your article was taken on Thursday, November 21st, the day before the tragedy when I accompanied my children and a few of their friends to a local fair. I was hoping to win them a prize at the shooting gallery.

"After the death of the President, my husband, the Prince, declared a week's period of mourning in the Principality and a Requiem Mass was said at the Cathedral of Monaco on the day of the funeral.

"As an American in Europe, I was very touched by the way Europeans showed a deep sense of personal loss and to see to what extent the President was respected and loved. Your criticism has wounded me greatly in its heartlessness and I want your readers to know, and I want to go on record saying that it is completely untrue and I bitterly resent being pictured in this fashion to my fellow Philadelphians, for whom I have great love and affection.

"Sincerely yours,

"Grace de Monaco."

In a postscript to the article the *Inquirer* had the final say.

"It will be noted that Princess Grace refers to her picture at the Monaco shooting gallery, which was published with the Cummings's column, as having been taken on Thursday, November 21st, 'the day before the tragedy.'

"The caption of the UPI Telephoto used in the Inquirer column is dated '11-26-63' and reads: 'MONACO: With steady hand and keen eye, Princess Grace of Monaco sights target at fairground shooting gallery here 11-25.' The date 11-25 was the Monday following the assassination of President Kennedy and the day on which he was buried."

The truth behind the story is, in fact, much more interesting. The reason that UPI's date line was Monday was that all news not concerning the death of President Kennedy was blocked for the four days from the time of the assassination until after the burial.

Whatever had piled up in the newsrooms of other events was released on Monday and updated for release on that day.

The hour of the assassination of President Kennedy was 1 P.M. in Texas which meant 8 P.M. European time. The Princess had been to the carnival with her children and their friends that afternoon, before the assassination.

The local paper, *Nice Matin*, printed the photograph the following morning, Saturday. The UPI date line and the *Philadelphia Inquirer* story caused a great deal of upset in Monaco and the photographers themselves offered to sign letters stating the exact time and date the photographs were taken.

From an American television personality who was at the Red Cross Ball in Seville in 1966 I have this on-the-spot coverage of the extraordinary occasion when Princess Grace met the President's widow. "Each of them had her own camp following," she told me. "There was Grace as a senorita driving in a carriage and looking incredibly pretty, and riding on horseback was Jackie looking absolutely stunning in a matador outfit. No two women could have looked more different.

"But the real crux came when Grace got up to open the Red Cross Ball in the evening and Jackie left the room."

In covering the even *Newsweek* reported, "The way it seemed to wondering newsmen, Jacqueline Kennedy all but snubbed Monaco's Princess Grace at the Red Cross Ball in Seville, Spain. At first a Madrid newspaper noted, Jackie walked past Grace without a word. Then there was a brief, 'cold' greeting, after which 'they not only didn't talk to each other, they didn't even look at each other.' A similar account in the European edition of the *New York Herald Tribune* referred to a 'cool conversation,' adding that 'reports blamed it on fatigue.' That fetched a sharp letter from Grace Kelly Grimaldi, as she signed herself. After complaining about the Trib's coverage, she wrote, 'I was delighted to meet Mrs. Kennedy again, for whom I have a great admiration and respect. If there was any coolness or fatigue that evening, it was caused only by some of the many dozens of photographers who pushed, shoved and relentlessly pursued us all night.' "

In addition to the reports given by these esteemed newspapers, Princess Grace was also on the defensive in an account run by *Time*. The Princess wrote that she was "deeply hurt" by the *Time* report.

213

"What you call my frostiness and pique was directed at some of the hundreds of photographers who spoiled the evening for many of us, and certainly not at Mrs. Kennedy, for whom I have admiration and respect.

"And let me add in refute to your snide and unnecessary remarks that I am delighted to be 'upstaged' by Mrs. Kennedy at any time."

When the de Gaulle altercation was at its height, the myth was that Princess Grace was brought in to charm the not too unsusceptible seventy-one-year-old president. A "cold war" had developed between France and the tiny principality born of France's edict that by October 11, 1962, Monaco had to accept fiscal alignment with France; that the people living in Monaco, as well as the international business organizations which had made their headquarters there, must pay French taxes. Prince Rainier was adamant.

There is no personal income tax in Monaco; nor does the owner of a business pay direct corporate taxes. Negotiations were begun in Paris and the Monegasque delegation offered to meet practically all the French demands except "fiscal alignment." They based their refusal on the grounds that it violated the "Declaration of the Rights of Man."

Had the precarious situation not had such serious undertones and threats to the Monegasques, on hindsight it had the ingredients of one of those delicious Ealing movies like *Whisky Galore* or *The Lavender Hill Mob*.

Undoubtedly Princess Grace was an asset during the visits that were exchanged between the Monegasque and French heads of state, but in such matters the Prince does not earn his title "the Benevolent Autocrat" without cause.

What Princess Grace did do—and what any other sensible woman would have also done—was to study a précis of the General's memoirs (which she had her lady-in-waiting prepare) inasmuch as she herself had not yet read the originals. At dinner she titillated de Gaulle's vanity by charming references to his great work. What man could resist that!

In answer to the various rumors that he would abdicate if the situation grew much worse, the Prince said, "The rumors are absolutely ridiculous and, it goes without saying, without any foundation. I have no reason to abdicate. I will never do it. Such an idea never came to my mind."

Nor did it to Princess Grace's. During that critical weekend in October, 1962, she went about the streets of Monaco doing her shopping. To anyone who asked about her feelings she replied, like Marshal MacMahon at Sebastopol in 1855, "J'y suis et j'y reste" ("Here I am and here I stay").

"Naturally we are very concerned, but I am optimistic that everything will turn out all right."

A few years earlier Princess Grace would not have been ready to face the crowds. This day, with her royal act superbly intact, she gave the Prince the best possible support by going among his people.

One piece of blatantly unkind reporting in the British press that deeply upset Princess Grace was the remark made after Princess Anne's wedding that it had been inappropriate for her to wear a white dress and try to upstage the bride.

As she already had the elegant cream-colored outfit and it was warm enough for the vagaries of the English climate, she chose it simply because she also had a mink toque to match. She had previously discussed it with both the Prince and some friends, who all advised her to wear it. "This has nothing to do with a wedding dress and is just the very thing as it is practical and chic," one woman friend suggested.

The truth is far stranger than the myth. The Princess had, in fact, intended to wear a blue outfit, but she did not have the right hat and there was not enough time to get one. As she was sitting watching the guests arrive at the Abbey on color television, just before she and the Prince left the Connaught Hotel, she turned to him and said, "There are plenty of off-whites and pale shades in the Abbey," and did not think a thing about it.

When she did arrive at the Abbey and saw the Queen was in the same blue that she had intended to wear, she felt relieved. The Princess was not only one of the most strikingly dressed women in the Abbey, but was, in fact, complimented on her outfit by several members of the royal family. Consequently, she was totally unprepared for the criticism she read in a newspaper the next day. She was so distressed that she hasn't worn the outfit since, and it hangs tucked away in one of her clothes closets.

Thirty-one

"She is such fun . . ." Paul Gallico said. "Being with her you laugh a lot," said Fleur Cowles. "You always knew that you would have a laugh with Grace . . ." said producer John Foreman. "We turn our differences into jokes," said Prince Rainier.

This, then, is the side of Princess Grace that the general public, alas, never sees.

This joyfulness in the family life of Princess Grace permeates through to the people who work around her. She and Prince Rainier both have the ability of enjoying the absurd and seeing the funny side of a situation.

Through the years that they worked in the palace both Phyllis Blum and Maureen King were to contribute to many hilarious escapades. That these two engaging girls were able to get away with so much flippancy only illustrates the humanity and sense of humor of their royal employers.

When Princess Grace went to Switzerland in 1959 with the Prince and Caroline to have her appendix out, both Phyllis and Maureen accompanied them. The whole entourage was installed in the Beau Ridage Hotel in Lausanne where Phyllis attended to the secretarial side and Maureen looked after Princess Caroline. Prince Albert, still a baby, had been left in Monaco.

Phyllis and Maureen were noted for their healthy appetites, so much so that Maureen earned herself the title "Killer King."

"The Prince always said that Phyllis and I cost him more on this trip than the whole of the Princess's clinic bill because we ate so much," she recalled.

"One morning we decided to really give him something to talk about. He had been teasing us about our breakfasts for so long. We called for the menu card and literally ordered everything on it. We told the waiter it was for a joke and said, 'Just put everything on it. We won't eat it but put it there.'

"The Prince normally came in when we were having breakfast with Caroline. There we were with a table groaning with food and Phyllis and I sat passively at either end.

" 'Good God!' he exclaimed. He was so amazed that he was almost speechless. He didn't really believe it so he rushed into his room and came back with a camera. Still in his dressing gown, he was leaping around taking pictures of Phyllis and me having this fantastic breakfast. He said the Princess would never believe him unless he could show her proof.

"When the Princess, who was convalescing in the hotel, saw them she laughed so much we were worried that she would burst her stitches."

During the same visit to Switzerland Prince Rainier happened to mention to the girls that he was worried that the laundry was starching his shirts. Maureen immediately suggested that she would wash them for him. The Prince was slightly apprehensive about her ironing and begged her to be careful not to burn them.

That was sufficient for a joke to be born in Maureen's mind. She acquired a piece of old white linen that at a distance resembled the Prince's fine poplin shirts, and made a large scorch mark on it. She then waited for the moment when she knew that the Prince would be in his room. Filled with apologies, she took the scorched fabric into the Prince, who on seeing it exploded with anguish. Only after a few minutes did she let him see that it was just another joke.

While his real shirts were hanging up to dry in their bathroom, the girls took a series of photographs of how to wash shirts, step by step.

Long after, when they had returned to Monaco, they presented the Prince his birthday gift—a do-it-yourself washing kit, with a clothesline, soap powder, detailed instructions and the photographs from Switzerland showing the step-by-step process.

It was a battle of wits between the Prince and the two girls as they vied with each other to devise new pranks. Prince Rainier, in fact, won on points, but the girls took the cake for invention. One of his best efforts was the Hungarian pianist episode. Here is the story as Phyllis Earl remembered it.

"In the bar playing every night at the hotel was a Hungarian pianist. One night we had gone into the bar and said to each other, 'Let's be rash and have a sherry,' and somehow we talked to him just for a minute or two. A few days later I had a day off and went to see a school friend in Geneva. When I returned, there in a vase in my room was a single red rose with a note tied to it.

"I've kept this note to this day. It was a declaration of love from the Hungarian to me and asking me to go downstairs and meet him in the bar carrying the rose. Of course I immediately recognized the Prince's handwriting, but Maureen was so excited about the whole thing I thought I would carry on and see what happened.

"I arrived downstairs with the rose and, of course, the poor Hungarian didn't know what was going on. But there standing in another doorway appearing to be preoccupied was Prince Rainier, waiting to report it all back to Princess Grace.

"Prince Rainier carried the joke on for a long time, constantly asking me, 'How is your friendly Hungarian?' so I decided to play along. About a year later when we were in Paris, Maureen and I did a whole long thing where we made out that the Hungarian had re-appeared on the scene and was taking me out. I think the Prince was never quite sure whether it was true or not."

While the Princess was still recuperating, she asked Phyllis Blum to go out for a short walk with her as she felt some fresh air would do her good.

"We came back and I could see that she was suddenly very tired. I thought the best thing to do was to get her upstairs as quickly as possible, so we came in through the side door of the hotel. As we walked in she immediately noticed that the Prince was sitting there talking to a tall, very portly man. As we drew nearer we realized that it was ex-King Farouk with one of his daughters at his side. The Princess stopped to talk to King Farouk and asked me to talk to his daughter.

"After five minutes Maureen came running down and said, 'The Queen of Spain is upstairs,' so the Princess excused herself as she did not know exactly what Caroline, left alone with the elderly Queen, might be doing or saying. When the Princess arrived in the room, there was tiny Caroline quietly showing the aged Queen how to master the hula hoop, the Prince having bought her one in a Lausanne shop.

"But the remark that I will always remember is when the Princess turned to me in the elevator and said, 'Kings to the right of us, Queens to the left of us. We don't know which way to turn.' "

On their last evening in Lausanne, the girls decided to have a "really good spread." When the wine steward came over to ask what they were drinking, they jokingly said, "Whatever His Serene Highness would like to offer us."

With horror they watched the waiter go over to the Prince, who was dining with some business friends, and whisper in his ear. About ten minutes later a jumbo bottle of chianti arrived back at their table with two red tulips stuck on it and tied to the top of the bottle was a note: "And bloody well see that you drink it to the last drop."

The girls drank what they could before going off to the cinema. When they arrived back at the hotel and returned to their room, the bottle was standing outside their bedroom door with another note: "Please finish."

There was always plenty of fun on the Swiss holidays, with everyone ready to join in. Far from palace protocol and duties, the Grimaldi family is probably the most relaxed of all the European royal families.

One year Prince Rainier rented a chalet at Gstaad for the family, including Oliver and one of the other dogs. On arrival the Princess, always considerate of other people, became anxious about the thick white carpet covering the floor and how the change of environment would affect the dogs and their house-training. The moment she mentioned this to Phyllis and Maureen, the temptation was too great.

During their day off, the girls found a "gag shop" and bought a selection of accessories necessary for their joke—"plastic puddles and 'big jobs.' "

As Mrs. Wood now remembers, "We waited for a convenient evening when we knew they would be coming home late. We went into their bedroom and dropped our props in appropriate places . . . a large puddle on the sheepskin rug by the Princess's side of the bed just where she would step to climb in and the 'big jobs' scattered round the place.

"We went upstairs and waited for them to come back. It was a wooden chalet so you could hear everything and suddenly we heard a shriek, 'Rainier . . . Rainier, come and look at this!' The Prince rushed in but quickly spotted what it was. He got a brush and pan and handed it to the Princess, telling her to 'get on with it'. There she was in the dim light cleaning it up and it wasn't until it was all in the pan that she realized it was plastic. Of course, we were convulsed with laughter, as were the Prince and Princess.

"They were so marvelous to play jokes on simply because they always responded in the right way."

On another occasion in the same chalet, the incorrigible two were feeling bored one night, and with them boredom was an invitation to play a practical joke. When the Prince and Princess had gone out, they decided to make a couple of bodies and put them in their beds.

"We borrowed one of the Princess's nighties and stuffed it with paper to look like two enormous bosoms and we whipped out a pair of the Prince's pajamas and stuffed them also. I remember making the faces with paper and covering them with a white tea towel and putting specs on them," Maureen Wood recalled.

"I think we gave the woman a headscarf like something she might wear over curlers and we propped them up in bed. We made the man look as though he was reading some sexy magazine propped up in front of him. It looked terribly realistic—it really did.

"They came home very late and we heard the Princess go into the room, which had a very dim light. She let out a blood-curdling shriek for the Prince to come. He dashed in and put on the light. 'Oh, those girls upstairs' we heard him saying as they doubled up laughing.

"I suppose looking back that we were both very naughty, but I think for the Princess we were almost a link with 'family' and because of this she obviously enjoyed our jokes very much."

One of the best practical jokes that the King-Blum team ever played on the Princess concerned a dinner party to be given by one of the palace staff.

"She had invited the Prince and Princess to an Indonesian dinner," Mrs. Earl recalled, "and would have liked to have asked me but explained that already there were too many women and too few men. There and then we decided that I should go as a man. Maureen was only too willing to help, as was Louis Chiron, the famous former racing motorist.

"Louis and his wife, Didi, were invited to the party and they were also great practical jokers. He promised to 'take me in hand.'

" 'First of all,' he said, 'we'll have to take you to Nice and get you a man's wig,' as I had to have something to cover my long blonde hair. Because I didn't have much time, he suggested that he drive me there on my lunch hour because when I finished working the shops were all closed. You can imagine driving to Nice from the palace, getting fitted and driving back all in two hours. When I got back, shaking, I turned to Louis and said, 'Now I know why you were world champion.' "

From one of the male dancers at the Casino she borrowed a black suit, because he was the only man they could find who was tall and thin. Chiron lent shoes and socks, and shirt and jacket came from the dancer.

"It was summertime and I was very tanned, so Didi insisted on my taking off my ring and with make-up erased the white mark around my finger. They were so thorough that they made me file down my fingernails. The final touch was a pair of slightly tinted glasses and sticking on a stubbly sort of beard.

"We arrived at the dinner a bit early and I still remember our hostess coming up to me and saying, 'You really make a very attractive man—I could go for you myself,' " Phyllis Earl continued.

They had all decided that Phyllis was to be introduced as a Polish pianist cousin of Didi Chiron's, and as she was of Polish extraction and this was the International Chopin year, it all fit into place. This also made it conceivable why the Pole did not speak English and only spoke a few words of German, which Phyllis could manage. Princess Grace was the only other one there who knew any German, but it was not really sufficient to test Phyllis.

The Prince had, in fact, his own private joke by arriving at the party dressed as a down and out seaman. As their hostess opened the door, she took one step back before she realized that it was the Prince.

Phyllis Earl took up the story. "As the only 'stranger' present I was presented to the Princess. I bent over her hand, being careful not to kiss it, clicked my heels together and she passed on. I stood there by myself because, of course, no one could speak to me. Over drinks I did hear the Prince say in French to Louis, 'Your cousin, he's a little bit on the effeminate side.' And Louis replying, 'Well, yes, but you know how it is with these musical people.' "

They all sat down to dinner. The first course was clear soup with noodles. Louis noticed that a few got caught in his "cousin's" beard but worse—it had begun to peel off. Pretending he was giving the musician a pat on the cheek, he pushed it back into place. Phyllis continued:

"All the time the Princess was smiling at me and trying to put me at my ease. Leaning towards me at the table she said in her best German, *'Die Suppe ist gut,'* and then aside to her neighbor because I didn't answer, 'Maybe he doesn't like soup.' "

Suddenly the conspirators knew that the joke was getting stale, as the whole dinner party was being ruined, especially when Princess Grace whispered to her hostess, "This young man is spoiling everything. You should have warned us that we would not be alone. The Chirons should not have brought their cousin with them."

From across the table Louis Chiron said, "Don't you know who it is? Don't you know who this is sitting next to me?"

The Princess left her seat and went to have a good look. Even then she did not recognize her secretary. Finally Phyllis Blum took off her glasses. The Princess screamed with joy and took her face in her hands and kissed it. She admitted that the make-up and everything had been "absolutely fantastic."

On another occasion it was the Princess who dressed up. Alexandre, the hairdresser, had sent her a brown wig from Paris so that she could wear it when traveling incognito during her trips abroad.

One evening when they had invited some friends to see a film, the Princess put it on and was introduced to everyone as a friend of the Princess's. Madame Banac, a delightful elderly lady and mother of Vane Ivanovic, the consul general for Monaco in London, was perturbed as she thought that it was improper of the guest to be wearing one of the Princess's dresses. Prince Rainier entered into the whole spirit of the affair and kissed Princess Grace's hand. It was some time before anyone guessed the identity of the flirty young woman with the lovely brown hair and Wedgwood blue eyes.

The Prince has a collection of practical jokes which all his friends send him from various countries. When their old friend the actress Jessie Royce Landis went to dinner with them once, the Prince bent tenderly over her and pinned a red rose on her bosom. Miss Landis was enchanted and bent to smell it when out popped a plastic snake.

On another occasion when guests were invited to dinner, there seemed to be a particularly bumbling old butler who bumped into things and mumbled to himself all the time. This, of course, was Prince Rainier.

Princess Grace can also be one of the most amusing of guests. Once she is in the mood, she can tell stories in every kind of dialect as well as any professional. No one who has heard her can ever forget how she tells stories in the Jewish and Irish idioms and reduces her audience to near hysteria with laughter.

All the family have this gift of laughter when things get out of hand, but none more than Princess Grace. As Fleur Cowles remembered, "When she was staying in Spain last Easter with us at our restored Spanish castle, she was followed by the police, the Guardia Civil, the riot squad, photographers and mobs. She viewed it with a detached calm when in public and with peals of laughter when safely private in our garden."

Among the intimate staff of the palace there is a freedom of manner. When Maureen King once pointed out to Princess Grace, the minute before she was to make an official appearance on the balcony of the palace, that her petticoat was showing, she slipped into the next room and re-appeared in a few seconds.

"It's in the Chinese vase," she murmured out of the corner of her mouth.

Christmas in Monaco is a tremendous occasion as it combines the best of American tradition with the best of French. There is the tinsel and fun of the New World balanced with the religious aspect of the Roman Catholic Church. The Princess devotes the entire month of December to preparing for their official and private Christmas.

There are seven hundred Christmas cards to be sent out, seven hundred parcels for the children of Monaco, parcels for the children of the palace staff and Red Cross parcels for the aged. In the palace there are two women busy on knitting machines making sweaters for the staff children.

Four big Christmas trees are brought in which begin the Christmas palace decorations. There is one in the middle of the twin seventeenth-century staircase in the court of honor in front of the palace, one in the formal living room where official guests are received, the family one in the children's playroom and one in the servants' dining room. Princess Grace personally decorates the trees with the help of her children, and the palace electrician.

The preparation also means wrapping hundreds of Christmas

parcels and filling the family stockings. In the Kelly family the stockings were always hung on the mantel, but as Prince Rainier was brought up by an English nanny his was hung at the end of the bed. The family agreed on the British way simply because it was also a way for the Prince and Princess to get another hour's sleep when the children were young.

After Midnight Mass there is always a buffet supper in the formal living room to which close friends and a handful of officers from any American warship who may be in port are invited.

All this was too much one Christmas for Phyllis and Maureen. They concocted a plan to enliven Christmas Eve in their own special way. They decided to give themselves to the Prince and Princess in a Christmas stocking! In telling the story today Phyllis Earl remembered, "It would have looked very funny if we had not gone to the midnight service in the chapel so we sat way back. All our plans had been made several days before. The women in the *lingerie* had sewn up a huge red Christmas stocking big enough to contain even me, and I am 5 feet 10½ inches, and Maureen, who is 5 feet 6 inches.

"On this particular Christmas the captains of the ships in the Sixth Fleet of the American navy had been invited to the Mass and supper and the sailors from one of the ship's choirs were going to sing carols after the Mass, serenading the party as they walked back to the palace for the supper.

"As Maureen and I left the church just before the end of the service, they immediately thought that this was the signal that the service was over and began singing *Silent Night*. We almost jumped on them to shush them up, but fortunately inside the chapel the singing was so loud that they did not hear the false start."

Back in the formal sitting room the girls were slid into the stocking, which was propped against the tree by the roaring log fire. The top was covered with white cotton wool and the only air they got was through peepholes that had been carefully placed in the stocking.

As the royal party entered the room there was a cry of surprise from the Princess, who later confessed to the culprits that she thought it could only have come from Aristotle Onassis.

Tied to the top of the stocking was a note which read something like, "We thought hard what to give you but as you have everything we decided to give ourselves," but the Princess was too busy with her guests to look. It was not until the stocking began to bulge and wobble that anyone was suspicious and then, of course, the joke exploded. No one laughed harder than Princess Grace. It was just the kind of thing she might have done herself.

Maureen King and Phyllis Blum probably would not have gotten away with as many pranks as they did if they had not been two very pretty, intelligent and charming girls. It is highly unlikely that any French members of the palace staff, with their traditional values and attitudes, would have dared to play these jokes.

All these pranks are naturally kept within the family circle or among close friends, but they do reveal that this is a very unconventional, intimate and happy family.

Thirty-two

Will Princess Grace ever act in a feature movie again? This is the question that has been asked countless times over the past twenty years.

It all began when Prince Rainier went to Hollywood after their engagement and, unbeknownst to his fiancée, made the announcement that she would not be making any more pictures.

"Now what would make him want to say that?" Miss Kelly is reported to have said when she heard the news.

The other interested party was, of course, M.G.M., which still had an option on a further picture from her. When Grace Kelly had called on her agent to tell him of her good news, he immediately asked how it would affect her working arrangements. As he explained, "She said, 'I guess it will have a rather profound effect on my working arrangements.' I got the message, but many still hoped."

Finally M.G.M. did waive her contract on the grounds that had she planned to continue her career, they would have had first option within the period of time covered by her contract.

A month later it was reported in the *Daily Sketch*, "Her Hollywood studio has stopped Grace's $1085-a-week salary because 'she does not feel like returning.' A studio official said, 'She might come back in a couple of years. We'll wait.' "

Hollywood had left the door open. "I never say 'never' and I never say 'always,' " Grace Kelly had said enigmatically and thus a hope still flickered in the hearts of some movie directors—and one in particular, Alfred Hitchcock.

During the next few years after her marriage, it was well known that her agents, M.C.A., had often sent her scripts with the hope of luring her back. It had also been reported that His Serene Highness had "desired" that the Princess turn down a Hollywood offer to play the Virgin Mary in *King of Kings*.

It was Alfred Hitchcock who nearly pulled off the picture deal of the decade. In 1962, after weeks of telephone calls and leters, Mr. Hitchcock had put the idea to Princess Grace that he would like her to play the title role in a film to be made called *Marnie*.

It was a strange story of a beautiful, poised, bewitching girl who substitutes safe cracking and lying for passion and love. It was a part that Hollywood's Grace Kelly could have played superbly and Monaco's Princess Grace even better. It required enormous sensitivity and style.

For many weeks there had been negotiations between Hitchcock and the Princess. They had not only an intelligent working rapport, but there had been a cozy friendship between the two families over many years.

The plan was that the film would be made during the two-month summer vacation of Prince Rainier and Princess Grace in America which had already been planned. Hitchcock had offered to find a suitable location so that it could be a holiday combined with work and Prince Rainier would most likely be present during part of the shooting.

Princess Grace's fee, according to Hitchcock, would have been around $732,000 plus a percentage of the profits.

When the final commitment had to be made, Mr. Hitchcock himself went to Monaco. With great tact Princess Grace let the producer tell Prince Rainier about his plans as she knew that he was a man of tremendous discretion, wisdom and selling power.

It may also have been a much more womanly wile in that she was making it easier for Prince Rainier to say no to Hitchcock rather than to her. Everyone, including Prince Rainier, knew how much she longed to make this film.

It was on March 19, 1962, that a minor bombshell hit Monaco. Earlier that day Princess Grace had invited four court officials to her study and told them, "Gentlemen, I have news for you." She then proceeded to tell them that she had accepted an offer to appear in a film to be made during the summer.

227

Within an hour the news was relayed all around the world. No one, least of all the Princess, could have foreseen the chaos that followed. The message read as follows:

"A spokesman for the Prince of Monaco announced today that Princess Grace has accepted to appear during her summer vacation in a motion picture for Mister Alfred Hitchcock to be made in the United States stop The Princess has previously starred in three films for Mister Hitchcock bracket Dial M for Murder Rear Window and To Catch a Thief bracket stop The film to start in late summer is based on a suspense novel by the English writer Winston Graham stop It is understood that Prince Rainier will most likely be present during part of the film making depending on his schedule and that Princess Grace will return to Monaco by the beginning of November stop"

What was not included in the message released by the Palace Press Office was the fact that the Princess had intended to donate all monies received to her favorite children's charity.

Looking back at the whole episode from a distance of fourteen years, the Princess realized that what she did with the proceeds was surely her business and no one else's. But had the news that she intended to use it for her special children's charities in Monaco been made patently clear, the announcement might have had a different effect.

As it was, when the news broke in the principality the people were stunned. They felt abandoned, deceived and shocked. Into what should have been a joyous summer experience they read all kinds of sinister motives. Why was their Princess going back to Hollywood? Was the marriage in danger? Why had they not been consulted on such an important step? It was reduced to such trivia as declarations of horror that their Princess might be required in the script to kiss another man.

Princess Grace was appalled at the reaction to such an extent that she became physically ill. First and foremost she was a princess of Monaco, and it pained her deeply when she heard of the bad effect her decision could have not only on her own position in Monaco but, because of the bad publicity, on an already delicate situation which existed between France and Monte Carlo. But what worried her most of all was the suggestion that she was abandoning her role as wife and mother and preferring, instead, to return to a Hollywood career.

Hitchcock was consulted; then suddenly, while the air was still thick with speculation, it was all over. From the producer came a terse announcement that "his busy schedule" would not allow him to shoot during the Princess's summer vacation.

A simultaneous announcement, "The Princess regrets . . . ," was also given from the palace.

At the time it was conjectured that President de Gaulle, the Pope, or even Prince Rainier had persuaded the Princess to abandon her plans when, in fact, it had been the wishes of the 3,000-odd Monegasques. She would never let them down.

When asked recently if she had ever regretted her decision she answered noncommittally in a voice devoid of emotion, "I don't look back. When people are maturing they all have certain things to conquer and we have to face our own inadequacies. The one thing to do is to improve and grow as a human being and this is what I have tried to do."

Twelve years after the *Marnie* fracas, in April, 1974, Princess Grace stood before an audience of 2,800 in Lincoln Center in New York at a gala tribute paid to seventy-four-year-old Alfred Hitchcock. On a night fraught with emotion and nostalgia, Princess Grace had flown over from Monaco to be there along with the other stars who had gained fame through his loving direction and superb craftsmanship.

She stood there all honey-haired and clad in white chiffon. There was not a person unaffected by her presence—the women wondering how she kept her flawless beauty, the men regretful that she had ever left Hollywood, and the police guard affectionately calling her "Kelly."

The Princess led the procession of stars onto the stage. In a short tribute she said, "Alfred Hitchcock took the thriller—once thought to be a second-class entertainment—and made it an art. He is the master of suspense."

She also brought ripples of unexpected laughter when she reminded the audience that when she arrived on his set for *To Catch a Thief* wearing a sensual gold lamé dress Hitchcock had whistled, "There's hills in them thar gold, Grace."

In 1963 Princess Grace did, in fact, play herself for the first time after her marriage in a film which was made in Monaco for Columbia Broadcasting Service television.

She was still smarting after the *Marnie* hubbub, but when it was pointed out that this was for Monaco she agreed. The film, which was called *A Look at Monaco*, was the forerunner of several similar films which have been made over the last years and shown all over the world.

Writer Cynthia Lindsay was brought in to supervise the dialogue, with Bill Fryer as producer and that great cameraman Lionel "Curly" Linden.

Such was the impact of the six weeks she spent working on the film that in Cynthia Lindsay's memory it is still bright and new. We walked and talked about it on Malibu Beach, where she now lives.

Prince Rainier and Princess Grace opened their palace—and their hearts—to the American television team. There were evening dinner parties and screenings of old American films. At one of these parties, Princess Grace wore a sheath of beige chiffon encrusted with silver sequins. She looked fabulous. As the guests arrived she told Fryer, "I'd better put on my glasses to see who's here."

One of the most vivid memories Mrs. Lindsay has is of Princess Grace's passion for children—all children—and animals.

"When we arrived at the children's home near the palace [Princess Grace changed the name from orphanage] the children plus their dog named Mélange all ran around her with a great sense of 'here comes a friend.'

"One little girl in an overwhelming burst of affection kissed her and perched a doll's hat on her head. The Mother Superior of the home immediately removed it. Princess Grace gently took the hat, pretended to study it and said, 'But, ma Mère, it's so pretty,' and put it back on again."

During the school recess, Princess Grace noticed the endearing scene of the children all sitting on their potties gossiping, reading or just thinking. She thought that this would make a charming sequence in the film, especially as all the chamber pots were different colors. She mentioned this to the producer, who did not want to film it in case it might be offensive.

"But this is an honest part of the day," the Princess insisted. And so it was filmed and was surely the most captivating shot in the whole film.

Princess Grace was also concerned that the image of Monaco be right. Despite all the enchantment and beautiful flowers of the principality, she and the Prince wanted to portray it as a place run seriously by serious people.

At the beginning of the filming, everyone was slightly apprehensive about Curly Linden, who, though one of the great cameramen in the business, was also a notable drinker. Linden, however, not only rose to the occasion, but became a lifetime friend of Prince Rainier and Princess Grace. It was a matter of three professionals recognizing and respecting one another.

Some time later Curly Linden returned to the South of France to make another film. The Prince and Princess invited the entire company to the palace for dinner. He was asked to stand with the Prince and Princess in the receiving line to introduce the rest of the company. It was just one of those thoughtful gestures that makes Princess Grace the special person she is.

During working hours the Princess was always prompt and professional, and only once did she fluff a line. For some of the crew, who were all decidedly nervous, it was a little difficult to remember to always address the Princess as "Your Serene Highness."

When the first scene began, director Douglas Heyes was so overcome when he saw the beautiful blonde in front of the cameras that he said, "Now, Your Highness, honey . . ."

"Princess Grace has a decent respect for herself as a human being," Cynthia Lindsay said. "She never tells a good story about herself. Rather she makes a light kind of joke. Although she is less rigid than other highly placed women, she can turn on authority, if necessary, very quietly. It just couldn't happen that anyone could go too far with her. By one quiet, almost invisible look, she can stop any nonsense—from adults or children. Actually she really looks astonished and *you* become surprised and wonder. She has a kind of 'this couldn't be happening' look and the other person responds immediately."

When *A Look at Monaco* was made, Prince Albert and Princess Caroline were still small children and were sometimes reluctant to take part in the filming.

One scene was filmed in the Prince's zoo, which is open to the public every afternoon. Prince Rainier was wandering around with a chimp on one shoulder and the children following. Prince Albert began to imitate the way the chimpanzee walked and Princess Caroline just looked and said, "Look at Albie's little bare behind," which is exactly what the chimp had at that time.

The director then turned to her and said, "Now you make like a monkey." But she was not to be made a fool of. Even then Princess

231

Caroline had her own mind. She just looked at the director very solemnly and said, "No, I am not going to. I don't like your games and I am not going to play them," and walked off the set.

Instead she insisted on taking Mrs. Lindsay to the small kitchen off the dining room where there were a lion and two cubs curled up in a cage which had been placed near the warmth of the stove. She was terribly proud as she pointed out the cubs which she said she was "helping to bring up."

The small girl stood and looked at the big cat for some time, then sighed, "Oh, Mrs. Lindsay, wouldn't you adore to sleep with that lion?"

"I said I'd kind of like to know whether he would like to sleep with me first," Cynthia Lindsay remembered.

Princess Caroline answered, "Think of the cold nights and you could put your feet in and out and all cozy and warm and you could cuddle up."

At that moment a lioness came out of the back and Princess Caroline asked, "Is that his wife?"

"Probably," came the answer.

Then, pushing her small eager face against the bars of the cage, she said, "What a fortunate lion you are to have such a lovely wife."

The film was shot with enormous warmth and gaiety and happiness. When the film unit arrived at the palace the first day Princess Grace took them on a small tour to show them what she and the Prince wished to be included in the film.

In the hall of mirrors the producer thought how wonderful it would be to have this beautiful woman reflected seventy-three times. Cynthia Lindsay made a note about the throne, the hall of mirrors and finally the subterranean tunnels which were once the palace's own aqueduct.

After the tour she realized she had lost the note and was horrified that one of the security guards might have found it. It read, "Shoot Princess in Hall of Mirrors and what shall we do with the throne?"

The late English racing driver Graham Hill also had a happy experience in filming with Princess Grace. In his brilliant career he won the Monte Carlo Rally five times. He related:

"I wrote to the Prince and Princess and asked them whether they would agree to take part in a film that was being made about me called *Graham*, which was to be shown on British television.

"We had a meeting after the Grand Prix in 1973 in their garden by the swimming pool, where we had a short chat. I was most impressed that she was so knowledgeable about the Grand Prix . . . very observant in discussing the start, for instance. The interviewer talked with Prince Rainier and Princess Grace separately and then we just sat around and chatted and they filmed it.

"One of the most charming things about her is that at the reception after the race given for a lot of officials and dignitaries, she is always there and circulates, remembering everybody's name. She always seems to be pleased to see them and is very frank and open.

"It seems that America is forming its own aristocracy that has nothing to do with line of blood. It is a very young country and in a few years' time these will be the aristocrats of America. They must be very proud of Princess Grace that she has brought to one of the royal families of Europe this frank and refreshing way and opened it right up. I think it is very nice for the Prince to have somebody like her. She is so in touch. . . .

"The one thing that surprised me is that after the official prize giving at the Hotel de Paris, which ends about 2 A.M. or something like that, a lot of us English types all flock down to a little bar called the Tip Top. It has nothing except a bar, but everyone goes there for a plate of spaghetti. She knew this and commented on it. I was so surprised that she knew."

The Princess is revered at the Grand Prix parties because of her concern for her guests. One year there was a big dance, at which as usual she danced better than anybody. A signal was given to one of the Italian drivers that the party was over and instead of there being a formal withdrawal he started a conga line and the entire group from all the nations who had been invited joined in and simply "conga'd" through the door and disappeared out into the night.

Standing enjoying it all until the last guest had disappeared were Prince Rainier and Princess Grace.

Years later Mrs. Lindsay had taken her own ten-year-old daughter with her to the South of France, and on hearing this Princess Grace invited them to the palace so that she could play with Princess Caroline. She had brought with her as a gift some small dolls, which were welcomed. Previously Princess Grace had spent a lot of time with Princess Caroline making shoe boxes into beds and using cut-outs and pasteboard and any other little things that were around. Happily the dolls just fit.

When Cynthia Lindsay's daughter left, well brought up as she was, she curtsied as she would have done to anyone older, and thanked the Princess for a lovely time. Once they were outside the door she asked her mother, "When are we going to meet the Princess?"

"But, darling, you just have," Mrs. Lindsay answered.

"Oh, that cozy lady . . . was *she* the Princess?" the child replied.

Thirty-three

"I've had an interesting and wonderful life, and I like to think I have made it so. If I've had unhappy moments, I've probably made that so, too. We do it to ourselves," Princess Grace recently said.

This sentence embraces much of her philosophy of living. She abhors self-pity and places loyalty high on her list of priorities. Friends who have known her right through from those early Hollywood days find her totally unchanged.

"Grace has the capacity for friendship, and once you gain her trust she never lets you down," John Foreman said, and he has known her for twenty-five years.

"She is a real friend and she takes that situation seriously. She never says 'no' when a 'yes' would be helpful or give pleasure," said Fleur Cowles, who was first introduced to her in 1950 by Cary Grant.

There are lesser known friends, too, who have experienced the depth of her friendship. In Monte Carlo recently an elderly Englishwoman, Lady Doverdale, passed away. But she did not die alone. Princess Grace sat with her for almost two days.

The point was not that Lady Doverdale had lived as a revered citizen of Monaco for many years—it was more personal. She had no one of her own to be with her, so the Princess filled the gap, sitting with her and comforting her day and night.

Most of Princess Grace's friends are scattered around the world and can only be cherished on her many travels. But she has her own captivating way of "keeping in touch." On her many trips abroad whenever she sees something that reminds her of someone—a handkerchief for Edith Head, a scarf for Vera Maxwell, a crazy invention for David Niven—she buys it and sends it off.

"These things are so spontaneous, so individual," Edith Head observed. "For instance, she knows that I collect handkerchiefs as she used to collect shoes and gloves. Attached to a beautiful lace one she sent me from Africa once was a little note, 'Here is a pretty for you.' A lot of people would write, 'Here is a pretty thing for you,' but Grace has a very special way of expressing herself and here she uses pretty as a noun."

Near neighbors and friends at Cap d'Antibes are Virginia and Paul Gallico, whose friendship with Prince Rainier and Princess Grace is a close and meaningful one. One senses that here are two couples with the same sort of happiness who wish to share it with each other. In addition to this, the men have a common bond in their love of animals.

Friends are constantly amazed that Princess Grace finds time to make special presents for them in a life already packed with too many busy hours. For Paul's birthday once she made him a tapestry in the Leo sign, which is his birth sign; and for Virginia she embroidered a cushion copying the famous medieval tapestry *La Dame à la Licorne* ("the lady with the unicorn") now in the Cluny Museum in Paris. It is kept today in the dining room at the Gallicos' house in Antibes. Fleur Cowles has a piece of Princess Grace's embroidery, one of her own delicate flower pictures transferred into petit point.

Perhaps the most beguiling proof of the friendship between Gallico and Grace is a small book called *Manx Mouse* (Victor Gollancz), which Gallico wrote and dedicated "For Grace."

Manx Mouse is the charming consequence of ceramic lessons Princess Grace was taking. When she told Gallico about these classes at dinner one night, he promptly said, "I want to give you your first commission. I want you to make me a mouse."

The next day the Princess went back to her class in Monaco and began making "a teensy weensy" mouse. She gave it big ears and a skinny little tail which it held in its minute hands. She wanted it to be grey with pink ears. The teacher pointed to some coloring "over there" and Princess Grace mixed it up and applied it to her clay before firing. When the mouse came out of the kiln, it turned out to be bright blue and the tail had fallen off in the firing. It was the most pathetic mouse and she decided then and there to make him another one.

Some weeks went by and Paul had a birthday, which he quite often shares with Prince Rainier and Princess Grace. She arrived with the funny little broken mouse.

"It is only a small mouse," she said as she put it on his plate. "I am so ashamed because he lost his tail, he is the wrong color and everything's wrong about him."

Paul Gallico insisted that he did not want another mouse.

"No," she said, "I made you another mouse."

"Well, this funny little one will be Manx Mouse and the new one Mrs. Mouse," replied the writer, who gained a kind of immortality with his delightful book *The Snow Goose*.

Today Manx Mouse and Mrs. Mouse, together with a small silver one given by Prince Rainier, sit on Paul's desk where he writes every morning.

Nor does the story finish here. The following year for her birthday Princess Grace received the book *Manx Mouse*, written by Paul Gallico for children of all ages. The book begins, "There was once rather an extraordinary old ceramist who lived in the village of Buntingdowndale in the heart of England. Ceramics is the art of making pottery into tiles or dishes or small glazed figures. What was unusual about him is that he only made mice."

Princess Grace is much too sensitive and realistic not to recognize that in her royal position she has the power to make people happy or to disappoint them. For this reason she is, perhaps unconsciously, extemely careful to keep any promise she makes to a child. It may take years to fulfill but her promise is a bond.

When Virginia Gallico's daughter by a previous marriage, Ludmilla von Falz-Fein, was a child of eleven she came to know the Princess through her parents' friendship. From the age of six she had always sewn, first making flower-patterned tapestry cushions and later fabric collages filled with mystery and fantasy.

"One day when you have enough of those pictures for an exhibition, I will come and open it," the Princess told the child. By 1973 Ludmilla Nova, as she now called herself, was not only a promising young actress in London, but she had enough collages to give her first exhibition. Remembering the Princess's promise, she wrote and received back two dates on which Grace was free to come to London and open it.

The result was twofold: she had kept her promise to a child and, more important, by her presence an exhibition that might have been lost in the limbo of London's countless exhibitions was given maximum press coverage.

On opening night, there was a multitude of people in the gallery as Princess Grace and Princess Caroline arrived and a radiant Ludmilla went out onto the pavement to greet them. She was wearing the stage costume that she wore twice daily as one of the bel canto singers in *Babes in the Wood* at the London Palladium. The picture of this greeting made every newspaper next day.

The following day Princess Grace had lunch with the Gallico family. When Ludmilla arrived home from the show, there was a small box on the stairway. Inside was a pretty flower-shaped piece of jewelry in gold with a turquoise center to be worn on a fine chain. With it was a happy appreciative note "From Grace." Again it was a very special choice of gift, as Ludmilla signs her name (even on her printed checkbook) with a small flower dotting the *i* in Ludmilla. The gold flower was an exact copy and had been made by a jeweler in Monte Carlo.

Princess Grace's influence on Ludmilla has been profound. Ludmilla sat amid bundles of materials in her studio, which was once a garage, in Belgravia, and told me about her.

"In this modern world, women like her are to be admired. She is so disciplined. I don't know how she fits in as much as she does in a day. She once told me, 'Never stand when you can sit down.' But she is so feminine and graceful and doesn't mind wearing gloves to go out shopping, or getting up early to do her exercises.

"In show business, people look at you if you bring out your sewing and say, 'You must be mad,' but in fact I have watched Princess Grace do just that and when I first started in the business I thought, 'Well, there's nothing wrong with it if she does it,' and it became part of me by just watching her."

For Easter one year Princess Grace made Ludmilla a white ceramic Easter egg topped off with her own tiny signature flower. The egg divided in two and inside one half was her Easter greeting. Virginia Gallico also received an egg which opened to reveal a tiny fantasy bird amid a personal message.

It was the Gallicos, too, who suggested to the Prince that he enter his Dion Bouton 1903 in the London-to-Brighton veteran car rally in 1968. The Gallico family went to England ahead of the Grimaldis and made a dry run in three hours.

On the morning of the run, only Scotland Yard and the Royal Automobile Club were aware of their celebrity contestants. In the first car was Prince Rainier, Princess Grace, Princess Caroline and Prince Albert. Following was the Gallico family.

Princess Grace, who looked fabulous muffled up for the part in a thick coat and a large fur hat, had organized a picnic to be eaten en route and the whole party had arranged to stay the night in Brighton.

The Prince was making such good time on the route that, despite the fact that Princess Grace was so cold that she transferred to the Gallicos' car, he arrived in one hour and twenty minutes.

To celebrate, they decided to have the picnic in the hotel suite. There was a funny moment when the hotel manager opened the door to inquire when Their Serene Highnesses would like lunch served, to find everyone sitting on the floor enjoying the picnic amid much laughter.

The whole outing was topped off with a visit to the celebrated Lanes and the return trip to London and the *Brighton Belle* singing American camp songs.

The David Nivens were also close friends of the Prince and Princess. David Niven's friendship with her began during her days in Hollywood, but he and the Prince share more than memories. They both have a zany sense of humor and are constantly playing gags on each other.

Once when the Prince and Princess went to dinner at the Nivens' villa Lo Scoglitto—"the little rock"—they were confronted by a grave and consummate butler who wore with ponderous aplomb a startling ankle-length frock coat, originally white and many sizes too large. The butler had acquired his summer uniform from the milkman and could not be persuaded to remove it, even for royal guests. Princess Grace thought he was the doctor and could not understand why he was serving dinner.

One of Princess Grace's closest friends is Vera Maxwell, the distinguished dress designer in New York. Theirs is typical of the lasting quality of Princess Grace's friendships. It began in 1955, when they traveled to Dallas to receive an award each had been given by Neiman Marcus for her contribution to fashion.

Sitting in her unique little office above the belting traffic of New York's Third Avenue, and surrounded by bolts of material and fashion drawings, Vera Maxwell talked of this friendship which has spanned twenty-one years.

In their own special ways, these two women have the same kind of elegance. Vera Maxwell with her porcelain skin; grey hair pulled back into an unobstrusive little knob; face devoid of make-up; eyes clear, frank and alert. Her artist's smock becomes chic because of the way she wears it.

"I was old enough to be her mother and here we were thrown together in the same hotel suite. We each had our own bedroom and shared the drawing room. There were wonderful parties going on and I watched the sheer genius of this girl of twenty-three, then at the height of her film career, in the way she handled people. There were flashy smiles and mini actresses around, but I never once saw Grace give a false smile.

"I remember at the time thinking what a remarkable young woman. Not because she was a supreme actress but just because she was such a marvelous person. We invariably left the hurly-burly of the parties and went upstairs to our rooms with a glass of milk.

"The real bond came when I discovered that she liked Shakespeare's sonnets. We discovered that we both carried copies with us, the only difference was that Grace knew many by heart. I was so impressed by this young girl reciting Shakespearean sonnets that one of my first gifts to her was a tiny, very old copy of them and I always think of her in this connection. I am a great reader of eighteenth-century literature and we also had a common interest there, although I think she only has time to read biographies now."

Despite being a dress designer, Vera Maxwell has a healthy respect for Princess Grace's squirrel-hoarding of her clothes.

"I think it is heavenly that she keeps clothes, and the last time we met I said, 'Don't throw away anything you have of Zuckerman—a well-known American designer of the fifties. You must give them to the Smithsonian."

Princess Grace's shoe closet is also a cupboard filled with memories. At Roc Agel every summer she brings out and wears the blue and white sandals that she had made in a village during her stay in Africa for the filming of *Mogambo* over twenty years ago.

For many years Vera Maxwell had a small flat in Monaco and regularly went there, and whenever Princess Grace is in New York she invariably stays in the small guest unit in Vera Maxwell's apartment. Here she can have complete privacy, which is difficult when staying in New York hotels where she is constantly recognized and stared at.

Princess Grace's fortieth birthday was celebrated as a Scorpio party because of her blind confidence in the stars. As a struggling young actress her climb to movie stardom and her later role as a royal princess were all foretold in her horoscope.

In his book *Astrology and Prediction* (E.T. Bastsford) Eric Russell defines the Scorpionic character thus:

"It is, if anything, more prone to schizophrenia than Geminian. Mars rules it and Mars can indicate either great strength or great cruelty; it is watery and fixed, indicating great possibilities of great depth of character. In sum, the Scorpionic native could either be a person of immense will-power and ambition, sensitive but forceful, or a person delighting in his power over others and using that power sadistically. All astrologers agree in crediting the Scorpionic native with great sensuality, which can amount to eroticism."

It is intriguing to find not only Princess Grace but Martin Luther, Mata Hari, Queen Elizabeth the Queen Mother, Goethe, Grandma Moses and Maurice Chevalier all born under the sign of Scorpio.

Guests were sent crimson red invitations in the form of a horoscope reading:

Day for travel . . . journey to Monte Carlo is indicated. You are being invited by H.S.H. Princess Grace of Monaco, High Scorpio, to come to her Scorpio party in Monaco. Miss this at your own risk.

Love . . . Venus enters your sign

Romance is favored and may become highly inspirational by mid-November.

Social Activities . . . You may meet many interesting people who might influence your career.

     —Saturday, November 15, 9 P.M.
          Dinner and dancing
          Hotel Hermitage, Monte Carlo
     —Sunday,   November 16, 12:30 P.M.
          Brunch
          Hotel de Paris swimming pool

Health . . . If you survive these two events, you are a very healthy person and can look forward to an untroubled old age.

Advice . . . Ladies: Do not ignore the colors of your sign—red, black or white only

Dinner jackets propitious for gentlemen
For brunch: Studied Casualness
Hotel de Paris wholly converted for Scorpion occupancy. Your
private nest awaits you . . . Courtesy of the High Scorpio. Other
signs married to Scorpions tolerated.

It is easy to spot whose hand was behind the preparation of this
invitation and the many giggles that must have ensued during its
conception.

The dinner was splendidly festive in the newly decorated dining
room of the Hermitage. Because I believe that most people love to
know what the ''Beautiful People'' eat in festive mood here is the
complete menu:

Coulibiac de Saumon
Consommé Chaud aux Profiterolles
....
Coeur de Carolais
Bouquetière de Légumes
Fond d'Artichaut Florentine
Yorkshire Pudding
....
Plateau des Fromages
....
Crêpes Suzette
....
Corbeille de Friandises
....
Tasse Moka

And the wines, even more splendid:

Chevalier Montrachet 1964
Chateau Margaux 1945
Pommery & Greno Brut Rose 1961
Cognac, Liqueurs,
Marc de Champagne.

Among the notable Scorpions present was Richard Burton, who
had just given the Cartier diamond to Elizabeth Taylor and this was
to be its first official wearing. The story behind the delivery of the

diamond to Monaco is in itself worthy of a movie script, especially when viewed in the context of their on-and-off marriage.

The actual sale of the stone had been completed in the first-class section of a Pan American aircraft over the mid-Atlantic between a representative from Cartier's and Aaron Frosch, the American lawyer for the Burtons. This had been done to avoid American or British taxation.

When news that Elizabeth intended to wear her diamond to Princess Grace's birthday party reached Monaco, a whole security plan had to be put into operation. First Miss Taylor had to be reassured that she would not have to pay any sales tax if she brought the jewel into Monaco. Then she and Burton requested, of the French préfecture at Nice, a police escort to accompany the real stone and a copy which they carried with them.

There was a slight hitch when it was discovered that no police escort is allowed for material goods but only if a life is in danger. The French police also pointed out that they could only be responsible for the jewel until it reached the Monaco border and then the Prince's police would have to take over. All this in the name of friendship—Elizabeth Taylor and Princess Grace have been friends for many years—and publicity value, which was arranged even down to procuring two safes in which to keep the real stone and the fake.

As Elizabeth Taylor entered the restaurant all eyes were riveted on her bosom where the diamond quivered between two white cushions of flesh as smooth as satin.

During the afternoon prior to the party she had been playing ping-pong with Burton, and the match became quite intense. Richard thought he could beat her and naturally Elizabeth decided to win. In the heat of the game he had said, "If you win this match I'll buy you another diamond."

So with that incentive Elizabeth naturally won and Richard kept his promise by presenting her with a second diamond. Only this one was about 1/10 carat, the smallest diamond that can be set in a ring.

During the evening when asked to show her diamond Elizabeth said, "You want to see my latest diamond?" She then showed everyone the ring.

Princess Grace wore an emerald and a ruby ring and quipped, "I like to know which is my starboard and port side."

243

Princess Grace, who is now forty-five years old, makes no effort to conceal her age.

"It's cozy and not so bad," she says.

She rates thirty-five as the best age for a woman simply because "she is old enough to know a lot of things, yet still young and fit."

Thirty-four

The royal palace at Monaco with its two hundred or so rooms is a kind of village within a village. It has a distinctly medieval ambiance about it which is expressed not only in the charming buildings and courtyards, but in the almost feudal set-up of the palace staff, which numbers one hundred fifty.

Within the palace many families of the senior members of the staff live in their own apartments. There are the Prince's aide-de-camp and gentleman-in-waiting, the head of the Carabinier unit, the private secretaries of the Prince and Princess, the palace chaplain, majordomo, head butler, ladies-in-waiting as well as the usual live-in staff in any household of this stature.

A *régisseur* takes care of the palace logistics—the store rooms, laundry, food buying and so on. All the household bills are paid by the secretary to the Prince, and his Cabinet handles budgetary matters. One of the most important additions Princess Grace made to the domestic staff early in her marriage was the appointment of an English housekeeper, Miss Christine Plaistow. She had formerly been a guide, but grew into the household duties and has remained there for the last fifteen years.

Like most husbands the Prince takes a cursory interest in the household accounts, and when they become too high there is an economizing. In most Continental households of any size, the *chatelaine* keeps a small pad and pencil beside her place at the table for recording any remarks about the food, which are then forwarded to the chef. But in the Monaco palace the Prince holds this office and has since his bachelor days. It is probably true also that along with the notes on the menu are small personal reminders for his busy life.

One of the most handsome decorations in the living room of the flat in Avenue Foch, which the family used until they moved into their new Paris house last autumn, was, in fact, a direct result of one of the Prince's economies.

In remodeling the apartment, the Princess wanted to have a proper fireplace where she could burn logs. The Prince thought that this was too extravagant. Instead an aquamarine ceramic stove which had been buried and dug up in the palace garden was installed. Much of it was missing or broken, and with painstaking craftsmanship the potter at the ceramic school repaired it. Today it looks perfect, despite the fact that it does not work. As the centerpiece in the blue-green room, it is exceedingly handsome.

In the Prince and Princess's own personal quarters at the palace the staff usually number about ten. For everyday work they wear green striped jackets and trousers and red waistcoats with gold buttons. Formal official protocol is rigidly observed in Monaco and for State occasions the staff wear full livery with velvet knee breeches, white silk stockings and buckled shoes. All the staff get one month's holiday a year and are well cared for if they fall ill.

Both the chef and his assistant are French, and most of the food is therefore French or Italian; but the Princess occasionally manages to persuade the chef to bake American cakes. Her greatest triumph was the day he cheerfully made pumpkin pie from a recipe from one of her own books.

Lunchtimes are usually busy during the summer season, with parties of anywhere between six and twenty guests every day. The menu is simple but delicious with plenty of salads and fresh fruit, and is served at round tables in the tropical garden by the swimming pool. It is a beautiful, fragrant setting with orange and lemon trees and splashes of bougainvillaea and other flowering trees. Cages with tropical birds are often set amid the trees, turning it all into a kind of fantasy garden. Now that the children are growing up, they often join their parents for these semi-official luncheon parties.

"One thing I enjoy in France is that people take the time to live in a pleasant way," the Princess has said. "They are not rushed, not as hurried as in the United States. I think the midday meal when the whole family is together is very pleasant."

Within the Grimaldi family life is as informal and cozy as could be imagined within the confines of a royal household. There is a free flow between parents and children, who come and go as they wish.

During the summer, instead of being served a stuffy afternoon tea offered by a butler, a guest is just as likely to be offered a Coca-Cola by one of the children.

Early evenings for the Prince and Princess in Monaco are usually taken up with people to be received, exhibitions to visit or projects to be inspected. Prince Rainier usually does not get home from his "office," which is in one of the towers, until 7:30 and dinner is at 8 P.M. The children often eat earlier simply because there is lots of homework to be done as in any other French family.

After dinner, if the Prince and Princess are alone, she goes to her desk or does one of her hobbies and the Prince looks at television or writes his personal letters. They both try to leave official work behind them, but often there are mutual things to be discussed and the work schedule overlaps with their time together.

The Princess likes to retire at 10:30 and often reads late, but these are rare treats during the busy months. Sleep recharges her strength and all through her life has been her refuge in times of stress. Today whenever she can, she takes a couple of days off and "gets lost." Her only concession to age—and she is the youngest-looking forty-five-year-old one has ever seen—is that she appears to conserve her energy and sits whenever possible.

Mondays are always busy days for the Princess when she is at the palace because then she does all the housekeeping chores. There is the governor of the palace to see and guest lists for the week to study, as Princess Grace does most of the placing of guests at the tables. The chef makes his suggestions for the menus, usually three days in advance, and the Princess studies them thoughtfully, altering them if she feels that she can bring a better balance to the meal. The flowers, which are a feature of the private part of the palace, are cheerfully discussed with the housekeeper, Miss Plaistow, who often arranges them with the gardener simply because the Princess does not physically have the time.

Even in their private entertaining, Princess Grace prefers to sit her guests at small round tables with cloths that fall to the ground. In her early days at the palace this idea, beloved of American interior decorators, caused some concern among the palace butlers, who were accustomed to the conventional long table. But now, as with everything else in which she persists, it is an accepted fact and is even proudly acknowledged as a feature of the palace hospitality. The tablecloths are in a range of soft pastel shades, with small bouquets of flowers to match, but at Christmas they are holly-red. Each year Princess Grace herself makes the centerpieces for the Christmas tables from white- and silver-sprayed cones, tinsel, artificial Christmas roses, spruce, holly and candles.

Throughout the year informal entertaining can also take place in the recreation room, which was originally one of the old coach rooms and converts to a cinema. Here movies are regularly shown, and it was once the home of the Prince's electric trains. Nowadays with the children growing up, friends are asked to bring their families and it ends up with a party-for-all-ages. There are pinball machines and a bowling alley, where teenagers and fathers are to be found. A bar and buffet at one end of the room is laden with all the delicious cold food and salads that can be found in France. Female guests usually follow the lead of the Princess and wear long skirts and shirts or caftans, while the men are informally elegant.

On one occasion when Sir Winston Churchill and Mr. Onassis went to the palace, boef bourguignon and champagne were served in this room. An amusing aisde was that after the event, Sir Winston and the Princess's secretaries compared notes and discovered that each of their employers had been "very excited and very nervous" to meet the other.

That the Prince is totally aware of the difficulties of running such a large establishment as the palace household was evident when he commented, "No woman can really feel at home running a palace. For example, if she wants to make a change she is often faced with tradition. Moreover it is difficult for a woman to run a house that has one hundred fifty employees."

The Princess's "office" is in the twin tower to the Prince's. It is a pleasant airy room, nostalgic and personal. The walls are soft green and the furniture French Provençal. It is a gay room filled with sunshine and flowers and personal memorabilia, such as the gold record presented to Grace Kelly and Bing Crosby for their successful hit song "True Love," the Film Critics' Award, a painting of New York in a snowstorm and dozens of pictures of the Kelly family and of her own.

The Princess's large antique desk looks lived in. There is a French saying that she applies to her desk: *L'ordre est le plaisir de la raison et le désordre est le délice de l'imagination*—"Order is the pleasure of reason and disorder is the delight of imagination." But with her extraordinary ability for total sight recall, she knows where everything is, down to such details as a small blue button hidden at the bottom of a pile of papers.

Most of her mornings are taken up with answering letters and the routine work of the palace. The Prince and Princess both take their royal roles with dedication and sincerity. As in that other absolute monarchy, Saudi Arabia, there is a rule that permits any Monegasque with a problem to bring it to his ruler in person. With the Princess, the request is more likely to be contained in a letter.

One of the most poignant letters she received was one written in 1973 by Emile Mangiapan, a Frenchman who was incarcerated for life after a conviction for killing a policeman during a robbery in Nice in 1949.

After twenty-four years in prison, on the basis that his family once lived in Monaco, he wrote to Princess Grace.

"Emile's letter touched me," the Princess said at the time. "He told me how he loved to paint and how painting materials were sometimes difficult to get in prison. He also asked me to check on his case."

For ten years the Princess corresponded with Mangiapan and sent him Christmas gifts and money to buy painting materials. Mangiapan said that it was the Princess who took his case to the president of the Monaco Court of Appeal—"a move that finally got me paroled. In France when you get a life sentence, it means exactly that . . . a life behind bars. I'd still be in prison if she hadn't decided to help me."

From newspaper photographs, Mangiapan painted a portrait of the Princess which now hangs in the palace at Monaco. After leaving prison, Emile went to live in a commune of painters in Lille.

"I'm a free man and I owe it all to the Princess," he said.

Whenever the children have birthdays, the palace is inundated with letters from children of the same name from all over the world. These all have to be organized and acknowledged. The daily requests for a photograph of the royal family are answered with a colored postcard of the now famous family group taken by the Italian photographer Gianni Bozzacchi.

After lunch, for the Princess there is always Red Cross or other charity work to be done. It is also during these hours that she attends to the hairdresser and personal shopping.

Several of the Paris couture houses have dummies of the Princess so that when she is in residence in Monaco, she can shop by post in between her regular seasonal visits to the collections in Paris. She buys from the houses of Lanvin, Givenchy, Dior and used to patronize Balenciaga. She also acquires many of her leisure clothes from New York, where she is guided by her close friend Vera Maxwell, who dressed her in her private life all through those early years when she was a movie star. Other clothes she buys in Nice and Monaco, and some of her dresses are made to her own design by the seamstress in the *lingerie* at the palace.

"I am nostalgic about clothes," she said and this seems to be the case. "If you think that I am a hoarder, you should see my husband and his sister," she told friends when accused of being a miser with her possessions. An amusing result of the Princess's painstaking garnering is that with the fashion swing last year to clothes of the fifties, Princess Caroline was in luck.

"I never give her my clothes . . . I only lend them" is how Princess Grace explained her daughter's appearance in clothes from her mother's early wardrobe. One of the most successful "loans" last year was a suit, complete with square shoulders and pleated skirt, made for the Princess twenty years earlier by the English tailor Huntsman. Another shared triumph was the Dior white crêpe pajamas, which did double duty with mother and daughter wearing them on alternate occasions.

The much-photographed silver crocheted cloche which Princess Caroline wore to nightclubs last year was not bought at a Paris boutique, but had been crocheted by Princess Grace for a few francs.

Princess Grace chooses her wardrobe with extreme care, mindful of official functions where she is liable to wear the same dress many times if it pleases her. In no way is she a slave to fashion and prefers the same classic styles that made her one of Hollywood's best-dressed stars.

Gardner Cowles has a charming story of Prince Grace which, though twenty years old, is just as relevant today as then.

"I used to live in Des Moines, Iowa, and at this time I had moved to New York just after my wife, Fleur Cowles, and I had separated. In a feeling of nostalgia I invited eight of my Des Moines friends to see the Iowa University football team play in Los Angeles and they were to be my guests at the Beverly Wiltshire. I asked the four wives who they wanted to see most in Hollywood and they all answered, 'Joan Crawford and Grace Kelly.'

"I arranged a cocktail party on the Sunday afternoon after the Rose Bowl game. Joan and her late husband, Al Steele, head of Pepsi Cola, arrived first. She fascinated everyone with her flamboyant dress, flamboyant fur coat and flamboyant stories about everyone. She held forth for about three quarters of an hour and then the telephone rang, which I picked up to answer.

"Joan turned to me and said, 'Who was that?'

" 'Oh, nothing, it's just Grace is on her way up,' I answered.

"Joan turned to her husband and said, 'Darling, it is later than I thought and we must leave,' and just as they did, Grace came through the door. Now the point of the story was that Joan Crawford was quite well along in years and was not going to get caught next to Grace Kelly, who was so young, fresh and beautiful. Grace was so demurely dressed with her hair in a simple style and little white gloves. The impression that she made on this crowd from Des Moines was immense—the contrast between one of the most flamboyant females in Hollywood and one of the best dressed and most successful."

Today wherever she goes, Princess Grace is the center of attraction. It is neither her immaculate and pretty clothes nor her indestructible beauty, but a kind of inner tranquility that seems to radiate from her. She masks her great sense of fun by a dignified but easy exterior—the sort expected of a princess.

She has also acquired more confidence over the years, since she is surely aware of being a success at her job. When she and the Prince were present at the gala celebrations at Persepolis, which were given by the Shah of Iran and the Empress Diba to mark the two thousandth anniversary of their dynasty, Princess Grace was talking to Prince Philip and happened to mention, "Oh, Tito's an interesting man."

"How did you meet him?" Prince Philip asked eagerly. "I'd love to speak to him."

"Oh, I just went up to him and said, 'I'm Grace of Monaco,' and he said, 'I'm Tito,' and from then on we went on talking."

This could not have happened earlier on in her marriage. She would have been too shy.

"Being a princess was a job I accepted to take on and spent a while trying to learn how to do it," she explains.

Being the wife of Prince Rainier, a complicated, indulged Gemini, cannot always have been easy. Talking with Leslie Bennetts of the *Philadelphia Bulletin,* Princess Grace gave one of her rare insights into her attitude toward marriage.

"Today there is so much talk about freedom and finding oneself. I'm all for the dignity of the individual, but I don't think anyone has a successful marriage or a career or anything without sacrifice. Discipline seems to be a word that has almost disappeared from today's vocabulary. I learned discipline in Catholic schools, by being brought up in a strict family, and in the theater."

When asked about deference to her husband, the Princess replied, "You can't wait for the sacrifice of another person. You have to develop your own terms of sacrifice. It's a woman who keeps the family together. She is the heart of the home and thereby must be the strongest person in the family structure. . . . It is the man who must be the head of the household. I would say it is the Prince who makes the ultimate decisions."

Though not an active women's libber, Princess Grace has strong views of women's place in society today. In one of the few press interviews given in Monaco, she recently said to a reporter from *Nice Matin,* "Woman's first vocation is to be a wife and mother. In this domain no one thinks of disputing her supremacy, do they?

"More than ever women have an important role to play in modern society, only it is, perhaps, not the role people think it is . . . they can be the moral regulators of society. This is linked with the role of educators. Our civilization is passing through a period of upsets which we all know about and that sometimes give strange consequences—in the field of sex, for instance.

"It's not for me to express a view on the role of censorship for theaters or publications. After all, everyone is free to go and see any film he wants or read his favorite 'specialized' magazine. But what I do think is intolerable is the aggression committed against our children by advertising which is displayed in public places. Not because I'm excessively puritan, but because I consider that this amounts to destroying—and in what a sordid fashion—the element of mystery without which love, whether physical or sensuous, loses its magnificent charm . . .

"I know that many mothers secretly agree with me. Because it's fashionable nowadays to proclaim the opposite, woman's major role—and her real role—might, perhaps, be to demonstrate her opinions effectively. One of the most important things in life is to act according to your conscience."

252

To mothers whose children discard them and find them outdated, Princess Grace has these words to say, "In her time, my mother was considered to be a woman of very advanced ideas. That didn't prevent me from finding her old-fashioned. I think we are all inevitably a bit old-fashioned in comparison with our children, but I must add that up to date we have had nothing but satisfaction from our children."

Last year Princess Grace was not particularly interested in Women's Year, although she thought it was an opportunity for countries where women live in inferior conditions. In Western society, she wants to see women fight against certain injustices, such as unequal pay, but she does not believe that the way in which women should fight for female conditions is by opposing masculine ones. "I find it rather ridiculous." One of her firmest convictions is that women ought to found a new organization to smooth out the differences between working women and women in the home, as this is an area where much misunderstanding occurs.

Thirty-five

Roc Agel is not only a place; it is a state of mind. For the Grimaldi family it means complete happiness. In 1957 Prince Rainier bought a small farm at Roc Agel, 2460 feet above the sea, in the mountains over the border in France. It was to be a retreat so that the family could escape from the artificiality of Monte Carlo and live a normal life. The Prince and Princess also have a theory that children benefit from a change to sea and mountain air.

Roc Agel was originally built in the Provençal style of a *mas* (farmhouse), with sturdy stonework and massive beams. In 1959 the *mas* was enlarged until now it looks more like an American ranch and is referred to by the Monegasques as "The Ranch." Even the plumbing, which the Princess supervised with the French architect, is functional and American!

George Stacey, the American interior decorator who had previously worked for Princess Grace and was acquainted with her taste, helped turned the farm into an extremely comfortable family home.

"It is a sort of playground for everyone" is the way Prince Rainier described the sixty-acre estate. Here the entire family does *their* thing as *they* wish. The Prince has enjoyed turning Roc Agel into a pleasant home farm. In addition to raising chickens, he has had a small model dairy installed where several cows are kept. He believes that home-produced milk is much more nutritious than commercial milk, and they even make butter for their own use.

The Prince also takes pleasure in getting behind the tractor; and in addition to planting four hundred fruit trees—apple, cherry, apricot, pear—he likes to work in the vegetable garden. All the salad makings and small vegetables for the palace are grown there in

254

organic gardening conditions. The vegetables are fertilized by manure that is collected from the few horses on the farm, and as Prince Rainier tells friends, "My vegetables taste a lot better than those in the shops."

It has not been easy cultivating this rocky area, but with his tractors, the Prince has scooped out large areas in the rock and used them for pocket cultivation. This not only shelters the gardens from the stringent winds, but conserves water, which is scarce up in the mountains.

Princess Grace has her own garden. She plants the bulbs and looks after the roses and climbing vines on the house. She is such a bemused gardener that she was absolutely delighted when her former publicist, Rupert Allen, sent her some special tapes that must be merely twisted to attach plants to the wall. Costing only a few cents each, these tapes are prized by the Princess as if they were gold.

Her main joy, however, is puttering around the superb American-style, aquamarine-colored kitchen. Here she sometimes cooks for the family and the few very close friends who are allowed to share Roc Agel. The Princess loves experimenting with all kinds of Provençal dishes, which include the Monaco specialty pisaladière (a dough base covered with onions, tomatoes and black olives), canneloni, and, when the aubergines are ripe, ratatouille.

The Prince is fastidious about food and dislikes slabs of meat, such as American king-sized steaks. Instead, he prefers the delicate flavor of foods found in Indonesian and Provençal cooking, as well as in Chinese, Indian, Mexican and Polynesian cuisine. Princess Grace has her own favorite collection of these types of recipes, especially curries.

On her return from America once, the Princess brought back with her a quantity of American T-bone steaks as a treat for some of their friends. They were invited to the palace, where the Prince had set up his barbecue in the courtyard. But it rained that night and everything had to be moved into a covered part of the palace building.

"It was not the sight of the Prince in his apron and asbestos gloves that amused us, but the palace staff in their white cotton gloves as they solemnly took the steaks from the Prince as they were cooked and handed them round. They clearly thought we were all mad," one of the guests told me.

Since then barbecuing is mainly done at Roc Agel. The children and their friends particularly enjoy barbecuing and making hamburgers, hot dogs and waffles with maple syrup.

Life at Roc Agel is joyously informal and is much more like that of a well-off American family than its French counterpart. For both the Prince and Princess, who are normally tied to official duties, it means complete relaxation.

The Prince plays golf at the nearby course in the afternoon. Sometimes they leave Roc Agel in the evenings to try out small restaurants further along the coast or, during the month of August, to go down into Monte Carlo if there is some international artist they particularly want to see.

Hours are flexible, with meals when it suits everyone. The only help in the house comes from an Italian couple who see that the house is in order for the family's arrival. After that they more or less look after themselves.

Just as the Kelly children had their own play houses at the bottom of the garden in Germantown, so did the Grimaldi children each have his or her own house at Roc Agel. When friends came to stay, Prince Rainier would often put up tents on the ground so that the children could play at camping.

For two summers, the whole family went to the States, where the children attended a typical summer camp while their parents took a house nearby in New Hampshire. The girls learned a good selection of camp songs, but the Prince doesn't care for them much and makes disparaging remarks when he hears them.

Prince Rainier has a strange and interesting theory that, like human beings, animals need holidays, too. Each weekend he likes to take some of the animals from his private zoo up to Roc Agel so that they can get a change of scenery. It is quite a performance moving the large "cats," which are loaded in their cages onto a motor truck that has a special drop side. Once up at Roc Agel, if they are in the least bit tame, they are allowed out of their cages—sometimes tethered or roaming free.

Lion cubs have always been a problem for Princess Grace as not only does Prince Rainier enjoy them but the young Grimaldis have collected them as other children do puppies and kittens.

"Whenever they went to a circus, they were always presented with a baby chimpanzee or lion cub," said Princess Grace. And the same discussion always ensued. She would say, "I am not having anything to do with this. I'm simply not cleaning up after this one.

I'm not feeding it. I'm not doing anything. If you want the cub, it is your responsibility." But always in the end the children won, and the cubs stayed.

At Roc Agel, it was nothing to enter the large family sitting room and find two lion cubs growling and playing on the rugs or scampering over the chairs. As house training was not included in the lions' or chimps' schedule, there were other difficulties, too.

They once had a friend there who was doing some sculpting. Every time she got her clay ready for use, a baby chimpanzee would scuttle along and steal the clay, and then sit and eat it. It happened so often that in the end the sculptor had to give up.

Like her father, Princess Caroline has no fear of animals whatsoever. As a thirteen-year-old, she handled her lion cubs as another child fondles a kitten. At one period she had a cub which she called Elsa. She played with it all day, cuddled it like a doll and fed it from a bottle. There was only one problem: Elsa was a young male lion. He soon began growing a mane and finally had to be put in a cage. Princess Caroline was heart-broken. It took all Prince Rainier's parental persuasion to prevent her from sneaking into the cage to be with her pet.

Princess Grace has taken many home movies of their life at Roc Agel and of the animals on holiday, with the cubs playing with the children. Her favorite one is of the dogs' birthday party she gave.

At the time there were seven dogs in the family, and the Princess thought that they should have a communal birthday party. Incidentally, it was also a way of using up all the cake mixes that had accumulated in the kitchen cupboards.

Everyone helped as the Princess organized making paper hats for the dogs with elastic bands to fit under their chins. The invitation list included four poodles—Oliver's widow, Cannella, and daughter, Gamma; Chester; and Lindy—the Prince's Labrador, called Kim; a pointer named Bella, which was the most neurotic dog they have ever had; and a Rhodesian ridgeback called Fanny.

Princess Grace spent the morning baking the cakes—chocolate, angel, devil's food and so on—and setting the lawn with paper napkins. The party was extremely funny simply because each dog behaved according to its character. Cannella was very grand in powder blue and would not have any part of it at all, while the others came and stole their bits of cake and ran away.

After the food was finished, the children played games with the dogs just as at any proper children's party. All the time the party was going on, Princess Grace, in stitches of laughter, was making a home movie, which they now run through from time to time.

Oliver had died tragically in Switzerland. The Prince and Princess had taken him there while they were on winter sports. On returning to their villa, Princess Grace heard a terrible scream from nearby and rushed to find that Oliver had been attacked by another dog and was dead.

Her grief was almost unbearable. Oliver had been like a human being to her, knowing her every mood and understanding her every word. Moreover, he had been her constant friend during those early and difficult transitional days when she arrived in Monaco. She asked Father Boston, the palace almoner who was on holiday with the family, to bury Oliver.

Seeing the Princess's grief, which was all the more difficult to bear as there were other guests in the house, the Prince ordered, as a surprise, a black poodle called Chester, the same size as Oliver, to be sent by air from Paris as soon as possible.

The thought was meant kindly, but the Princess was inconsolable. She was even more bitter about the whole incident and resented the new dog terribly. She said that foisting a new dog on her, especially so soon after Oliver's demise, was the worst thing to do.

"I don't think my husband would have done it except that he was influenced by our friends and he thought it might comfort me. He is very knowledgeable and sensitive about the relationship between human beings and animals," the Princess commented afterward.

As pet lovers the world over know, many strange telepathic happenings occur in the animal world. Gamma, Oliver's daughter, who had always been the wicked one rushing about and chasing the chickens, went straightaway after the accident to lie at Princess Grace's feet; and that same night when the Princess went to bed, Gamma was lying in the same spot which Oliver had previously occupied. From that day on, she selflessly and devotedly did her best to replace Oliver in Princess Grace's life.

When Princess Caroline was small, she was given a first-aid kit for animals. Gamma bore the brunt of this with fortitude. When the mood came over her, Princess Caroline did a complete first-aid job on the dog. She must have been the only healthy dog in the world who, from time to time, was bandaged from nose to tail.

Today Princess Grace has as her special pet—a tiny, beguiling little apricot poodle called Timmy, which the Prince gave to her. His color is so rare that at the time of his birth, it was not recognized by the American Kennel Club.

Roc Agel is a wonderful house with its own special atmosphere of freedom and happiness as the dogs, children, chimpanzees, birds and lion cubs all live together in total acceptance. Few children in the world have such a heritage.

Prince Rainier also has his own stables. He and Princess Caroline love to take a couple of Carmargue ponies out for a gallop far away over the blue-hazed hilltops, the wind in their faces and below them the dropcloth of an azure-blue Mediterranean fringed by Monte Carlo. Princess Grace does not ride as much as she used to, but when she does she prefers side saddle and has her own hunter.

In the evenings, there is television and each family member has his or her own hobbies. Princess Grace disappears to press flowers for her collages. Princess Caroline loves to play pop music and often has discussions of jazz versus pop with her father. Prince Rainier is a hi-fi expert and has a vast collection of jazz records. He has everything that Al Jolson ever recorded and many Negro spirituals.

Prince Rainier also has his own workshop where he likes to do metal sculpture. Some of it is abstract art, others are modernistic, whimsical flowers. One of his pieces stands in the modern sitting area in their apartment in the palace. He is also clever at carpentry and tries to encourage his children to use their hands because he firmly believes, as does the Princess, that in doing so they will be more balanced and happier people.

Princess Grace always has needlework at hand. Apart from the waistcoat she made for Prince Rainier, she has also embroidered him slippers and a carpet for Princess Stephanie's bedroom which depicts Winnie-the-Pooh characters and is inscribed "To Stephanie . . . with love . . . from Mother." Princess Caroline is at present going through a non-embroidery phase, but little Stephanie often sits with her mother doing hers. Twice a week at school she takes lessons in sewing and embroidery.

It is in this relaxed and unpretentious atmosphere that Prince Rainier and Princess Grace try to instill in their children the fundamentals of living today.

Among the American virtues which Princess Grace would like to have superimposed on her children's European culture is the openness that Americans have—their forthright self-reliance. Life at Roc Agel, she hopes, will give them just this.

The relationship between Princess Grace and her children is a wondrous thing. She is endlessly patient with them and treats them with gentleness and grown-up understanding. People who surround her say that she is seldom impatient, but can be firm if the occasion arises. A Kelly family endearment which is used constantly is "Lamb." As said by Princess Grace, it is exceedingly pretty. She uses it as other mothers use "darling."

In the early days of their marriage, before the modern wing of the palace was built, Princess Grace regarded Roc Agel as her real home. Here she felt comfortable, happy and self-sufficient in the family life she enjoyed.

Yet, no matter how hard she tried, the Princess always felt that the original apartments which she and the Prince occupied upon their return from their honeymoon could never be a real home. There was nothing there that she had created—the structure and atmosphere had been formed by someone else. Also, the sleeping quarters were cramped. At one period, Prince Albert and baby Stephanie had to share the day nursery while Princess Caroline slept in the night nursery. Princess Grace had to store her clothing in cupboards alongside the nursery.

Now Princess Grace feels that the modern addition to the palace, which was completed in 1969, has become her real home. She and the Prince have a large airy bedroom plus a dressing room and bathroom for each, and the children all have their own rooms.

In spite of its marble floors and two-storied living area, the new wing has a homelike quality. The whole effect is light and contemporary, with lots of glass counterbalanced by a large fireplace made of smooth stones taken from the sea below. There is a large, squashy, American-style sofa in a clotted cream color and occasional tables of glass and metal. Set amidst a wall of glass is a huge brass telescope which the Prince uses constantly to scan the harbor. He can recognize all the yachts of well-known international celebrities as they enter it into his principality.

Besides his private zoo, which he visits most mornings, the Prince likes to have some of the animals and birds actually living in cages within the house. In the first apartment, he kept his favorite pet, a black and white lima, in the dining room. The Prince would go over to the animal, putting his arms through the cage and give him a hug and a kiss. All through dinner the lima would sit on the top of his tree, hanging on to it with his six-foot-long tail. If he was ignored too long, he would reel in his tail like a fisherman reeling in his line and sit cradling it in his arms and singing to it. No guest could resist him.

As the dining room in the present apartment is like a cool, pretty tent in blue and white cotton ticking and seats only eight, alas there is no room for the lima. Instead, on the walls hang a sketch of Prince Pierre (Prince Rainier's father) and three Vidal Quadras portraits of the three children all done when they were three and a half.

Another talented pet is Coco the parrot. His party trick is that he can not only sing the national anthem and the theme song from *The Bridge on the River Kwai,* but he can imitate the drawing of a cork superbly. Furthermore, whenever the telephone rings he begins, ''Hello . . . hello . . . hello.'' He also calls all the various dogs by their right names—a most engaging bird.

There is not another royal household in the world where animals and birds are accepted so naturally and fit so well into the family pattern.

The Princess was once standing in the old library talking to her secretary when the Prince rushed in, terribly impatient. He waited for the Princess, who did not hesitate while giving instructions to the secretary. Finally he burst out, ''You don't seem to understand how important it is. Tanagra is pregnant! It is very rare for a chimpanzee to breed in captivity.''

''All rightie,'' quipped the Princess. ''I'll knit her something.''

Thirty-six

To families not only in Monaco, but all over the world, Prince Rainier and Princess Grace present an attractive picture of family life.

"I don't much like the word 'example' as it gives a terrifying responsibility, but if the picture of our family gives help and confidence to others I am very pleased," Princess Grace once commented.

For a royal family in a golden goldfish bowl, Princess Grace has managed her job as a mother with miraculous skill. To see how all four members of her family dote on her—and she on them—is a lovely experience.

Right from the beginning of their family life, Prince Rainier and Princess Grace vowed that they would be caring and concerned parents. Within the structure of royal life—with its advantages and disadvantages—they have managed to give their children as balanced and normal a life as possible. The result is three charming, intelligent, uninhibited young people. The Prince and Princess's present concern is to be able to carry through over the next expansive years until their children are self-sufficient adults.

The popular press all over the world has found in Princess Caroline a constant headliner. With the looks of Ali McGraw and the vitality of Liza Minnelli, she could not be otherwise; but the Prince and Princess are fiercely protective of their children, who are unable to fight back at incorrect publicity. When an Italian newspaper falsified photographs to make it look as though Princess Caroline was sunbathing in the nude, Prince Rainier sued it. When an Englishwomen's magazine ran a story under the sensational headline "Why Mother Doesn't Know Best, by Princess Caroline of Monaco," the Centre de Presse de Monaco immediately notified the editor that the story was a complete fake, which indeed it was.

One of the most exacerbating untruths in recent years concerned the story that Princess Caroline was alleged to have had a secret romance with Prince Charles.

The truth was that at that stage, Princess Caroline had never met Prince Charles nor was likely to in the immediate future. Apart from a difference in age, which, of course, is not insurmountable, the religious differences would make a union highly unlikely. Princess Caroline is Roman Catholic and Prince Charles will one day be head of the Church of England.

Princess Grace herself takes a remarkably modern and philosophical view about her daughter's future. As she said to one American reporter, "I would like to see Caroline marry a Catholic. It makes it easier. But I guess if she really had her heart set on marrying somebody who wasn't Catholic . . . well, Caroline is a strong character and she probably would end up doing it no matter what we thought. Like all parents we wish for her happiness."

When another newspaper scurrilously wrote that Princess Caroline's studies for the Institut d'Etudes Politiques in Paris were falling behind because of her gay night life, Princess Grace was angry. She immediately wrote to the editor and gave a factual account of her daughter's educational achievements. Princess Caroline did in fact fail the entrance exam a few weeks later.

Princess Grace has many acute and original observations to make on the bringing up of children—something she totally understands.

"Children need to be told constantly—over and over again by their parents—that they are loved. This French parents do so well while American ones tend to take it for granted that the children know. I think this is a very subtle difference," Princess Grace has said. From the shining open looks of the Grimaldi children, they are suffering no lack of being told of their parents' affection. They have given their children a childhood overspilling with the goodness of security, fun and love.

All the children have pocket money but "it is not nearly as much as some of their friends'," Princess Grace has said.

The decision made last year between Prince Rainier and Princess Grace that a more permanent home had to be created in Paris during the period of their children's education did not come easily. For both it means a tremendous sacrifice in living apart for much of the time.

Even before his marriage the Prince had always had an apartment in Paris, and during the last few years he and the Princess acquired a much larger one on the Avenue Foch. But with the children needing more space for entertaining their own friends, the Prince has now bought a permanent house in Paris into which the family moved last autumn.

For the Princess, who dislikes traveling (especially by air), the present arrangement means almost weekend commuting to Monaco, but this she feels is necessary and worthwhile until her children are old enough to stand on their own feet.

"Caroline is too old for a governess and too young for a lady-in-waiting, so it seemed the only solution," the Princess explained to inquirers.

Had it been in America or had the Prince and Princess had members of their own families, with children of a similar age, living in Paris, undoubtedly Princess Caroline would have stayed with them.

Prince Albert, with the clean good looks of his mother, will remain at school in Monaco until he is ready for college. The Prince, especially, is concerned that Prince Albert will not have the same experience as he had by being educated abroad. However, when Prince Rainier finally returned to Monaco as a grown man, he knew few people of his own age. Prince Albert, on the other hand, is growing up among the boys who will one day help him in the ruling of the principality. Last summer he spent at a camp in America teaching swimming to other children.

It is unlikely, too, that Prince Albert will be sent to an American university for any long period. His destiny lies in the new Europe.

Although Prince Albert is remarkably like his mother in character, as well as looks, the Prince and his son have an excellent rapport.

"Albie is much too keen on swimming and keeping fit to ever be bothered with the drug problem," a family friend told me. "He and the Prince are like a couple of brothers when they lock themselves away in the palace gymnasium. He will make a fine ruler one day. He is intelligent, dependable and trustworthy, with a great deal of compassion."

Prince Albert is already being gently eased into his royal role and attends various functions with his parents. As Prince Rainier has said, "Albert should have time to enjoy himself and not be parachuted into the job. I should like him to work alongside of me for at least a year or so to get the feel of the ropes."

It is generally conceded in Monaco that Prince Rainier will step down from the ruling position when in his early sixties.

Princess Stephanie is a beguiling little girl. She is bright, indulged and has the quick wit of her father.

Although both are aware of the generation gap, Prince Rainier and Princess Grace have tried to minimize it as much as possible in their relationship with their own children. They go out for meals together, sit around in the evenings together and play together, just like millions of other families.

In 1973 when Princess Caroline turned sixteen and started to go to grown-up dances, with felicitous concern Princess Grace felt that it was time that all the family knew how to dance properly in addition to disco-dancing. She did a most astonishing thing to rectify this. A telephone call was put through on her behalf to Peggy and Frank Spencer from the tulle and sequin world of the BBC's television program *Come Dancing*. They were invited to Monaco for ten days to teach the whole family what Frank Spencer quaintly calls "Couple Dancing."

A class of young people, friends of the royal children's, and Princess Grace, met daily in the Hermitage Hotel, where they were given a ten days' crash course in the waltz, quick-step, fox trot, jive, tango, Viennese waltz and Zorba dance. The Spencers brought a collection of the top band records out with them.

On the first day, the children turned up in jeans and casual clothes. By the second day, the Grace-line was working and they all arrived immaculate in party clothes.

The climax and test came at the Red Cross ball which Princess Caroline attended that year for the first time. As the music commenced an extremely proud—and elegant—Prince Rainier took the floor with his daughter for the first waltz while the rest of the dancers stood and watched. They did not put a foot wrong.

Neither the Prince nor the Princess is concerned with the constant speculation in newspapers that their marriage is in danger of breaking down. They have learned to live with such gossip.

They have an unequivocal closeness which becomes even more

apparent as the marriage entered its twentieth year this April. Neither has ever tried to minimize the differences which occur in any marriage at its onset.

For a marriage that began with so few interests in common, it is a remarkably successful one. The Prince's hobbies include shooting, boxing, underwater swimming, soccer, skiing, automobiles, fishing and yachting, none of which the Princess especially enjoys. Nor does the Prince share her genuine enjoyment of walking.

The common denominator is the family plus an engaging sense of humor. Princess Grace is quick to point out that her husband is wittier than she is and finds it easier to talk to people than she does. However, this is not the impression among her friends. Her humor can be devastatingly pungent and individual.

Another bond between Prince Rainier and Princess Grace is their deep religious conviction. At a table by his bedside Prince Rainier keeps the *Cardinal Spellman Prayer Book*, which he takes everywhere, and a small crucifix belonging to a German which he picked up on a battlefield.

Princess Grace has expressed the view that, like many Catholics, she is concerned with the changes in the Church. Some she can accept and others she cannot.

"We are all looking for answers. But your answers don't apply to other people—and that may account for the generation gap. Life is constantly changing. What was valid and true five years ago is not true any more. My ideas are constantly changing. . . . As a Christian I think I've improved over the years. . . . I may not be the best Catholic."

All the children have been brought up with an awareness of and an involvement in religion. There was never any question of allowing them to drift until they were old enough to decide for themselves.

As the Princess has said, "It's like telling children to wait until they are twenty-one before they brush their teeth. By then their teeth might have fallen out."

Next to the birth of her children, Princess Grace says that her trip to Ireland was one of the most profound experiences of her life.

In memory of that trip in 1961, the Princess wears, along with her platinum wedding ring, an old Irish ring in the design of the cladagh which was given her on that trip. She also bought a collection of five hundred books, including Irish literature, poetry and plays, which she is astutely reading.

She has a spiritual as well as physical identification with Ireland. She was overjoyed when she heard that her friends the Gallicos had bought the Shannon Pot in Derrylahan, Glangevlin, County Leitrin, in 1968, purely for the romance of owning the source of the Shannon River, and by doing so hopefully protecting it from the evil promotors and constructors who love to ruin nature.

Before going on a visit to make the final arrangements, Virginia Gallico had told the Princess that she intended to take an Hermès scarf to Mrs. Maguire, from whom they were buying the Shannon Pot.

"Perhaps she may not know who I am, but would you take her one of my scarves?" Princess Grace asked. "Please tell her to use it and not to put it in a drawer."

It so happened that Mrs. Maguire had two American heroines— Princess Grace and Mrs. Jacqueline Kennedy. When the Gallicos arrived with the pretty scarf Princess Grace had designed and gave it to Mrs. Maguire, she took it and held it in front of the crucifix. At least one of her heroines had not let her down. And doubtless today the scarf lies alongside one of her religious relics.

During the years Princess Grace has lost much of her initial shyness. In the early days she suffered agonies before any great event on their official trips abroad. Besides being nervous—and it always went to her stomach and she could not eat—she found the endless protocol boring. Now she masks her ennui beneath bemused resignation.

Both Prince Rainier and Princess Grace take the principality seriously, including its standards of princely protocol and behavior. In the colorful soldiers guarding the palace, who are drawn from the principality's army of eighty-nine, they recognize a powerful piece of tourist propaganda. Ditto the galas and the big names Princess Grace lures there every summer for the various fêtes.

Among the Monegasques the royal family is held in tolerant affection. They have brought stability and permanence. "We have no drug problem, no serious crime, no taxes, a fine health system and our children are well educated . . . what more do we want? If we were to be a republic or part of France all this might disappear. We are well satisfied," an elderly Monegasque told me. "The royal family, poof, they are harmless."

To the thousands of foreigners warming their aging bones in the golden sunshine, there is also a strict code of behavior. If they have any criticism of either the Prince or Princess they keep it to themselves. "We are guests here," they say conspiratorially. "We don't discuss any problems with anyone."

They are all aware that the Prince is the supreme authority in all Monegasque matters, with the power to suspend the Constitution and disband the elected legislature (which he did in 1959)—and also to expel any undesirable foreigners!

In *Nice Martin*, the newspaper which circulates to the whole of the Riviera, one is conscious that little crime is reported in the section from Monaco. Perhaps it does not exist or perhaps it is suppressed in the hope of giving Monaco a crimeproof image for its many rich residents.

There is also another facet to this interesting little principality. The scientific work being done there is stretching out into the world. On my television screen recently I watched Jacques Cousteau in a program concerning the mystery of an unknown poison affecting the fish on Lake Titicaca in South America—an economic factor as serious to the Indians there as drought is to the Ethiopians. Samples of fish were taken back to the laboratory of the Oceanographic Museum in Monaco and there a diagnosis resulted. In this way both the Prince and Princess feel that the small nations have a positive contribution to give to the world and they want Monaco to be in the lead.

To Princess Grace, with no inbred royal hang-ups, the role of princess is just another job. "I work hard in social work, public relations and raising the Grimaldi heirs. But that's what I get paid for," she says.

For a woman whose entire life was wrapped up in her work as an actress, she has made the transition to full-time princess with ease and credibility.

"Most women want to be married and have a family and I found that I was no different from anybody else," she says with disarming honesty.

At forty-five years of age, Princess Grace is still at her prime as a woman. She has phenomenal beauty, health, diversified talents and professionalism. With one career as a world film star behind her and midway in her role as a reigning royal princess, she is well on her way to completing her third one—that of a conscientious mother to a lively, growing family.

In addition to this, I feel that there is still an untapped source of energy and creativity that may well provide further surprises. The "act" is far from complete.

When asked once if she was happy, she replied, "I have peace of mind and occasional moments of happiness. Happiness isn't a perpetual state. Life isn't that way."

Index

274

O'Donnell, Cathy, 40
Oechsle, Jack, 32, 33
Olivier, Laurence, 94
On the Waterfront, 90
Onassis, Aristotle, 126-27, 150,
    158, 164, 210, 224, 248; and
    S.B.M., 207, 208-9
Onassis, Jacqueline, 209. *See also*
    Kennedy, Jacqueline
Onassis, Tina, 209

Pamp, Maree, 118
Panton, Margaret, 105
Paramount, 85, 87, 89, 100
Paris Match, 104, 112-14
Parnis, Mollie, 146
Parsons, Louella, 100
Pascal, Gisèle, 113, 124, 167
Patachou, 95
Penn, William, 13
Perette, Suzy, 146
Perlberg, William, 85, 87, 89
Perrie, Ernestine, 50-51
Philadelphia Story, The, 50, 137
Philip, Prince, of England, 251
Pierre, Prince, of Monaco, 123,
    139, 150, 152, 154-55, 162,
    174, 261
Plaistow, Christine, 245, 247
Playhouse in the Park, 52, 73-74
Polignac, Duke Pierre de. *See*
    Pierre, Prince
Portanier, Marcel, 154, 180
Prêtre, Georges, 196
Prince and the Showgirl, The, 4
Prince Rainier of Monaco
    (Hawkins), 163
Princess Grace Foundation, 190-
    92
Pursuit of Destiny, The, 117

Quadras, Vidal, 261
Quentin Durward, 91-92

Rainier, Prince of Monaco, 118,
    162-64, 167-69; and animals,
    231, 256-57, 260-61; daily life
    of, 245-49; family life of, 198-
    205, 254-69; family of, 122-24;

and gardening, 193-94, 254-55;
    and Grace, 4, 104, 112-16, 172-
    77, 180-81; and Monaco, 207-
    9, 214; and staff, 216-25; in
    United States, 129-34
Rampo, Maree, 160
Ratoff, Gregory, 46-47
Ray, Harry, 103-5
Rear Window, 45, 77-78, 81, 85,
    119
Red Cross, 6, 185-91
Red Dust, 60, 61
Redford, Robert, 36
Renaud, Madeleine, 95
Reybold, Carolyn, 118, 131, 160
Reybold, Malcolm, 131
Rhine, J. B., 118
Richards, Lexford, 50, 152
Richardson, Sally, 141, 160
Righter, Carroll, 135-36
Ring Round the Moon (Anouilh),
    184
Riva, Maria, 51
Roc Agel (ranch), 254-60
Roosevelt, Franklin Delano, 11
Rose, Helen, 119, 140, 146
Rostropovitch, Mstislav, 196
Russell, Eric, 241
Russell, Jane, 138

Saadia, 68
Schary, Dore, 92, 139-40
Schlee, George, 126-27
Schoenbrun, David, 124
Schraffenberger, Nancy, 186
Schwarzkopf, Elisabeth, 196
Scott, Lizabeth, 49
Scott, Sir Walter, 91
Seaton, George, 85, 87-89
Segonzec, Baroness Gladys de,
    112
Selznick, David, 87
Seton, Lady Julia, 192-93, 194
Seton, Sir Alexander, 192
Showoff, The (Kelly), 11
Simpson, Adele, 146
Sinatra, Frank, 61, 63, 65, 67, 99,
    137, 140
Sinclair, Mary, 51

275